NOTHING COULD BE *Finer...*

CLASSIC SOUTH CAROLINA RECIPES FROM THE PALMETTO CABINET

The Palmetto Cabinet, first organized in 1974, is comprised of spouses of current and former General Assembly members and Constitutional Officers, current and former General Assembly members and Constitutional Officers, and current and former First Ladies of South Carolina.

Our purpose is to learn more about South Carolina: the people, places and the functions of government. Throughout the year, we are involved in various fundraising efforts to benefit the South Carolina Governor's Mansion. We have assisted the Governor's Mansion Foundation in purchasing items for the mansion and with restoration projects. All proceeds from the sale of this book will be used for our Governor's Mansion projects.

For additional copies, please use the order form at the back of this book
Or send a check for $24.95 plus $5.00 shipping and handling to:

The Palmetto Cabinet
P.O. Box 593
Columbia, SC 29202

ISBN: 978-0-9795378-0-6

First Printing:
November 2007 5,000 copies

This cookbook features recipes that are tried and true, but not necessarily original.

Photography by Mr. Sam Holland and Mr. Jay Vaughan

WIMMER
COOKBOOKS

A CONSOLIDATED GRAPHICS COMPANY

800.548.2537   wimmerco.com

DONATIONS TO THE GOVERNOR'S MANSION BY THE PALMETTO CABINET

Our projects have funded the following restorations and purchases for the Governor's Mansion complex.

* The dolphin fountain, two urns and two planters in the Charleston Garden located off the Palmetto Dining Room in the Governor's Mansion

* A landscape portrait, Young Man and Dog and Young Girl with Flowers, by Charleston native, James H. Shegogue (1806-1872)

* Two pastel portraits c.1717 by one of America's first pastel artists, Henrietta Dering Johnston. One portrait is of Mrs. Robert Brewton and the other is Mrs. Charles Pinckney

* Repairs to patio fountain in Mansion Courtyard

* Pair of Sheffield sterling candelabra c.1823, made in Sheffield, England

* Framed (in antique frames) the photographs of all first ladies (that are available) which are on display in the Governor's Mansion and the Caldwell-Boylston House

* Purchased Gorham Crystal (50 iced beverage glasses and 32 water goblets)

* Antique chandelier and medallion in bedroom in Lace House

* Antique mirror in the Lace House entrance

ACKNOWLEDGEMENTS

The creation of a cookbook, or any large project for that matter, requires the cooperation and coordination of many individuals. We would like to thank all those involved in the development of this cookbook.

Those who contributed recipes are especially important, for, absent recipes, there is no cookbook. The names of those who submitted recipes are listed below their recipes. Thank you so much for sharing your favorite recipes with us.

Thanks to our very talented professional chefs and restaurateurs who so gladly provided delicious recipes for us to share with you. We are fortunate to have such extraordinary culinary talent in our state. We hope you will take the time to visit these fabulous restaurants located around the state.

In addition to our hard-working testing committee, there were many volunteers who assisted us in recipe testing. Their willingness to ensure the accuracy of the recipes contained in this cookbook proved invaluable. For their efforts, we extend our sincere appreciation. They are individually listed on the following committee page.

Cookbooks like this require funding for publication. We are very grateful to our sponsors for their generosity and support of this project. Their confidence in us and in this project is greatly appreciated. We acknowledge their contributions on the following pages.

We must thank our exceptionally talented photographers. Mr. Sam Holland, who so generously provided the beautiful photographs of our state used on the cover and on the divider pages. Also, Mr. Jay Vaughan kindly allowed us to use his artistic images of the waterfall and Shem Creek featured on the cover. Seeing South Carolina through their camera lens, you will appreciate our great state even more.

We appreciate the support from our Palmetto Cabinet members and the South Carolina Governor's Mansion. Their patience in seeing this project through and willingness to lend a hand when possible helped make the project move along more smoothly.

Last, but not least, thanks to all the committee members who contributed their time to this project. It was two years in the making, but they never wavered and are the ones who deserve the credit for this truly special book.

Vickie Skelton
Cookbook Chair

4

COOKBOOK COMMITTEE

Chair & Editor
Vickie Skelton

Assistant Chair
Amelia Cotty

Treasurer
Alinda Mahaffey

Testing Coordinator
Kathy Koon

Testing Committee
Norma Jean Barfield
Anne Elliott
Alinda Mahaffey
Lynn Owens
Ruth Rice
Vickie Skelton
Reba Stille
Kelly Talley
Linda Witherspoon

Sidebar Committee
Amelia Cotty
Lisa Courson
Marie Land
Vickie Skelton

Sponsorship Committee
Shelvie Belser
Amelia Cotty
Reene Gambrell
Joyce Hearn
Alinda Mahaffey
Betty Ryberg
Joan Scott
Vickie Skelton

Art & Design Committee
Ginger Huggins
Evelyn Ritchie
Betty Ryberg
Vickie Skelton

SPECIAL THANKS

Honorary Committee Member: B.R. Skelton

Photography: Sam Holland, www.scimages.com. Mr. Holland is a commercial photographer and has also been the photographer for the SC House of Representatives since 1997. Jay Vaughan, a freelance photographer from Spartanburg, provided the photographs of the waterfall and Shem Creek used on the cover.

Proofing and Editing: Jason Zacher, Zacher Media Strategies, www.zachermedia.com

Guest Testers: Kathy Bigham, Susan Talley, Evelyn Mack, Cheryl Koon, Janice Williams, Malissa Koon, Misty Koon, Anna Koon, Robin McKee, Susan Mahaffey, Lynn Weatherman, Jean Carlisle, Dot Carter, Emily Lesesne, JoAnne Kennedy, Zelda Oates, Elizabeth Ferguson, Vicky Cheek, Stephanie Owens, Dawn Rampey, Monique German, Frances Moore, Helen Owens, Terri Campbell, Joan Owens, Ann Thomas, Susan Gasque, Wanda Britts, and Claire Rice

Arrangements: Ann Martin

ACTIVE MEMBERS OF THE PALMETTO CABINET

Nancy Altman
Doris S. Anderson
Ann Bailey
Lynn Bales
Mary Margaret Bannister
Norma Jean Barfield
Katherine Battle
Shelvie Burnside Belser
Margaret Bennett
Jennie Bingham
Shelton Bosley
Tomilyn Bowen
Felicia Breeland
Alfreda E. Brown
Dorothy Brown
Ann B. Bryant
Lalla Lee Campsen
Floride Carter
Kris Cato
Maelda Chalk
Mona Chapman
Sharon Chellis
Joanne Clark
Joan Clyburn
Amelia Cotty
Lisa Courson
Becca Crawford
Linda Cromer
Betty Pauline Dangerfield
Barbara Dantzler
Becky Delleney
Debbie DeMint
Natalie B. Dennis
Melody Duncan
Ann D. Edwards
Dotty Edwards

Anne A. Elliott
Ginger Elwell
Jane M. Evatt
Judy A. Frye
Reene Gambrell
Joan Hamilton
Ginny H. Hammond
Marty Hardwick
Louise Grant Hartnett
Nancy Harwell
Joyce C. Hearn
Vera Helmly
Sharon B. Herdklotz
Lisa C. Hiott
Betty Holland
Arri Holt
Ginger Huggins
Cindy Kelly
Reba Kinon
Suzanne Kirsh
Betty Knotts
Katherine Koon
Marie M. Land
Jolene S. Lander
Marilynn Leach
Ellen L. Leventis
Alinda Mahaffey
Susan Martin
Sara McLeod
Julie H. McLeod
Kitty Mescher
Janet Moss
Pamela Mulvaney
David Neilson
Gayle O'Dell
Lynn Owens

Margie Patterson
Anne Perry
Janis Reese
Chessie Rhoad
Ruth Rice
Margaret Richardson
Evelyn Ritchie
Betty Ryberg
Willie C. Saleeby
Sandra Sandifer
Jenny Sanford
Joan Scott
Ada Jane Setzler
Vickie Skelton
Dot Smith
Linda L. Smith
Macaulay Smith
Peggy C. Smith
Dot Spears
Sharon Stewart
Reba Stille
Robin Stilwell
Kelly Talley
Emilie Theodore
Fran T. Thomas
Linda Toole
Patricia F. Townsend
Kim Verdin
Martha Walker
Blanche G. Weathers
Lois R. West
Margaret Williams
Roxanne Wilson
Linda Witherspoon
Amy F. Wright

The Big Palmetto, by Jim Harrison

There's no place like home.

When we opened Carolina First in 1986, our goal was simple: to become a premier bank by putting customers first. Twenty years later, we're still on that mission. And today, we're among America's Top 50 Financial Institutions, with more than 160 offices across the Carolinas and Florida. But no matter how we grow, South Carolina is still our home. Our corporate headquarters are here. And it's where we continue to offer every one of our customers the personal service of a community bank, coupled with the power of a leading financial institution.

There really is no place like home. And for Carolina First, home is right here with you.

CAROLINA FIRST

We take your banking personally.

www.carolinafirst.com   Member FDIC

Palmetto Sponsor

The South Financial Group
Carolina First Bank

Capital Sponsors

Spartanburg Regional

BMW Manufacturing Co.

www.bmwusfactory.com

Crescent Sponsor

Governor's Sponsors

McNair Law Firm

Rep. and Mrs. B.R. Skelton

Rep. and Mrs. Joseph G. Mahaffey

Nelson Mullins Riley & Scarborough LLP

House Speaker Robert W. Harrell, Jr.

Rep. Harry F. Cato

Rep. Robert E. Walker

Rep. Daniel T. Cooper

Ms. Laura M. Hewitt

Rep. James H. Harrison

Friends of the Cabinet

Cross Creek Plantation -
Jack & Angela Shadwick

SC Beverage Assn.

Senator Linda H. Short

The late Senator William C. Mescher
and Mrs. Kitty Mescher

Rep. Alan D. Clemmons

Rep. David R. Hiott

Felder & Associates

Lt. Governor Andre Bauer

First Monday Club of Spartanburg County

Rep. Phillip D. Owens

Capitol Strategies Inc.

Ms. Judy P. Hamer

Rep. W. Douglas Smith

Rep. Robert W. Leach, Sr.

Senator & Mrs. W. Greg Ryberg

Ms. Shelvie Burnside Belser

Rep. Rex F. Rice

Secretary of State and Mrs. Mark Hammond

Rep. J. Gary Simrill

Rep. Chip Huggins

Anderson/Abbeville County
Legislative Delegation

Kelley, McCain & Smith Owens LLC

Benefactors

Mrs. Iris Campbell

Mr. Fred Allen

Former Rep. and Mrs. Ralph W. Norman

Senator John C. Land, III

SunTrust Bank

Judge J. Mark Hayes, II

Ms. Mary Jane Holland

Mrs. Dorothy H. Brown

Senator & Mrs. Nikki G. Setzler

Former Senator & Mrs. Scott H. Richardson

Rep. & Mrs. John L. Scott, Jr.

Rep. G. Ralph Davenport

Rep. William F. Cotty

Mrs. Amelia Cotty

Dr. Deborah J. Davis

SC Farm Bureau Federation

Contributors

Senator John D. Hawkins

Mrs. Margaret Williams

Senator & Mrs. William H. O'Dell

Rep. & Mrs. Robert S. "Skipper" Perry, Jr.

Mrs. Emilie Theodore

Rep. & Mrs. Scott F. Talley

Mrs. Joan B. Clyburn

Mrs. Horace Smith (Dot)

Rep. & Mrs. Converse A. Chellis, III

Former Rep. & Mrs. David Wright

Mrs. Jane M. Evatt

Dr. Anthony L. Mathis

Mrs. Jolene Lander

Ms. Louise Grant Hartnett

Ms. Betty B. Holland

Mrs. William J. McLeod

South Carolina

COLUMBIA

INTRODUCTION

When we first embarked on this cookbook, we wanted it to be a successful fundraiser for our Governor's Mansion projects. But then it became so much more.

As we collected recipes and thought about the theme for this book, we realized that what connects us to our long-time favorite foods and our newly discovered favorite dishes are the memories or stories behind them. Whether the memory of a dish lovingly prepared by a dear grandmother or a recipe shared by a best friend or the innovative food of a talented chef, sharing the memory is what makes the food even more special.

We decided what better way to present this book to you than to share not only our love of food, but also our love of the places and people of South Carolina. "Smiling Faces, Beautiful Places" is not just a motto placed on our license plates, but a true reflection of our state. We are so blessed to have such wondrous natural resources and gracious, friendly people. We had to take a moment to share the stories of our people, the places we live and love to visit, where we like to celebrate and what we celebrate. South Carolinians love tradition, food, parties and above all, sharing the abundance of life with others.

You will perhaps notice from the recipes contained in this book that there are many old-fashioned recipes alongside recipes containing the latest ingredients. We think food is a lot like life – always evolving. You will find many "Southern" dishes in this book, but some recipes are just as likely to be from Southern Italy, the South of France or South of the Border. While we hold true to our roots, we are always willing to try new things. That is what makes food, and life for that matter, more interesting.

How fortunate we are to live in a state that produces so many delicious products. We encourage you to visit your local Farmers Markets and roadside stands to support our farmers. Alongside the recipes contained in this book, we have listed a few of the state's festivals that celebrate these products, but space would not allow us to list all. When you have the opportunity, attend as many of these festivals as you can. You'll be glad you did.

We thought a lot about the artwork we would feature in this book and we looked at many fabulous pieces from extremely talented South Carolina artists. But the more we contemplated the message we wanted to convey in this book, nothing beat the real thing. We could not have presented the state in a more breathtaking way than through the majesty of Jay Vaughan and Sam Holland's photography.

We hope this book will make you appreciate how fortunate you are to live in this wonderful state and if you are visiting, make you want to come back time and time again.

Because … South Carolina at its best - NOTHING COULD BE FINER!

My Favorite Recipes

RECIPE	PAGE NUMBER

TABLE OF CONTENTS

MAGNOLIAS	Charleston	*Chef Donald Barickman*
PENINSULA GRILL	Charleston	*Chef Robert Carter*
CHARLESTON GRILL	Charleston	*Chef Bob Waggoner*
THE DINING ROOM AT WOODLANDS RESORT & INN	Summerville	*Chef Tarver King*
MICHAEL ANTHONY'S	Hilton Head Island	*Chef Michael Cirafesi*
BLUE MARLIN/FOXFIRE GRILL	Columbia	*Chef Brian Dukes*
33 LIBERTY	Greenville	*Chefs John & Amy Malik*
DEVEREAUX'S	Greenville	*Chef Steven Greene*
RESTAURANT O	Greenville	*Chef Rodney Freidank*
SOBY'S NEW SOUTH CUISINE	Greenville	*Chef Shaun Garcia*

14

Appetizers & Beverages

Appetizers & Beverages

The South Carolina Governor's Mansion in Columbia, SC

Orange Nuts

MAKES 4 CUPS

My sister-in-law, Betty Crick, gave me this recipe a few years ago. I love making the nuts at Christmas to have for guests or to place in festive containers and give as gifts. This recipe is very different from most party nut recipes and is so delicious!

4	oranges	½	cup milk
2	cups sugar	1	quart pecan halves

Cut oranges in half and remove pulp. Save pulp for another use such as ambrosia. Cover orange halves with water. Bring to boil. Cook 45 to 60 minutes or until tender. Remove from heat, drain and cool. Scrape all of white pith out. Slice peel into thin slivers. Combine sugar, milk and orange slivers. Bring to boil. Cook until mixture reaches soft ball stage on candy thermometer. Place nuts in large bowl. Pour on sugar mixture and quickly toss to evenly coat. Pour nuts onto a baking sheet and separate. Cool completely. Store in airtight container.

Vickie Skelton
(Representative B.R. Skelton)

Our State Bird is the Carolina Wren. The Mockingbird had that official honor until it was replaced. Perhaps it was the Wren's sweet song or its small size that won over the legislators, but in 1948, the 1939 Act, which designated the Mockingbird, was repealed and the Wren was made the Official State Bird.

Rosemary Cashews

MAKES 4 CUPS

3	tablespoons butter	½	teaspoon cayenne pepper
1½	tablespoons dried rosemary	4	cups roasted unsalted cashews
3	teaspoons salt		

Preheat oven to 350 degrees. Melt butter in a large saucepan. Remove from heat. Add rosemary, salt and cayenne. Stir in cashews, tossing to coat well. Spread nuts on a baking sheet. Bake for 10 minutes, stirring occasionally. Serve warm.

Cookbook Committee

South Carolinians love pecans. The City of Florence honors this delicious nut at their annual Pecan Festival held in November.

Hot and Spicy Pecans

MAKES 3 CUPS

3	tablespoons unsalted butter	½	teaspoon freshly ground black pepper
1	teaspoon chili powder	3	cups whole pecans
1	teaspoon salt		

Preheat oven to 350 degrees. Melt butter in a large skillet over medium heat. Stir in chili powder, salt and pepper. Mix well. Remove from heat. Stir in pecans, tossing to coat well. Spread nuts on a baking sheet. Bake for about 8 to 10 minutes or until just browned. Cool. Pecans can be made 2 days ahead and stored in an airtight container.

Cookbook Committee

Almond Brandy Mold

Great for bridal luncheons and afternoon teas!

SERVES 8-10

½ cup golden raisins

¼ cup brandy

1 envelope unflavored gelatin

¼ cup cold water

12 ounces cream cheese, softened

½ cup butter, softened

½ cup sugar

½ cup sour cream

Zest of 2 lemons

1 cup slivered almonds

Frosted grapes for garnish

Ginger or lemon cookies

Place raisins in a small container and pour brandy over to cover. Soak for at least 30 minutes. Drain well. In a small bowl, sprinkle gelatin over cold water and set aside for several minutes to dissolve. Beat cream cheese, butter, sugar and sour cream until smooth. Add gelatin, lemon zest, almonds and raisins to creamed mixture. Mix well. Pour mixture into a well-greased 1-quart ring mold. Refrigerate for several hours. When ready to serve, invert mold onto a serving plate. Place frosted grapes in the center. Small champagne grapes look especially nice. Serve with ginger or lemon thin cookies.

Katherine Battle
(Representative James A. Battle, Jr.)

Summerville has been called the "Flower Town in the Pines." Tourists flock to the town in spring to view the millions of beautiful blooms - especially the azaleas - in Azalea Park.

Boiled Peanuts

MAKES 8 CUPS

3	pounds (about 8 cups) fresh green peanuts in the shell	3	tablespoons salt
		3	quarts water

Combine peanuts, salt and water in a large stockpot. Simmer peanuts uncovered for 1 to 2 hours or to desired consistency. Softer peanuts require a longer cooking time. The saltiness is determined by how long peanuts sit in water. Sample peanuts until reach desired saltiness.

Senator Catherine C. Ceips

In 2006, the South Carolina General Assembly designated boiled peanuts to be the Official State Snack. Boiled peanuts can be found in stores, in roadside stands all across South Carolina and at most sporting events.

Baked Brie in Puff Pastry

SERVES 8

1	(8 ounce) wheel Brie cheese	½	(17 ounce) package frozen puff pastry, thawed
3	tablespoons apricot or peach preserves	1	egg white
			Assorted crackers

Preheat oven to 350 degrees. Slice Brie wheel in half. Spread preserves on the cut side of one half. Place second cheese half on top. Wrap Brie with one puff pastry sheet. Place seam side down on a lightly greased baking sheet. Brush puff pastry with the egg white. Bake for 30 minutes or until pastry is golden browned. Serve immediately with crackers.

Debbie DeMint
(US Senator Jim DeMint)

Bruschetta with Tomatoes and Basil

Bruschetta is usually eaten as an antipasto, but is also good as an accompaniment to salads.

SERVES 8

BRUSCHETTA

1	loaf good quality crusty bread, cut into ¼ inch slices		Extra virgin olive oil
		6	garlic cloves, halved

Preheat broiler. Place bread slices on a baking sheet and drizzle with oil. Toast until lightly browned. Rub with garlic.

TOPPING

3	fresh ripe tomatoes, finely chopped	2	tablespoons extra virgin olive oil
1	garlic clove, pressed		Salt and pepper to taste
2	teaspoons minced fresh basil		Freshly grated Parmesan cheese

In a medium bowl, combine tomatoes, garlic, basil, oil, salt and pepper. Place a spoonful of topping on toasts. Sprinkle with Parmesan cheese.

Marie Land
(Senator John C. Land, III)

In 1775, Colonel William Moultrie was asked to design a flag for the South Carolina troops. He chose the uniform color of blue and added a crescent to represent the silver emblem worn on their caps. Later in 1861, this flag was adopted as the state flag with the addition of the palmetto tree to honor Moultrie's defense of the palmetto log fort at Sullivan's Island against British forces.

South Carolina has not one, but two State songs. "Carolina" is a poem by Henry Timrod, which was set to music by Anne Custis Burgess and adopted by the General Assembly as the Official State Song in 1911. In 1984, "South Carolina on My Mind" by Hank Martin and Buzz Arledge was also made an Official State Song.

Bruschetta with Apple and Goat Cheese

SERVES 16

¼ cup goat cheese, softened

¾ teaspoon minced fresh thyme or ¼ teaspoon dried thyme

¼ teaspoon freshly ground pepper

8 (¾ inch thick) slices firm crusty bread

8 thin slices prosciutto (about ¼ pound)

1 Fuji apple, cored and very thinly sliced

Preheat broiler. Combine goat cheese, thyme and pepper. Set aside. Place bread on baking sheet. Broil about 6 inches from heat until lightly toasted. Loosely pleat prosciutto onto bread. Cut each bread slice in half. Place apples over prosciutto. Spread cheese mixture over apples. Broil until cheese softens. May serve as first course or pass as hors d'oeuvre.

Representative Joan B. Brady

Pimiento Cheese Spread

Great spread for sandwiches or serve as a party dip with crackers.

MAKES ABOUT 4 CUPS

1½ cups mayonnaise

2 (4 ounce) jars diced pimiento, drained

1 teaspoon Worcestershire sauce

¼ teaspoon cayenne pepper

2 (8 ounce) packages shredded sharp Cheddar cheese

Blend mayonnaise, pimiento, Worcestershire sauce and cayenne. Stir in cheese until well blended. Refrigerate until ready to serve.

Sandra Sandifer
(Representative William E. Sandifer, III)

Hudson's Cheese Ball

MAKES THREE 1 POUND BALLS

1	(32 ounce) package processed cheese loaf	1	teaspoon Worcestershire sauce
3	(3 ounce) packages cream cheese, softened	2	teaspoons cayenne pepper
½	pound pecans, finely chopped		Paprika
1	garlic clove, minced		Assorted crackers

Combine cheese loaf, cream cheese, pecans, garlic, Worcestershire sauce, and cayenne. Shape mixture into 3 balls, approximately 1 pound each. Roll balls in paprika to coat. Cover and refrigerate until firm. May freeze balls and thaw in refrigerator. The longer balls are frozen the spicier balls will be. Serve with crackers.

Ginny Hammond
(Secretary Of State Mark Hammond)

Favorite Beer Cheese

MAKES 1½ CUPS

1	(8 ounce) package shredded sharp Cheddar cheese	1	garlic clove, crushed
		⅛	teaspoon salt
1	(3 ounce) package cream cheese, softened	¼	teaspoon Tabasco sauce
		⅓	cup beer
2	tablespoons minced parsley		Assorted crackers or pita wedges

Beat Cheddar cheese, cream cheese, parsley, garlic, salt and Tabasco. Add just enough beer to reach a spreading consistency. Cover and refrigerate for several hours. Remove about 30 minutes before serving. Serve with crackers or pita wedges.

Kelly Talley
(Representative Scott F. Talley)

The SC Governor's Mansion was originally built as officers' quarters for a military academy. It has been the governor's official residence since 1879. The 9-acre complex includes the Governor's Mansion built in 1856, the Lace House built in 1855 and the Caldwell-Boylston House built in 1830.

21

Blue Granite was adopted as the State Stone in 1969.

The first Yoshino cherry trees were planted in Edisto Memorial Gardens in Orangeburg to honor Palmetto Cabinet member Mrs. Marshall (Margaret) William's birthday. She has since raised the money to add trees to the Gardens. There are now approximately 90 large trees. They bloom from mid-March to April and attract attention to rival that of Washington, D.C.

Old-Fashioned Cheese Ring

SERVES 10 TO 12

1	pound sharp Cheddar cheese, grated	⅛	teaspoon garlic salt
1	cup chopped pecans	1	(20 ounce) jar strawberry jelly
¾	cup mayonnaise		Assorted crackers
1	medium onion, grated		

Combine Cheddar cheese, pecans, mayonnaise, onion and garlic salt until well blended. Refrigerate for 1 hour. Shape cheese mixture into a ring on a serving platter. Spoon jelly into center. Serve with crackers.

Kelly Talley
(Representative Scott F. Talley)

E.V. Leventis
(Senator Phil P. Leventis)

Chunky Vegetable Spread

MAKES ABOUT 3 CUPS

2	cucumbers, grated	1	envelope unflavored gelatin
1	small onion, grated	¼	cup cold water
1	small bell pepper, finely chopped	¼	cup boiling water
2	tomatoes, seeded and chopped	2	cups mayonnaise
			Assorted party breads

Drain vegetables in a colander. Dissolve gelatin in cold water. Add boiling water to dissolved gelatin. Stir in vegetables and mayonnaise. Cover and refrigerate overnight. Spread on bread of your choice.

David Neilson
(Representative Denny W. Neilson)

Cheese Buttons

MAKES 110 BUTTONS

2 cups all-purpose flour

2 cups crisp rice cereal

1 cup butter or margarine, softened

1 (8 ounce) package grated sharp Cheddar cheese

¼ teaspoon cayenne pepper

Salt to taste

Preheat oven to 350 degrees. Combine flour, cereal, butter, Cheddar cheese, cayenne and salt until well blended. Shape into small marble-sized balls. Place 1 inch apart on a lightly greased baking sheet. Gently press down on tops to flatten. Bake 15 minutes or until lightly browned.

Sue Kirsh
(Representative Herb Kirsh)

Reba Stille
(Former Representative Harry Stille)

David Neilson
(Representative Denny W. Neilson)

It was made official in 1939 that the palmetto tree should be the State Tree. The honor was earned when the spongy tree held up against the cannonballs from the British troops at the fort on Sullivan's Island.

23

Parmesan Toasts

This is a very easy appetizer to make when you are in a hurry. During the Christmas holidays, I like to use cookie cutters to make fun holiday shapes.

MAKES 24 TOASTS

¾ cup freshly grated Parmesan cheese	¼ teaspoon ground white pepper
½ cup mayonnaise	24 slices extra-thin white sandwich bread, crusts removed
2 tablespoons finely grated onion	

Preheat oven to 425 degrees. Combine Parmesan cheese, mayonnaise, onion and pepper in a small bowl. Cut bread in half or use cookie cutters to make decorative shapes. Evenly spread cheese mixture on bread. Place bread on nonstick baking sheet. Bake for about 5 minutes or until lightly browned and bubbly. Serve immediately. Great with cocktails.

Vickie Skelton
(Representative B.R. Skelton)

The 250 varieties of Japanese Iris in full bloom are the centerpiece of the Sumter Iris Festival held each Memorial Day weekend. Thousands of irises bloom across the 150-acre garden. The festivities, held since the 1940s, include pageants, tournaments and parades to go along with the food, music and crafts that attract families.

Southern Fried Green Tomatoes

These fried green tomatoes are delicious with a dollop of pimiento cheese on top.

SERVES 6

1 cup all-purpose flour	1 cup crushed saltine crackers
1 teaspoon salt	2 eggs, beaten
1 teaspoon pepper	4 tablespoons butter
5 green tomatoes, sliced ½ inch thick	4 tablespoons canola oil

In a small shallow container, stir together flour, salt and pepper. Place cracker crumbs in another shallow dish and egg in a third dish. Melt butter and oil in a large skillet on medium heat. Dip each tomato slice in egg to coat and dredge in flour mixture. Dip tomato in egg again. Dredge in cracker crumbs. Fry tomatoes until golden browned on each side. Be careful not to burn. Adjust heat and add more oil if necessary. Serve hot.

Debbie DeMint
(US Senator Jim DeMint)

Anderson Motor Company in Rock Hill was one of the most successful early automakers in this country. Between 1915 and 1924, over 6,000 vehicles were made. One of those vehicles is on display in the SC State Museum in Columbia.

25

Cheesy Artichoke Squares

MAKES 60 SMALL SQUARES

4	eggs, slightly beaten	½	teaspoon salt
1	(8 ounce) package shredded Cheddar cheese	½	teaspoon dried oregano
¼	cup dry bread crumbs	½	teaspoon garlic powder
1	(14 ounce) can artichoke hearts, drained and finely chopped	½	teaspoon dried basil
		1-2	dashes Tabasco sauce
		1	tablespoon finely chopped onion

Preheat oven to 325 degrees. Combine eggs, Cheddar cheese, bread crumbs, artichoke, salt, oregano, garlic powder, basil, Tabasco and onion. Pour mixture into a greased 11x8x2-inch baking dish. Bake for 30 minutes. Cut into squares. Serve hot or at room temperature.

Iris Campbell
(The late former Governor Carroll A. Campbell, Jr.)

New Mexico Salsa

SERVES 8

1	(28 ounce) can whole tomatoes		Dash of crushed red pepper
⅓	cup chopped onion		Salt and pepper to taste
1	garlic clove, chopped	¼	cup chopped fresh cilantro
¼	cup chopped green chilies		Tortilla chips

Combine tomato, onion, garlic, green chiles, red pepper, salt and pepper in a food processor. Pulse until all ingredients are chunky but partially smooth. Pour into a serving bowl. Stir in cilantro. Serve with tortilla chips.

Marie Land
(Senator John C. Land, III)

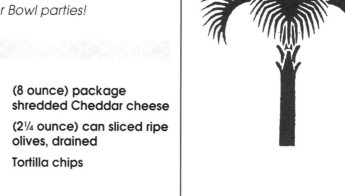

Mexican Dip

Great for tailgating or those Super Bowl parties!

SERVES 8-10

1 (8 ounce) package cream cheese, softened	1 (8 ounce) package shredded Cheddar cheese
1 (10 ounce) can chili, no beans	1 (2¼ ounce) can sliced ripe olives, drained
1 (16 ounce) jar of salsa, hot or mild	Tortilla chips

Preheat oven to 350 degrees. Spread cream cheese on bottom of 10-inch deep dish pie plate. Spoon chili over cream cheese. Layer with salsa and Cheddar cheese. Top with olives. Bake for 30 minutes. Serve with tortilla chips.

Sharon Herdklotz
(Former Representative Richard Herdklotz)

Baked Pimiento Cheese Dip

SERVES 6-8

1¼ cups mayonnaise	¼ teaspoon Tabasco sauce
1 (4 ounce) jar diced pimiento	1 (8 ounce) package shredded extra sharp Cheddar cheese
1 teaspoon seasoning blend or salt and pepper to taste	1 (8 ounce) package shredded sharp Cheddar cheese
2 teaspoons finely grated onion	Crackers or bread sticks

Preheat oven to 350 degrees. Mix mayonnaise, pimiento, seasoning, onion, Tabasco and cheeses together. Spoon mixture into a greased 11x8x2-inch baking dish. Bake for 20 minutes or until bubbly and golden browned. Serve with crackers or bread sticks.

Jean Littlejohn
(Representative Lanny F. Littlejohn)

South Carolina is one of three states where good quality amethyst stones are found. That's why it was made the State Gem Stone in 1969. An early stone from South Carolina is in the Smithsonian collection.

27

Southern Bell introduced phone service to Charleston in 1879 and to Columbia in 1880.

Pirates Blackbeard, Stede Bonnet, and Mary Ann Townsend are all said to have hidden their treasure in the marshes along the South Carolina coast.

Feta Cheese Spread

SERVES 6-8

1	(8 ounce) container soft cream cheese	7	ounces crumbled feta cheese
½	cup plain yogurt	½	cup sun-dried tomatoes in oil, drained
3	tablespoons toasted pine nuts		Crackers or crudités
2	tablespoons freshly chopped basil		

Combine cream cheese, yogurt, pine nuts and basil in a food processor. Pulse until smooth. Add feta cheese and tomato. Pulse until well mixed but still chunky. Serve with favorite crackers or crudités.

Emilie Theodore
(Former Lt. Governor Nick Theodore)

Hearts of Palm Spread

MAKES ABOUT 2 CUPS

1	(14 ounce) can hearts of palm, drained and chopped	½	cup grated Parmesan cheese
1	cup (4 ounces) shredded mozzarella cheese	¼	cup sour cream
¾	cup mayonnaise	2	tablespoons minced green onions
			Crackers

Preheat oven to 350 degrees. Combine hearts of palm, mozzarella cheese, mayonnaise, Parmesan cheese, sour cream and green onions. Spoon mixture into a greased 9-inch quiche pan. Bake for 20 minutes or until bubbly. Serve hot with crackers.

Lynn Owens
(Representative Phillip D. Owens)

Ole' Dip

I make homemade guacamole for this dip, but you can certainly use store bought. Great hit with the guys, especially if there is a sporting event involved.

SERVES 10-12

GUACAMOLE (MAKES ABOUT 2 CUPS)

4	ripe Haas avocados	1	large garlic clove, minced
3	tablespoons fresh lemon juice	1	teaspoon kosher salt
6	dashes Tabasco sauce	½	teaspoon freshly ground pepper
¼	cup finely chopped Vidalia onion		

Cut avocados in half and remove pit. Score inside of avocado and scoop out pulp into a medium-sized bowl. Mash pulp with a fork or a potato masher. Add lemon juice, Tabasco, onion, garlic, salt and pepper. Mix well. Adjust salt and pepper. If not serving right away, press plastic wrap against surface of guacamole. Refrigerate. Plastic wrap will keep guacamole from turning dark.

ASSEMBLE

2	(16 ounce) cans refried beans	2	large fresh tomatoes, seeded and chopped
2	cups guacamole	1	(12 ounce) jar sliced jalapeños (optional)
1	(1 ounce) package taco seasoning mix	1	cup finely grated Cheddar cheese
2	cups sour cream	1	cup finely grated Monterey Jack cheese
1	(3.8 ounce) can sliced ripe olives, drained		Tortilla chips
4	green onions, sliced		

Spread beans on bottom of a 9-inch pie plate or in center of a serving platter. Top with guacamole. Blend taco seasoning and sour cream. Spread over guacamole. Sprinkle with olives, green onions and tomatoes. Top with jalapeños. Sprinkle with Cheddar and Monterey Jack cheeses. Serve with tortilla chips.

The first treaty between states took place at DeWitt's Corner between Georgia, South Carolina and the Cherokee Indians. The counties of Oconee, Pickens, Anderson, and Greenville were obtained through the treaty.

Vickie Skelton
(Representative B.R. Skelton)

Southern Onion Dip

MAKES ABOUT 3 CUPS

¼ cup canola oil	½ cup cream cheese, softened
¼ cup butter	½ cup mayonnaise
2 medium Vidalia onions, thinly sliced	½ cup sour cream
1 teaspoon kosher salt	Dash of Tabasco sauce
½ teaspoon freshly ground pepper	Salt and pepper to taste
¼ teaspoon cayenne pepper	Chopped chives for garnish
1 garlic clove, minced	Assorted crackers, chips or crudités

Horry County (pronounced "O-ree") was named after Peter Horry, a French Huguenot planter, who was born in the mid-1700s in South Carolina. He served in the South Carolina militia during the Revolutionary War.

Heat oil and butter in a large heavy skillet over medium high heat. Add onion, salt, pepper and cayenne. Sauté for about 7-8 minutes. Do not burn. Add garlic. Reduce heat and cook for 15-20 minutes longer, stirring occasionally. Combine cream cheese, mayonnaise, sour cream and Tabasco in food processor. Pulse until well blended. Add onion mixture and pulse about 5-6 times. Add salt and pepper. Spoon into a serving bowl and refrigerate. Bring to room temperature about 1 hour before serving. Scatter top with chives. May serve with crackers, chips or crudités.

Cookbook Committee

Black Bean and Feta Dip

SERVES 10-12

2	(15 ounce) cans black beans, drained	1	sweet red or bell pepper, finely chopped
1	(15¼ ounce) can whole kernel corn, drained	1	(6 ounce) package feta cheese, crumbled
1	small onion, finely chopped	1	(16 ounce) bottle Italian dressing
			Tortilla chips

Mix black beans, corn, onion, pepper, feta cheese and dressing together. Refrigerate until ready to serve. Serve with tortilla chips

Robin Stilwell
(Former Representative Sam Stilwell)

Red Pepper Hummus

Easy and stores in the refrigerator for a week.

MAKES 2 CUPS

⅓	cup tahini (sesame paste)	2	roasted red peppers, coarsely chopped
2	large garlic cloves, minced	6	dashes of Tabasco sauce
1	(19 ounce) can chickpeas, drained and reserve 2 tablespoons liquid	1½	teaspoons kosher salt
¼	cup fresh lemon juice (about 2 lemons)		Pita wedges

Combine tahini, garlic, chickpeas, lemon juice, peppers, Tabasco and salt in food processor. Pulse until puréed. Adjust seasonings and place in a small serving bowl. Refrigerate until ready to serve. Drizzle a little olive oil over top and serve with pita wedges.

Vickie Skelton
(Representative B.R. Skelton)

Man's best friend, or should we say in this case, hunter's best friend, is the Boykin Spaniel. This dog was adopted as the Official State Dog in 1985. It was originally bred for hunting, but also makes a wonderful pet.

31

Clemson Blue Cheese Dip

I especially love Keebler Toasted buttercrisp crackers with this dip. Great for tailgating! Go TIGERS!

MAKES 2 CUPS

1 (8 ounce) package cream cheese, softened	4 ounces Clemson Blue cheese, crumbled
4 ounces feta cheese, crumbled	1 large garlic clove, minced
	Crackers or crudités

Combine cream cheese, feta cheese, Blue cheese and garlic in food processor. Process until smooth. Transfer to small serving bowl. Refrigerate until ready to serve. Bring to room temperature about 1 hour before serving. Serve with crudités or crackers. Best prepared a day in advance.

Vickie Skelton
(Representative B.R. Skelton)

Stumphouse Mountain Tunnel located in northern Oconee County was started in the 1850's as part of a railroad to connect South Carolina to the Midwest. Because of the Civil War, the work on the tunnel was stopped and it was never finished. Clemson University purchased the tunnel in the 1950's and used it for several years for its blue cheese curing process. The tunnel is now listed in the National Register of Historic Places.

Creamy Corn Dip

SERVES 6-8

1   (16 ounce) package frozen corn (any variety you prefer), thawed

1   (8 ounce) package cream cheese, softened

½   cup butter or margarine, softened

1   (12 ounce) jar chopped jalapeño slices, drained (or amount you prefer for degree of heat)

Corn chips

Preheat oven to 275 degrees. Combine corn, cream cheese, butter and jalapeño. Spoon mixture into a pie plate or small casserole dish. Bake for 20-25 minutes. Stir and serve with corn chips.

Ginger Huggins
(Representative Chip Huggins)

Mary Margaret Bannister
(Representative Bruce W. Bannister)

The State Butterfly is the Tiger Swallowtail. Its image was first captured in a painting done in 1587 by John White, a member of Sir Walter Raleigh's expedition. This butterfly is a friend to many a gardener.

Hot Spinach Dip

SERVES 6-8

2	teaspoons extra virgin olive oil	¼	teaspoon Worcestershire sauce
1	medium onion, diced	4	dashes Tabasco sauce
1	large garlic clove, minced	¼	cup plus 1 cup shredded part-skim mozzarella cheese, divided
2	(10 ounce) packages frozen chopped spinach, cooked and well drained		Salt and pepper to taste
½	cup milk		Crackers or toast points
1	(8 ounce) package cream cheese		

Preheat oven to 425 degrees. Sauté onion and garlic in oil until translucent. Drain spinach well. I squeeze in a dish towel to make sure all water is removed from the spinach. Place spinach in small bowl and add onion mixture. Heat milk in saucepan on low heat until just boiling. Stir in cream cheese until melted. Remove from heat. Add spinach mixture, Worcestershire sauce, Tabasco and ¼ cup of mozzarella cheese. Add salt and pepper. Pour mixture into a greased casserole dish. Top with the remaining 1 cup mozzarella cheese. Bake for 20-25 minutes until bubbly and cheese is golden browned. Serve with crackers or toast points.

Vickie Skelton
(Representative B. R. Skelton)

Horry County is the largest county in South Carolina at 1,134 square miles.

The last full weekend of April brings the Festival of Roses covering 150 acres at Edisto Memorial Gardens. Join the 40,000 visitors who come to see the 4,000 rose plants in every variety and color at their peak. They continue to bloom until the first frost. The garden is a haven for rose lovers.

Caviar Egg Mold

SERVES 6

½	cup plus ½ cup butter, divided
1	cup chopped green onions
6	hard-cooked eggs, finely chopped
	Salt and black pepper to taste
	Dash of cayenne pepper
2	cups sour cream
	Chopped parsley for garnish
1	(1¾ ounce) jar of black caviar
	Cracker or toast points

Melt ½ cup butter in medium skillet over medium-high heat. Sauté green onions until tender. Combine onions with eggs, remaining ½ cup softened butter, salt, pepper and cayenne. Pour mixture into a small round bowl and lightly pack down. Refrigerate until firm. Unmold onto serving dish. Spread sour cream over top. Sprinkle parsley around dish. Make a well with back of a tablespoon in top of the mold. Spoon caviar in well. Serve with crackers or toast points.

Marie Land
(Senator John C. Land, III)

The Pavilion at Myrtle Beach, an 11-acre amusement park, was a very popular tourist destination for many years. Many young people learned to shag in the Pavilion building which went through several reincarnations through the years due to fires. In 1948, a final structure was built by owners, Burroughs & Chapin, and endured until the park was closed and demolished in 2006. The "Last Ride" event to mark the closing was held on September 30, 2006.

Pawleys Deviled Crab

Served in crab shells, this makes a wonderful first course for a dinner party.

SERVES 4-6

1	pound crabmeat	2	teaspoons grated onion
1	cup mayonnaise		Dash of Tabasco sauce
1	tablespoon Worcestershire sauce	1	tablespoon butter, cut into pieces
2	eggs, beaten	½	cup fresh bread crumbs

Preheat oven to 350 degrees. Combine crabmeat, mayonnaise, Worcestershire sauce, eggs, onion and Tabasco. Spoon mixture into greased crab shells or baking dish. Sprinkle with bread crumbs and dot with butter. Bake for 15-20 minutes.

Representative Vida O. Miller

North and South Carolina were at one time one. "Carolina" was granted by Charles II of England to eight Lords Proprietors. The states officially parted ways in 1729.

E.V.'s Easy Crab Dip

SERVES 6-8

1	(8 ounce) package cream cheese, softened	½	teaspoon cream style horseradish
1	tablespoon milk	¼	teaspoon salt
1	(8 ounce) can crabmeat, flaked		Dash of pepper
2	tablespoons finely chopped onion		Crackers or toast points

Preheat oven to 350 degrees. Combine cream cheese, milk, crabmeat, onion, horseradish, salt and pepper. Spoon mixture into a small baking dish. Bake for 15 minutes or until bubbly. Serve with crackers or toast points.

E.V. Leventis
(Senator Phil P. Leventis)

Little River Crab Dip

SERVES 12-14

6	tablespoons unsalted butter	1½	cups plus ½ cup grated Swiss cheese, divided
½	cup finely chopped green onions	1	tablespoon prepared horseradish
2	tablespoons all-purpose flour	2	teaspoons Worcestershire sauce
2	cups bottled clam juice	½	teaspoon cayenne pepper
1	cup half-and-half	1	pound jumbo lump crabmeat
1	(8 ounce) package cream cheese, softened		Crackers

Preheat oven to 350 degrees. Melt butter in a large saucepan. Add green onions and sauté for about 2 minutes over medium heat. Stir in flour and cook for about 1 minute. Gradually whisk in the clam juice. Bring to boil over medium heat and continue to boil until thickened and bubbly. Whisk in half-and-half and stir constantly. Reduce to low heat. Add cream cheese and 1½ cups Swiss cheese. Stir in horseradish, Worcestershire sauce and cayenne. Stir until cheese melts. Remove from heat. Fold in crabmeat. Spoon mixture into small baking dish. Sprinkle remaining ½ cup Swiss cheese on top. Bake for about 10 to 15 minutes or until bubbly and cheese is slightly browned. Serve hot with crackers.

Cookbook Committee

Little River, located north of Myrtle Beach near the state line, celebrates both blue crab and shrimp harvests with parties in May for delicious blue crabs and in October for their Shrimp and Jazz Festival. Seafood and jazz: Who can beat that?

Zesty Marinated Shrimp

SERVES 6-8

1¼ cups canola oil

¾ cup white wine vinegar

2½ tablespoons capers

2½ teaspoons celery seeds

1½ teaspoons salt

Dash of Tabasco sauce

5-6 bay leaves

1 small Vidalia onion, thinly sliced

2½ pounds medium shrimp, cooked, peeled and deveined, tails on

Whisk together oil, vinegar, capers, celery seeds, salt and Tabasco. Add bay leaves, onion and shrimp. Toss to mix well. Cover and refrigerate overnight. When ready to serve, remove bay leaves, drain and place in serving dish.

Cookbook Committee

Shrimping is important to the economy of South Carolina and is a key ingredient in many lowcountry dishes. You will find shrimp boats docked along the coast waiting for their next harvest. Shrimp festivals are held in McClellanville in May, Yemassee in September and Beaufort in October.

Lowcountry Shrimp Ball

SERVES 10

2 cups shrimp, cooked and peeled

½ cup butter, softened

1 (8 ounce) package cream cheese, softened

3 tablespoons mayonnaise

1 tablespoon lemon juice

3 tablespoons garlic powder

¼ cup chopped parsley

2 teaspoons Tabasco sauce

½ teaspoon cayenne pepper

1 teaspoon Worcestershire sauce

Crackers or toast points

Mince shrimp in food processor. Add butter, cream cheese, mayonnaise, lemon juice, garlic powder, parsley, Tabasco, cayenne and Worcestershire sauce. Pulse until blended. Shape mixture into ball. Refrigerate until firm. Serve with crackers or toast points.

Marie Land
(Senator John C. Land, III)

Shrimp Aspic

SERVES 8-10 AS A SALAD

OR CAN BE SERVED AS AN APPETIZER

2 cups South Carolina creek shrimp	2 (3 ounce) packages cream cheese, softened
1 (10¾ ounce) can tomato soup	1 cup finely chopped celery
1 (10¾ ounce) can water	1 cup finely chopped bell pepper
2 packages unflavored gelatin	1 small onion, minced
½ cup cold water	1 cup chopped pecans
	Assorted crackers

Boil, clean and devein shrimp. May use larger shrimp and cut into smaller pieces. Bring soup and water to boil. Dissolve gelatin in cold water. When soup boils, stir in cream cheese until melted. Remove from heat. Add gelatin, shrimp, celery, pepper, onion and nuts. Refrigerate until set. May serve as a salad or an appetizer with crackers.

Josephine R. McNair
(Former Governor Robert E. McNair)

Robert E. McNair was a State Representative and Lieutenant Governor. He served as Governor from 1965-1971.

Camellias and azaleas were brought to this country from China. Middleton Gardens, near Charleston, is world famous for its landscaping which features these plants. Both are found in many varieties all over the state. Camellias are especially loved for the color they bring during the winter months.

Classic Shrimp Mold

SERVES 6-8

2   cups shrimp, cooked, peeled and deveined

1   (10¾ ounce) can tomato soup

2   packages unflavored gelatin

1   (8 ounce) package cream cheese, softened

½   cup minced celery

1   cup finely chopped onion

1½   cups mayonnaise

Salt and Tabasco sauce to taste

Chop cooked shrimp into small pieces. Heat soup over medium high heat. Remove ¼ of soup and add to gelatin in a small bowl. Set aside to dissolve. Stir cream cheese into remaining soup until melted. Let cool. Add gelatin mixture, celery, onion, shrimp, mayonnaise, salt and Tabasco to soup. Mix well. Pour mixture into a greased 4-cup mold. May line mold with plastic wrap to make unmolding easier. Refrigerate until firm. Unmold and serve on a plate surrounded by lettuce leaves.

Kitty Mescher
(The late Senator William C. Mescher)

E.V. Leventis
(Senator Phil P. Leventis)

The Battle of Sullivan's Island on June 28, 1776 was the first major victory for the Patriots. "Carolina Day" marks the anniversary of South Carolina's contribution to the cause of independence. South Carolinians celebrate this day with parades and other festivities.

Savory Smoked Salmon Cheesecakes

This is a delicious recipe from the chefs at the United States Ambassador's Residence in Ottawa, Canada.

SERVES 8

1 cup ricotta cheese	4 eggs
1 cup cream cheese, softened	1½ tablespoons all-purpose flour
1 cup freshly grated Parmesan cheese	2 tablespoons butter, melted
1 cup chopped smoked salmon	Salt and pepper to taste
1 cup sour cream	Chopped smoked salmon for garnish

Preheat oven to 325 degrees. Combine ricotta cheese, cream cheese, Parmesan cheese and salmon in a food processor. Blend until smooth. Add sour cream, eggs, flour, butter, salt and pepper. Process well. Divide mixture among 8 buttered and floured ½-cup size ramekins. Place ramekins in a baking pan with hot water to about half depth of the ramekins. Bake for about 30 minutes or until set like a cheesecake. Refrigerate until cooled thoroughly. May be easier to un-mold if slightly frozen. When ready to serve, unmold on a salad plate and garnish with salmon. Serve with a mixed green salad tossed with a light vinaigrette for a wonderful first course.

Chef Dino Ovcaric

Chef Dana Gosso
U.S. Ambassador's Residence
Ottawa, Canada

Submitted by Susan Wilkins
(Former House Speaker, US Ambassador David H. Wilkins)

Can-Am Days or the Canadian-American Days Festival began in 1961 in Myrtle Beach as a "warm" welcome for our Canadian visitors. The festival lasts about 9 days and includes many events to promote the Grand Strand and to show our northern neighbors our hospitality.

Swedish Meatballs

My mother was Swedish and this was one of her signature dishes. Our children love this recipe.

MAKES 48 MEATBALLS

1	egg, beaten
⅓	cup plus 1¼ cups half-and-half, divided
1	cup soft bread crumbs
⅓	cup finely chopped onion
2	tablespoons chopped parsley
¾	teaspoon salt
⅛	teaspoon plus ⅛ teaspoon ground nutmeg, divided
½	pound ground veal
½	pound lean ground beef
1	tablespoon butter or margarine
1	tablespoon all-purpose flour
1	teaspoon instant chicken bouillon granules

Preheat oven to 350 degrees. In a mixing bowl, combine egg and ⅓ cup half-and-half. Stir in bread crumbs, onion, parsley, salt and ⅛ teaspoon ground nutmeg. Add veal and beef and mix well. Shape mixture into forty-eight 1-inch meatballs. Place meatballs on a 15x10x1-inch baking sheet. Bake for about 20 minutes or until done. Remove meatballs to a paper towel lined plate. Drain well. Meanwhile, in large saucepan, melt butter. Stir in flour, granules and remaining ⅛ teaspoon ground nutmeg. Add remaining 1¼ cups half-and-half. Cook until thickened and bubbly, stirring constantly. Cook another 2 minutes. Place meatballs in sauce and stir to coat. Transfer meatballs and sauce to a serving plate or chafing dish.

Nancy Thurmond
(The late US Senator J. Strom Thurmond)

Ten former governors and five lieutenant governors hail from Edgefield County including "Pitchfork" Ben Tillman and Strom Thurmond. Is there something in the water?

Mushroom Cups

These are easy and always delicious. The mini filo cups are found in the frozen foods section. Just thaw and fill with the mushroom mixture and heat under the broiler.

MAKES 30 CUPS

2	packages frozen mini filo cups (30 total)	1	cup heavy cream
3	tablespoons minced shallots	1	tablespoon minced chives
¼	cup unsalted butter	1	tablespoon minced flat leaf parsley
1	(8 ounce) package fresh white mushrooms, finely chopped	½	teaspoon fresh lemon juice
		½	teaspoon salt
2	tablespoons all-purpose flour	⅛	teaspoon cayenne pepper
		2-3	tablespoons freshly grated Parmesan cheese

Heat filo cups according to directions on the package. Set aside. In a heavy skillet, sauté shallots in butter for 1 minute. Add mushrooms. Simmer mushrooms uncovered for about 10 minutes or until all liquid is absorbed. Remove from heat. Stir in flour. Add cream and return to heat. Bring to boil and cook 1 minute, stirring constantly or until thickened. Remove from heat. Add chives, parsley, lemon juice, salt and pepper. Divide mixture among filo cups. Top with Parmesan cheese. Broil until cheese melts. Serve hot.

Vickie Skelton
(Representative B.R. Skelton)

*It's all music to our ears...
The Official State Music is the
Spiritual which has a religious
or sacred theme. The Official
State Popular Music is Beach
Music which is associated with
the State Dance, the Shag.*

The last county organized in South Carolina was Allendale in 1919.

Goat Cheese Pinwheels

MAKES 48 PINWHEELS

1	(4½ ounce) can chopped black olives, well drained	4 ounces goat cheese, softened
1	(2 ounce) jar diced pimiento, well drained	6 flour tortillas
1	(8 ounce) package cream cheese, softened	1 bell pepper, finely chopped

Drain olives and pimiento well on a paper towel. Combine cream cheese and goat cheese until well blended. Spread about ¼ cup cheese mixture on each tortilla. Sprinkle evenly with about 1 tablespoon each of olives, pimiento and pepper. Roll up tortillas jelly-roll fashion. Place tortillas in a single layer in an airtight container. Place a damp paper towel over tortillas and cover. Refrigerate until ready to serve. Do not make more than one day ahead. Cut about ½-1-inch off ends. Slice each roll into 8 pieces.

Cookbook Committee

Proof that South Carolinians will celebrate anything and everything comes with the Governor's Annual Frog Jump Festival in Springfield held on the Saturday before Easter. The winner of this event travels to California for the Calaveras County Frog Jump—made famous by Mark Twain.

Carolina Caviar

This recipe is also delicious with grilled steak or chicken served as a salsa.

SERVES 8-10

3	**(15 ounce) cans black-eyed peas, drained and rinsed**
1	**cup finely chopped bell pepper, may use sweet red or yellow or a mixture**
1	**cup finely chopped Vidalia onion**
1	**(4 ounce) jar diced pimiento, drained**
½	**cup finely chopped banana pepper rings (from jar, use mild or hot)**

1	**ripe tomato, seeded and finely chopped**
1	**garlic clove, minced**
⅓	**cup red wine vinegar**
⅔	**cup extra virgin olive oil**
1	**tablespoon Dijon mustard**
	Salt to taste
	Freshly ground black pepper to taste
3	**dashes of Tabasco sauce or to taste**
	Corn or tortilla chips

Combine peas, pepper, onion, pimiento and banana pepper in a large bowl. Add tomato and garlic. Mix well. Set aside. In a small bowl, whisk together vinegar, oil and mustard. Add salt, pepper and Tabasco sauce. Pour vinaigrette over pea mixture and toss well. Serve with corn or tortilla chips.

Cookbook Committee

South Carolina was first known as the Iodine state, but was later changed to the Palmetto state. The earlier motto was derived from a public relations campaign to promote the state's high levels of iodine in its soil and therefore, the health benefits of South Carolina products.

Hot Spiced Cider

SERVES 8

1   (62 ounce) bottle of apple juice (you can substitute cranberry juice or ½ cranberry and ½ apple juice)

1   cup red hot candies

Heat juice and candy in heavy saucepan stirring until candy is melted. Transfer to carafe or coffee maker and serve warm. Leftovers can be refrigerated and reheated.

Marie Land
(Senator John C. Land, III)

Tea has been an important crop for South Carolina. It was given the distinction of State Hospitality Beverage in 1995. Tea was grown around 1799 at Middleton Place outside of Charleston. Today, descendants of those same plants are being grown at the Charleston Tea Plantation near Charleston.

Warming Chai Tea

SERVES 6

6   black tea bags

3   whole cloves

Dash of ground cardamom

Dash of ground cinnamon

6   cups boiling water

1   cup warm milk

Combine tea bags, cloves, cardamom, cinnamon and water in a saucepan. Steep for 5 minutes. Remove tea bags. Stir in milk. Pour into mugs and serve.

Marie Land
(Senator John C. Land, III)

Holiday Wassail

SERVES 25-30

2	oranges	½	cup honey or packed brown sugar
	Whole cloves		
3	quarts apple cider or apple juice	1	teaspoon whole allspice
		2	cinnamon sticks
5	cups pineapple juice		Dash of ground nutmeg
⅓	cup fresh lemon juice		

Stud 2 oranges with cloves. Combine apple cider, pineapple juice, lemon juice and honey in a heavy saucepan. Quarter the oranges and squeeze the juice into saucepan. Combine allspice, cinnamon sticks and nutmeg. Place in a spice ball. Heat apple cider mixture. Add spice ball and orange wedges. Slowly bring to boil. Simmer for 20 minutes. Remove spice ball and oranges. Serve very hot.

Nancy Thurmond
(The late US Senator J. Strom Thurmond)

J. Strom Thurmond was a State Senator and later Governor from 1947-1951. Elected to U.S. Senate in 1954. He was the longest serving and oldest Senator at the time of his retirement:100 years old and served 48 years.

Wedding Punch

SERVES 50

3	cups sugar	3	cups pineapple juice
6	cups boiling water	1	cup fresh lemon juice
3	family size tea bags	1½	quarts ginger ale
3	cups orange juice		Mint or lemons for garnish

Combine sugar, water and tea bags. Steep for 5 minutes. Remove tea bags. Combine tea mixture with orange juice, pineapple juice and lemon juice. Pour mixture into containers to freeze. When ready to serve, thaw slightly. May need to chop mixture until slushy. Pour in ginger ale. Garnish with lemons or mint.

Ginny Hammond
(Secretary Of State Mark Hammond)

Hot Afternoon Party Punch

SERVES 12

3   (12 ounce) cans frozen lemonade, thawed and diluted according to directions

1   (2 liter) bottle ginger ale

1   cup frozen orange juice, thawed and diluted according to directions

1   quart cranberry juice cocktail

1   orange, peeled and sliced for garnish

Combine all ingredients except for orange slices in a large container and mix together. Serve chilled in tall glasses with orange slice.

David Neilson
(Representative Denny W. Neilson)

Summer Party Punch

This is an old Manning recipe used at the Taste of Clarendon.

SERVES 50 (2 GALLONS)

1   cup boiling water

1   (6 ounce) package strawberry flavored gelatin

3   cups sugar

3   cups water

9   cups cold water

1   (46 ounce) container orange juice

1   (46 ounce) container pineapple juice

¾   cup lemon juice

1   (2 liter) bottle ginger ale

In a large stockpot, stir water with strawberry gelatin until dissolved. Stir in sugar and water. Bring to boil. Add cold water. Cool and stir in orange juice, pineapple juice and lemon juice. Pour into plastic containers and freeze. Remove containers from freezer about 1-2 hours before serving. Mixture should be soft at serving time but not fully thawed. Place mixture in punch bowl and add ginger ale. It makes a slushy mixture.

Marie Land
(Senator John C. Land, III)

South Carolina has not one, but two state mottos. Animis Opibusque Parati (Prepared in mind and resources) and Dum Spiro Spero (While I breathe I hope).

48

Apple Mint Julep

SERVES 3-4

2	cups cold apple juice	2	drops mint extract
1	pint lime sherbet, slightly thawed		Mint sprigs for garnish

Combine apple juice, sherbet and extract. Beat until smooth. Pour mixture into tall glasses. Garnish with mint sprigs.

Nancy Thurmond
(The late US Senator J. Strom Thurmond)

Cot-Coction of the Day

SERVES 24

1	(46 ounce) can cold apricot nectar	2	cups rum
1	(46 ounce) can cold Red Hawaiian Punch	1	quart raspberry sherbet
		2	(28 ounce) bottles cold club soda

Combine apricot nectar, Hawaiian Punch, rum and sherbet in a large punch bowl. Just before serving, stir in soda.

Nancy Thurmond
(The late US Senator J. Strom Thurmond)

The state legislature in South Carolina is called the General Assembly. There are 46 state senators and 124 state representatives.

Sunrise Bellini

SERVES 6-8

1	(750 milliliter) bottle cold sparkling wine or champagne	2½	cups cold apricot nectar
		3	tablespoons orange liqueur

Combine wine, nectar and liqueur in glass pitcher. Pour into champagne flutes and serve.

Vickie Skelton
(Representative B.R. Skelton)

49

Big Thursday refers to the football game between the University of South Carolina and Clemson University, which used to be played each year in Columbia on the Thursday during the State Fair week. The game grew in importance and attendance from the first game on November 12, 1896 until the last game in 1959. The next year the game was moved to the last game of the season and played alternately at each school. It continues to be a big rivalry with bragging rights on the line.

Tigertini

The name of this drink is attributed to the color - bright orange! Guess which state university this drink is named for? Hint, it's located in Clemson.

SERVES 2

| ½ | cup mango peach juice (I use V-8 Splash) | 2 | tablespoons peach schnapps |
| 6 | tablespoons vodka | | Orange peel for garnish |

Combine peach juice, vodka and schnapps in a glass pitcher. Add crushed ice. Strain into martini glasses. Garnish with an orange peel.

Vickie Skelton
(Representative B.R. Skelton)

Blushing Daiquiri

SERVES 4

2	cups sliced peaches	¾	cup light rum
2	cups sliced strawberries		Ice cubes
½	(12 ounce) can frozen limeade concentrate, thawed		Whole strawberries and peach slices for garnish

Combine peaches, strawberries, limeade and rum in a blender. Add ice cubes to fill container. Blend at high speed for 1 minute or until slushy. Pour into large glasses. Garnish each with a strawberry and peach slice.

Cookbook Committee

Breakfast,
Breads & Sauces

Breakfast, Breads & Sauces

Lake Hartwell, the largest lake in the Piedmont region of South Carolina

Rosey Banana Smoothie

Great way to start a morning!

SERVES 2

2	cups ripe strawberries	2	tablespoons honey
1	ripe banana	2	whole strawberries for garnish
1	cup plain non-fat yogurt		

Combine strawberries, banana, yogurt and honey in a blender. Purée until smooth. Pour mixture into two tall glasses. Garnish with whole strawberry on rim of glass.

David Neilson
(Representative Denny W. Neilson)

Good Morning Orange Smoothie

Excellent way to get your calcium and vitamin C!

SERVES 4

	(6 ounce) can frozen orange juice	½	teaspoon vanilla
1	cup milk	10	ice cubes
1	cup water		Orange, thinly sliced for garnish
¼	cup sugar		

Combine orange juice, milk, water, sugar, vanilla and ice cubes in a blender. Purée until smooth. Pour mixture into four tall glasses. Garnish with an orange slice.

David Neilson
(Representative Denny W. Neilson)

A replica of the Liberty Bell, one of only 53 cast in France, is located on the State House grounds.

Cranberry Orange Scones

SERVES 8

2	cups all-purpose flour	¾	cup cold unsalted butter, cut into small pieces and frozen
2	tablespoons plus 2 tablespoons sugar, divided		
1	tablespoon baking powder	1½	tablespoons orange zest
		1	cup dried cranberries
½	teaspoon baking soda	⅔	cup buttermilk
¼	teaspoon salt	2	tablespoons milk

Preheat oven to 425 degrees. Combine flour, 2 tablespoons sugar, baking powder, baking soda and salt. Mix well. Add cold butter and mix with a pastry blender. Stir in orange zest and cranberries. Stir in buttermilk until just combined. Knead once or twice until forms a dough. Turn out onto a floured surface. Flatten into a circle about ½-inch thick. Cut into 8 wedges. Place 1-inch apart on a greased baking sheet. Brush milk on top. Sprinkle with remaining 2 tablespoons sugar. Bake for 10-15 minutes or until golden browned. Remove from oven and serve immediately.

Cookbook Committee

South Carolina is the 40th largest state at over 30,000 square miles, from sea level on the coast to 3,560 feet at its highest peak, Sassafras Mountain.

Overnight French Toast

My sister Amy makes this dish for overnight guests. It is always a big hit!

SERVES 8-10

1	loaf white sandwich bread, cubed	2	cups milk
2	(8 ounce) packages cream cheese, softened	⅔	cups maple syrup
12	eggs		Ground cinnamon (optional)
			Maple syrup

Preheat oven to 375 degrees. Place half of bread cubes in the bottom of greased 13x9x2-inch baking dish. Slice cream cheese into ¼-inch slices and layer over bread. Scatter remaining bread cubes over cream cheese. In a large bowl, beat eggs, milk and syrup until well blended. Pour mixture over bread. Cover and refrigerate overnight. Remove from refrigerator and sprinkle with cinnamon. Bake for 45 minutes or until done. Best served with warm syrup.

Kelly Talley
(Representative Scott F. Talley)

One of the largest nesting grounds in the United States for sea turtles is located in Cape Romain National Wildlife Refuge located just north of Charleston.

53

Belgian Waffles

These waffles are so light and delicious! Can also be served with maple syrup, fruit syrup, warm fruit compote, fruit sauce, powdered sugar, ice cream, or chocolate sauce.

SERVES 6-8

2	cups all-purpose flour	2	cups non-fat buttermilk
2	teaspoons baking powder	½	cup vegetable oil
½	teaspoon baking soda	3	egg whites
1	teaspoon salt		Chopped fresh fruit and sweetened whipped cream for garnish
1	tablespoon sugar		
2	egg yolks		

Preheat Belgian waffle maker according to manufacturers instructions. Combine flour, baking powder, baking soda, salt and sugar. In a small bowl, blend egg yolks, buttermilk and oil. Mix well. Add egg yolk mixture to dry ingredients and stir thoroughly. Beat egg whites until stiff peaks form. Fold into batter. Ladle ¾ cup batter onto waffle iron. Cook to desired degree of doneness. Serve with chopped fruit and whipped cream.

US Congressman John M. Spratt, Jr.

The Grand Strand is the 60 mile stretch of coast from Georgetown to Little River on the NC/SC state line. Myrtle Beach is at the center. It has developed into one of the most popular tourist destinations on the East Coast.

Rise and Shine Coffee Cake

This cake smells so good while it is cooking that you will want to rise and shine!

SERVES 10-12

- 3 cups plus 2 tablespoons all-purpose flour, divided
- 1 tablespoon baking powder
- 1 teaspoon salt
- 1 cup sour cream
- ½ teaspoon baking soda
- 1 cup plus ¼ cup unsalted butter, softened and divided

- 1½ cups sugar
- 3 large eggs
- 2 teaspoons vanilla
- 1 cup chopped walnuts
- ¾ cup packed light brown sugar
- 2 teaspoons ground cinnamon

Preheat oven to 350 degrees. In a small bowl, combine 3 cups flour, baking powder and salt. Set aside. In a separate bowl, blend sour cream and baking soda. Set aside. Beat 1 cup butter and sugar with an electric mixer until fluffy. Add eggs one at a time, beating well after each addition. Stir in vanilla. Add flour mixture to creamed mixture, alternately with sour cream mixture, beginning with flour. Mix just until all ingredients are well combined. In a small bowl, combine remaining 2 tablespoons flour, walnuts, brown sugar, remaining ¼ cup butter (cut into pieces) and cinnamon. Pour one-third batter into a greased and floured 9-inch tube pan. Top with one-third nut mixture. Repeat batter and nut layers two more times with top layer being walnut mixture. Bake for 50-55 minutes or until toothpick comes out clean. Cool in pan for 15 minutes. Remove from pan and cool on a wire rack.

Cookbook Committee

North of Myrtle Beach is Ocean Drive Beach where many a South Carolina teen learned to shag in the numerous clubs along the beach. It has always been a very popular destination for spring breakers.

The World Grits Festival is held each year in St. George in April. In addition to the Miss Grits beauty pageant, there are grits eating contests and other fun grits related activities.

Grits are the product of milling dried corn kernels. During the 18th and 19th centuries, grist mills played an important role in South Carolina life. Before the invention of grist mills, corn and wheat were ground by hand. With the use of water as a power source for the mills, grains could now be processed much more efficiently. This had a positive effect on the state economy.

Special Ice Cream Grits

SERVES 6-8

2	cups heavy cream	½	cup butter
1	cup water		Salt to taste
1	cup stone-ground grits		

Bring cream and water to boil over medium heat, stirring frequently. Once boiling, add grits. Reduce heat and simmer, stirring constantly for 3-5 minutes to avoid grits from collecting on bottom and until grits plump up. Cover and cook for 35-40 minutes, stirring frequently. Stir in butter until melted. Add salt. Simmer for another 10 minutes until grits are creamy. If too thick, add more water. Serve warm.

US Congressman J. Gresham Barrett

Cheese Grits Soufflé

SERVES 8

2	cups milk	¼	teaspoon cayenne pepper
2	cups half-and-half	3½	cups grated white Cheddar cheese
1	cup quick grits		
½	cup unsalted butter	6	eggs, beaten
1	teaspoon salt		

Preheat oven to 350 degrees. Heat milk and half-and-half in a large saucepan over medium heat until small bubbles form around outside. Stir in grits. Reduce to low heat and simmer about 3 minutes, stirring constantly, until thickened. Remove from heat and add butter, salt, cayenne and Cheddar cheese. Stir until cheese melts. Whisk in eggs until well blended. Pour mixture into a greased 2½-quart baking dish. Bake for 1 hour or until lightly browned. Serve immediately.

Cookbook Committee

California Egg Casserole

Great for breakfast, brunch or as a side dish.

SERVES 8-10

6	eggs, beaten	1	(12 ounce) package shredded Monterey Jack cheese
⅔	cup all-purpose flour		
1	teaspoon baking powder	½	cup butter, melted
½	teaspoon salt	2	(4 ounce) cans chopped green chilies
¼	teaspoon pepper		
2	cups small curd cottage cheese		

Preheat oven to 350 degrees. Combine eggs, flour, baking powder, salt, pepper, cottage cheese, Monterey Jack cheese and butter until well blended. Stir in chilies. Pour mixture into a greased 13x9x2-inch baking dish. Bake for 35-40 minutes. Serve hot.

Ginger Huggins
(Representative Chip Huggins)

Sausage Cheese Casserole

SERVES 12

1	(8 ounce) can refrigerated crescent rolls	4	eggs, beaten
1	pound sausage, cooked and crumbled	¾	cup milk
			Salt and pepper to taste
1	(8 ounce) package shredded mozzarella cheese		

Preheat oven to 375 degrees. Press crescent rolls on bottom of 13x9x2-inch baking dish, sealing perforations. Spread sausage over dough. Sprinkle cheese over top. Blend eggs, milk, salt and pepper. Pour mixture over cheese. Bake for 20-25 minutes or until done. Serve hot.

Former Representative Becky R. Martin

F.G. Burroughs of Conway began to buy land and clear timber in the area known as the Great Swamp. He built a railroad to ship the timber. The shoreline terminal was named New Town until Burroughs renamed it Myrtle Beach after the evergreen shrubs that grow in the area.

Ham and Cheese Muffins

MAKES 3 DOZEN MINI MUFFINS

2	cups all-purpose flour	1	cup buttermilk
1	tablespoon baking powder	¼	cup vegetable oil
½	teaspoon salt	½	pound baked ham, diced
⅛	teaspoon cayenne pepper	1	cup shredded sharp Cheddar cheese
1	egg		

Preheat oven to 400 degrees. In a large bowl, combine flour, baking powder, salt and cayenne. In a medium bowl, whisk together egg and buttermilk. Whisk in oil. Stir in ham and Cheddar cheese until well mixed. Stir egg mixture into flour mixture and mix until just combined. Drop batter by spoonful into greased mini muffin cups. Bake for about 15-20 minutes or until lightly browned.

Cookbook Committee

Robert White was the first PGA president and built the first golf course at Myrtle Beach, Pine Lakes International.

Breakfast Sausage Pizza

SERVES 8-10

1	(8 ounce) can refrigerated crescent rolls	3	eggs
1	cup frozen hash browns, thawed	½	cup milk
1	pound sausage, cooked and crumbled	1	cup grated Cheddar cheese

Preheat oven to 375 degrees. Press crescent rolls over bottom of a 10-inch pizza pan, sealing perforations and crimping edges. Spread hash browns and sausage over dough. Beat eggs and milk. Pour over sausage. Sprinkle with Cheddar cheese. Bake for 20 minutes or until done. Serve hot.

Charm Altman
(Former Representative John Graham Altman, III)

Country Breakfast Casserole

This is a Cotty/Casson family favorite that my daughter Molly got from her sister-in-law, Hella.

SERVES 8

1½ cups water

2 cups chicken broth

½ teaspoon salt

1 cup quick grits

1 (8 ounce) package shredded sharp Cheddar cheese, divided

1 pound bulk sausage, cooked and crumbled

4 eggs, lightly beaten

¾ cup milk

¼ teaspoon pepper

¼ cup butter, melted

Preheat oven to 350 degrees. Bring water and broth to boil. Stir in salt and grits. Simmer for 5 minutes. Remove from heat and add 1 cup Cheddar cheese. Stir until cheese melts. Stir in sausage, eggs, milk, pepper and butter. Pour mixture into a greased 13x9x2-inch baking dish. Sprinkle with remaining 1 cup Cheddar cheese. Bake uncovered for 45 minutes. May be made ahead and also frozen after baking.

Amelia Cotty
(Representative William F. Cotty)

Golf Digest has designated South Carolina as the top golf destination in the U.S.

The last Saturday of October brings the Fall Steeplechase to Aiken. From the very elegant Friday night dinner and dancing to the tent party, children's stick horse race, Horse Carriage parade and hat contest-there is fun for all ages.

Special Brunch Strata

SERVES 8

3 tablespoons Dijon mustard	1 pound asparagus, cut into 1-inch pieces
12 (½-inch thick) slices French bread	3 tablespoons water
2 cups cooked and diced ham	6 eggs
2 bell peppers, diced (any color you prefer)	2 cups milk
1 cup finely chopped Vidalia onion	½ teaspoon salt
1 tablespoon olive oil	¼ teaspoon pepper
	1 (8 ounce) package shredded Swiss cheese

Preheat oven to 350 degrees. Spread mustard over bread slices. Arrange slices in bottom of greased 13x9x2-inch baking dish. Sauté ham, bell pepper and onion for about 1-2 minutes in a large skillet until onions and peppers are tender and ham is slightly browned. Spread ham mixture over bread. Add water to skillet and reduce heat to low. Add asparagus and simmer for 3 minutes or until bright green. Drain and place asparagus over ham mixture. Whisk together eggs, milk, salt and pepper. Pour mixture over asparagus. Sprinkle with Swiss cheese. Casserole can be made to this point, covered and refrigerated until ready to bake, up to about 8 hours. Bake for 45 minutes or until done.

Vickie Skelton
(Representative B.R. Skelton)

Walterboro is home to the Colleton County Rice festival which boasts to have the "World's largest pot of rice." The festival takes place in April.

Carolina Shrimp Quiche

SERVES 6-8

2 cups small shrimp, cooked (or larger shrimp chopped into smaller pieces)	1 (9-inch) deep dish pie shell, unbaked
8 ounces Gruyere cheese, grated	1 cup mayonnaise
⅓ cup chopped green onions	¼ teaspoon salt
	⅛ teaspoon cayenne pepper
2 tablespoons all-purpose flour	2 eggs
	½ cup milk

Preheat oven to 350 degrees. Combine shrimp, Gruyere cheese, green onions and flour in a large bowl and toss well. Spoon mixture into pie shell. Whisk together mayonnaise, salt, cayenne, eggs and milk. Pour egg mixture over shrimp mixture. Bake for 1 hour. If top browns, cover loosely with foil.

Katherine C. Battle
(Representative James A. Battle, Jr.)

South Carolina includes more swampland than any other state except Louisiana.

Cheese Garlic Biscuits

MAKES 1 DOZEN BISCUITS

2 cups biscuit baking mix	¼ cup butter or margarine, melted
⅔ cup milk	
½ cup shredded Cheddar cheese	¼ teaspoon garlic powder

Preheat oven to 450 degrees. Combine baking mix, milk and Cheddar cheese. Beat for 30 seconds until soft dough forms. Drop dough by tablespoonfuls onto ungreased baking sheet. Bake for 8 to 10 minutes until golden browned. Blend butter and garlic powder. Remove from oven and immediately brush butter over tops of biscuits. Serve hot.

David Neilson
(Representative Denny W. Neilson)

The Marion County Fox Trot Festival held in the spring invites locals and visitors to enjoy a parade, a street dance, fireworks, car show and helicopter rides under the spread of old trees draped with Spanish moss.

Sour Cream Drop Biscuits

MAKES 1 DOZEN BISCUITS

2 cups self-rising flour	¾ cup unsalted butter, melted
1 cup sour cream	½ teaspoon salt

Preheat oven to 350 degrees. In a large bowl, sift flour. Stir in sour cream until smooth. Add butter and salt. Drop batter by spoonfuls into ungreased muffin cups filling two-thirds full. Bake for 25-30 minutes or until golden browned. Serve hot.

Cookbook Committee

Charleston boasts the Four Corners of Law at Broad and Meeting Streets. On the four corners are: City Hall representing municipal government; County Courthouse for state government; United States Courthouse for federal law; and St. Michael's Church for God's law.

Sweet Potato Biscuits

MAKES 2-2½ DOZEN BISCUITS

2-2¼ cups all-purpose flour	½ cup vegetable shortening
⅔ cup sugar	2 cups cooked, peeled, mashed sweet potatoes
2 tablespoons baking powder	¼ cup milk
1½ teaspoons salt	
½ teaspoon ground cinnamon	

Preheat oven to 450 degrees. Sift together flour, sugar, baking powder, salt and cinnamon. Make a well in center of flour mixture. Add shortening, sweet potatoes and milk. Mix well until dough forms. Add a little more flour if dough is sticky. Roll dough on a floured surface. Cut with biscuit cutter. Place on a greased and floured baking sheet. Bake for 15 minutes. Serve hot.

Kelly Talley
(Representative Scott F. Talley)

Southern Angel Biscuits

MAKES 2 DOZEN BISCUITS

3	cups plus 1 cup self-rising flour, divided
1	teaspoon salt
2	teaspoons sugar
¼	teaspoon baking soda
½	cup vegetable shortening
1¾	cups buttermilk
¼	cup unsalted butter, melted

Preheat oven to 450 degrees. Grease and flour 2 (8-inch) round baking pans. In a large bowl, combine 3 cups flour, salt, sugar and baking soda. Add shortening and work in with hands until resembles small peas. Gradually add buttermilk until mixture is very wet but still dry enough to hold together. Spread remaining 1 cup flour on a cutting board. Place ¼ cup dough on board. Sprinkle a little flour on top. Shake off excess flour and pat into a round biscuit. Do not overwork the dough. Place biscuits close together in pan. About one dozen will fit in each pan. Place close together so dough will rise into thick biscuits. Bake for 10 minutes. Brush tops with butter. Bake for 5 minutes more. Serve hot.

Cookbook Committee

Edgefield pottery is world-renowned. In the early 1800s, potters moved to the Edgefield area to set up small businesses to make dishes for early settlers. The art form has continued. The series, face vessels, is a very well known type of Edgefield pottery. Most of these pieces are sought after by museums and collectors.

Skillet Cornbread

This is a recipe from my grandmother that has been in the Bigham family for generations.

SERVES 6-8

¼	cup vegetable oil	1¾	cups buttermilk
1	cup self-rising flour	1	egg
1	cup self-rising cornmeal		

Preheat oven to 400 degrees. Heat oil in a heavy, ovenproof 9-inch skillet (cast iron works great). Pour 2 tablespoons hot oil into a large bowl. Add flour, cornmeal, buttermilk and egg. Keep remaining 2 tablespoons oil in skillet. Pour mixture into hot skillet. Bake for 30 minutes or until golden browned. Serve hot.

Kelly Talley
(Representative Scott F. Talley)

Mexican Cornbread

SERVES 8-10

1	(14 ounce) can cream-style corn	½	teaspoon baking soda
¾	cup milk	1	teaspoon salt
½	cup vegetable oil	1	(4 ounce) can chopped green chilies, mashed
2	eggs, beaten	1½	cups grated sharp Cheddar cheese, divided
1	cup plain cornmeal		

Preheat oven to 400 degrees. Combine corn, milk, oil, eggs, cornmeal, baking soda and salt. Pour half of batter into a greased 8x8x2-inch square baking dish. Top with chilies and half Cheddar cheese. Pour on remaining batter and top with remaining Cheddar cheese. Bake for 45 minutes. Serve hot.

Reba Stille
(Former Representative Harry Stille)

South Carolina was the eighth state to join the Union on May 23, 1788.

Spiced Pumpkin Bread

This pumpkin bread makes a nice gift. May also make three (8½x4-inch) loaves.

SERVES 10-12

3	cups sugar	1	teaspoon ground nutmeg
1	cup vegetable oil	1	teaspoon ground allspice
1	(16 ounce) can pumpkin	1	teaspoon ground cinnamon
3	eggs, beaten	½	teaspoon ground cloves
3	cups all-purpose flour	½	cup water
2	teaspoons baking soda	1	cup chopped nuts
2	teaspoons salt		
1	teaspoon baking powder		

Preheat oven to 350 degrees. In a large bowl, beat sugar, oil and pumpkin until well blended. Add eggs and beat until well mixed. Sift together flour, baking soda, salt, baking powder, nutmeg, allspice, cinnamon and cloves. Add flour mixture to pumpkin mixture, alternately with water ending with flour. Stir in nuts. Divide batter between two greased and floured 9x5x3-inch loaf pans. Bake for 1 hour or until toothpick comes out clean.

Ann Edwards
(Former Governor James B. Edwards)

James B. Edwards served as Governor from 1975-1979. He was appointed United States Secretary of Energy in 1981. In 1982, he left to serve as President of the Medical University of South Carolina. He retired in 1999.

Where else would South Carolina celebrate pumpkins but in Pumpkintown, located in Pickens County. The annual Pumpkin Festival takes place there in October.

The annual SC Poultry Festival is held in May in Batesburg-Leesville.

Big, sweet, and juicy watermelons are a favorite summer treat all over the South. Something so wonderful simply must be celebrated. Both Hampton and Pageland do the honors. The seed-spitting contest is always a favorite.

Holiday Pumpkin Bread

My son's kindergarten class in Nashville, Tennessee made this pumpkin bread at Thanksgiving in 1971. He brought home one loaf and the recipe. It has been a family favorite ever since.

MAKES 3 LOAVES

3⅓ cups all-purpose flour	2 cups canned pumpkin
3 cups sugar	4 eggs
2 teaspoons baking soda	1 cup vegetable oil
1 teaspoon ground cinnamon	⅔ cup water
1 teaspoon ground nutmeg	1 cup chopped nuts
1 teaspoon salt	1 teaspoon vanilla

Preheat oven to 350 degrees. Combine flour, sugar, baking soda, cinnamon, nutmeg and salt. Make a well in center. Add pumpkin, eggs, oil and water. Mix until smooth. Add nuts and vanilla and stir until combined. Divide batter among three greased and floured 8½x4-inch loaf pans. Bake for 1 hour or until toothpick comes out clean.

Alinda Mahaffey
(Representative Joseph G. Mahaffey)

Nut Bran Muffins

These muffins freeze very well. Store them in plastic freezer bags. May take one out at a time and pop in the microwave for a few seconds and enjoy.

MAKES 4 DOZEN MUFFINS

7½ cups (about 15 ounces) wheat bran flakes cereal with raisins

3 cups sugar

5 cups all-purpose flour

4 teaspoons ground cinnamon

5 teaspoons baking soda

2 teaspoons salt

1 quart buttermilk

4 eggs, beaten

1 cup canola oil

4 teaspoons vanilla

1½ cups chopped pecans

Preheat oven to 450 degrees. Combine cereal, sugar, flour, cinnamon, baking soda and salt. Add buttermilk, eggs, oil and vanilla. Mix well. Stir in nuts. Spoon batter into paper-lined or greased muffin cups filling one-half to two-thirds full. Bake for 10-12 minutes or until lightly browned. Do not overcook.

Vickie Skelton
(Representative B.R. Skelton)

In 1924, South Carolina adopted the Yellow Jessamine as the State Flower. This vine-like plant with yellow flowers grows all over the state and is one of the first hints of spring.

Miss Evelyn's Squash Relish

Miss Evelyn is Evelyn Edmunds from York County. She is a former classmate of my husband, Herb. She makes wonderful homemade bread daily for her family and friends and raises turkeys on her poultry farm. She has raised turkeys for the turkey industry since the 1940s.

The Edisto River is one of the world's longest free-flowing blackwater streams.

MAKES 4½-6 PINTS

12 cups grated yellow squash	7 tablespoons salt
4 cups chopped onions	2½ cups white distilled vinegar
1 bell pepper, chopped	2½ teaspoons celery seed
1 jalapeño pepper, chopped	2 teaspoons pickling spice
1 (7 ounce) jar diced pimiento	1½ teaspoons ground turmeric
	4 cups sugar

Combine squash, onions, bell pepper, jalapeño and pimiento in a large bowl. Sprinkle with salt. Cover with ice and leave for at least 5 hours or overnight. Rinse with cold water and squeeze out liquid. Rinse 2 to 3 times. Combine vinegar, celery seed, pickling spice and turmeric in a large saucepan. Bring to boil. Add sugar and stir until dissolved. Add squash mixture and stir until well coated. Boil for 5 minutes. Seal in canning jars.

Sue Kirsh
(Representative Herb Kirsh)

Before the days of The Weather Channel, the Grey Man would walk the beach on Pawleys Island to warn residents of an impending hurricane.

Cranberry Relish

This recipe is from my sister, Robin McKee. Robin's favorite holiday is Thanksgiving. She hosts our family and her in-laws every year for a wonderful lunch. This is a relish she makes that I think goes so well with turkey and all the trimmings. Enjoy!

MAKES 2½-3 CUPS

1 large orange, quartered and peel left on	1 (8 ounce) can crushed pineapple, drained
1 pound fresh cranberries	2 tablespoons fresh lemon juice
1½ cups sugar	
½ cup apricot preserves	

Finely chop orange in a food processor. Combine cranberries and sugar in a heavy saucepan. Cook about 10 minutes over medium heat until cranberries just begin to pop, stirring constantly. Transfer cranberries to a bowl. Add apricot preserves and stir until preserve melts. Stir in chopped orange, pineapple and lemon juice. Cover and refrigerate until well chilled.

Vickie Skelton
(Representative B.R. Skelton)

Johnston, SC is called the Peach Capital of the World.

The official state snack food, the humble boiled peanut, is a staple at the never humble game of baseball. To recognize the importance of the peanut to the economy of South Carolina, the annual blessing of the peanut pots takes place at Pelion's Peanut Party during the late summer. Over 4½ tons of boiled peanuts are consumed during the festivities.

Tangy Barbecue Sauce

This sauce is especially good with chicken or pork chops.

MAKES ¾ CUP

1	tablespoon vinegar	3	tablespoons ketchup
2	tablespoons Worcestershire sauce	1	teaspoon salt
¼	cup water	1	teaspoon dry mustard
2	tablespoons butter, melted	1	teaspoon chili powder
3	tablespoons sugar		

Combine vinegar, Worcestershire sauce, water, butter, sugar, ketchup, salt, mustard and chili powder. Mix well. Serve with any cooked meat.

Mary Margaret Bannister
(Representative Bruce W. Bannister)

Susan's Mustard Sauce

This is a great recipe to be used with cheese and fruit. It is especially good with apples. Susan was one of my art buddies before she moved away. She always brought this to workshops for us to snack on with apples and maybe a little wine too. This is one of those little unexpected treats. Try it, you'll like it.

MAKES 1½ CUPS

½	cup dry mustard	½	cup sugar
½	cup cider vinegar	2	egg yolks

Blend mustard and vinegar in a small saucepan. Cover and let stand overnight. Next day, add sugar and egg yolks. Cook over low to medium low heat until mixture thickens to creamy consistency. Stir constantly as sauce will burn easily. Sauce thickens as it cools. Place in a glass or plastic container. Refrigerate until ready to serve.

Representative Vida O. Miller

There is the old debate over who has the best barbecue North or South Carolina. Well, we know it is South Carolina, but we even argue here in the Palmetto state about which is better, mustard-based, tomato-based, ketchup-based or vinegar-based. But no matter, we still celebrate that southern staple – barbecue.

Pesto

MAKES 1¼ CUPS

⅔ cup olive oil

2 large garlic cloves, coarsely chopped

½ teaspoon salt

¼ teaspoon freshly ground black pepper

2 tablespoons pine nuts or chopped walnuts

2 cups loosely packed fresh basil

½ cup loosely packed fresh parsley

½ cup grated Parmesan cheese

Combine oil, garlic, salt, pepper, pine nuts, basil and parsley in a food processor. Cover and process until smooth, scraping down sides as needed. Pour mixture into a bowl. Stir in Parmesan cheese. Serve with pasta, vegetables, chicken or pizza. Store refrigerated.

Marie Land
(Senator John C. Land, III)

Tomato Pesto

MAKES 1-2 CUPS

1 (8 ounce) jar sun-dried tomatoes in oil

1 large garlic clove

1 cup fresh basil, packed

¼ cup toasted pine nuts

1 teaspoon salt

½ teaspoon freshly ground pepper

½ cup freshly grated Parmesan cheese

Purée tomato, tomato oil, garlic, basil, pine nuts, salt and pepper in food processor until finely chopped. Add Parmesan cheese and pulse a few times until cheese is well incorporated. This pesto is great served on toasted baguette slices as an appetizer. May also toss pesto with pasta and add grilled chicken and crumbled goat cheese for a heartier entree dish.

Vickie Skelton
(Representative B.R. Skelton)

Sweetgrass baskets are a cherished art form in SC. The basket making technique has been handed down from generation to generation for almost 300 years. You will find many roadside or sidewalk stands in the lowcountry where the baskets are sold.

Jezebel Sauce

MAKES 3 CUPS

1   (12 ounce) jar apple jelly (or blackberry)

1   (12 ounce) jar pineapple preserves or jam

1   (5 ounce) jar prepared horseradish (or less, if desired)

3   tablespoons dry mustard

1   tablespoon cracked black pepper

In a large bowl, combine apple jelly, pineapple preserves, horseradish, mustard and pepper. Mix well. This sauce can be poured over cream cheese and served with crackers for an easy appetizer. It may also be served as a condiment with baked ham on a buffet.

Lynn Owens
(Representative Phillip D. Owens)

Riverbanks Zoo in Columbia is home to more than 500 animal species that live in areas created to look like their natural habitats.

Soups & Salads

Soups & Salads

Rural scene from the Upstate of South Carolina

Easy Vegetable Beef Soup

This soup is served daily at my parent's restaurant, Thursdays Too, in Rock Hill. It is a favorite among the customers all year long.

SERVES 6-8

1½ pounds lean ground beef

1 (46 ounce) can tomato juice

1 (15 ounce) can green peas, undrained

1 (15 ounce) can shoe peg corn, undrained

1 (15 ounce) can butterbeans, undrained

1 (15 ounce) can sliced potatoes, undrained

1 (10¾ ounce) can cream of onion soup

Brown ground beef in large saucepan. Drain and return beef to pan. Add tomato juice, peas, corn, beans, potatoes and soup. Cover and simmer for 3-4 hours.

Kelly Talley
(Representative Scott F. Talley)

Lake Keowee in Oconee County covers Keowee Town which was the capital of the Lower Cherokee Nation. It is the area visited by Spanish explorer DeSoto when he passed through in 1540. The lake covers over 18,500 acres.

Spicy Taco Soup

SERVES 8

2	pounds ground round	1	(12 ounce) can shoe peg corn, drained
1	large onion, chopped	1	(2¼ ounce) can sliced black olives
1	(1¼ ounce) package taco seasoning	1	(1 ounce) package ranch dressing mix
1	(16 ounce) can chili beans (I use Hormel)		Tabasco sauce to taste
1	(15 ounce) can black beans, drained	1	(16 ounce) jar salsa
1	(14 ounce) can diced tomatoes or diced tomatoes with chilies		Sour cream, shredded Pepper Jack cheese, tortilla chips for garnish

Brown ground beef and onion in a large skillet. Drain and stir in taco seasoning. Transfer beef mixture to a large stockpot. Add chili beans, black beans, tomatoes, corn, olives, dressing mix, Tabasco and salsa. Simmer for about 1 hour. May also cook in a slow cooker for several hours. Serve with sour cream, cheese and tortilla chips. This also makes a great dip, if drained. Freezes well.

Amelia Cotty
(Representative William F. Cotty)

Emilie Theodore
(Former Lt. Governor Nick Theodore)

Robin Stilwell
(Former Representative Sam Stilwell)

After 18 years of effort, Calhoun County was officially created in 1908 and formed from portions of Orangeburg and Lexington Counties.

Marie's Minestrone Soup

This is a good refrigerator clean-out soup. You can add whatever vegetables you have on hand or that are in season. I vary it by adding a handful of green beans or spinach.

SERVES 6

3	tablespoons olive oil	1	quart chicken broth
1	small onion, chopped		Salt and pepper to taste
2	garlic cloves, minced	1	bay leaf
1	large carrot, chopped	½	teaspoon dried basil or 2 teaspoons chopped fresh basil
1	celery stalk, chopped		
2	potatoes, peeled and chopped	1	(15 ounce) can cannellini or navy beans
3	large ripe tomatoes, peeled and chopped or 1 (28 ounce) can diced tomatoes with juice		

Heat oil in large saucepan. Sauté onions and garlic until translucent. Add carrot, celery and potatoes and cook about 2 minutes. Add tomatoes, broth, salt, pepper, bay leaf and basil. Bring to boil, reduce heat and simmer partially covered. Simmer for 30 minutes or until potatoes are tender. Add beans and cook a few more minutes until beans are heated.

Marie Land
(Senator John C. Land, III)

The City of Charleston, renowned for its history, culture, and architecture, has been repeatedly named Best Mannered City in America.

Five Hour Beef Stew

This recipe comes from Mom-Mom Talley who made this beef stew on cold winter days in Philadelphia. Her children and grandchildren still ask for this stew when the weather turns cold.

SERVES 10-12

2	pounds chuck beef, cut into 1-inch pieces	1	(10¼ ounce) can beef consomme
4	carrots, sliced	2	tablespoons tapioca (can substitute 3 tablespoons all-purpose flour)
4	celery stalks, large diced		
3	large potatoes, large diced		Salt and pepper to taste
1	large onion, sliced	1	tablespoon sugar
1	(12 ounce) can tomato juice	2	bay leaves

Preheat oven to 300 degrees. Combine beef, carrots, celery, potatoes, onion, tomato juice, beef consomme, tapioca, salt, pepper and sugar in a 13x9x2-inch baking dish. Place bay leaves on top. Cover and bake for 5 hours. Do not open oven or pan until 5 hours has passed.

Kelly Talley
(Representative Scott F. Talley)

Calhoun County was home to Colonel William Thomson (Old Danger) who was a hero at the Battle of Sullivan's Island during the Revolutionary War. He helped to pioneer this rich area by planting South Carolina's first commercial cotton crop in 1794.

Salmon Stew with Spiced Oysterettes

SERVES 2-3

SPICED OYSTERETTES

1   (1 ounce) package original ranch dressing mix

½   cup canola oil

½   teaspoon dried dill

½   teaspoon garlic powder

1   (10 ounce) package oyster crackers

Warm oil in a saucepan. Stir in dressing mix, dill and garlic powder. Mix well. Place crackers in a medium bowl. Pour hot dressing mixture over crackers and stir to coat well. Store in an airtight container.

SALMON

1   (14¾ ounce) can salmon, undrained

¾   cup ketchup

1   tablespoon butter

1   teaspoon dried onion flakes

    Salt and pepper to taste

1   cup milk

Place salmon in a medium saucepan. Add ketchup, butter, onion flakes, salt and pepper. Simmer mixture over low heat. Add milk and stir until bubbly. Serve with the oysterettes.

Sara McLeod
(Former Representative William J. McLeod)

The College of Charleston, founded in 1770, is the oldest municipal college and thirteenth oldest college in the United States. Among the founders are three signers of the Declaration of Independence and three framers of the United States Constitution.

Shortcut Gumbo

Robbie Sineath is my favorite butcher. He worked at a local grocery store until that chain closed all their stores in South Carolina. He now works in Anderson and I travel twice the distance each weekend to shop there. When you find a good butcher, he is a friend for life! Robbie shared this recipe with my husband one weekend when I was sick with a cold. My husband made this and nursed me back to health. Thanks Robbie!

SERVES 6-8

2-3 (14 ounce) cans chicken broth	2 boneless, skinless chicken breast halves, chopped
1 (16 ounce) package frozen vegetable gumbo mix	½ pound smoked sausage, cut into ¼-inch slices
1 (24 ounce) jar salsa	1 pound medium shrimp

Combine broth, vegetables and salsa in a large stockpot. Stir well. Add chicken. Cover and simmer for 30 minutes. Stir sausage and cook for another 30 minutes. Add more broth if needed. Stir in shrimp and cook for about 10 minutes or until shrimp turn pink. Serve with some crusty bread or over rice.

Vickie Skelton
(Representative B.R. Skelton)

Clarendon County Striped Bass Festival is held each spring around the historical Clarendon Court House Square. It is a special tribute to the striped bass, the species of fish that put the Santee Cooper Lakes on the fishing map. The lakes claim the first reproducing landlocked striped bass as well as the only significant self-sustaining population of fresh water striped bass in the world.

Beaufort Style Frogmore Stew

This is casual lowcountry eating at its best!

SERVES 8

3 tablespoons Old Bay Seasoning

3 tablespoons salt

1½ gallons of water

2 pounds hot smoked link sausage, cut into 2-inch pieces (you can also use kielbasa or polish)

10 ears freshly shucked corn, broken into 3-4 inch pieces

4 pounds South Carolina shrimp

Crushed red pepper (optional)

Combine Old Bay, salt and water in a large stockpot. Bring to boil. Add sausage and boil, uncovered, for 5 minutes. Add corn and boil another 5 minutes. Add shrimp and boil 3 minutes or until shrimp turn pink. Drain, add red pepper and serve immediately. Great served with cocktail sauce and hot French bread.

Senator Catherine C. Ceips

Charleston is home to the Southeastern Wildlife Exposition held each February. The City celebrates the fascinating world of nature with wildlife and nature paintings, sculptures, prints, crafts, and conservation exhibits.

Hessie's Gumbo

SERVES 3 QUARTS

½ pound bacon, diced

½ cup diced yellow onion

½ cup diced celery

½ cup diced bell pepper

2 garlic cloves, minced

1 teaspoon dried basil

1 teaspoon dried oregano

2 cups clam juice

2 cups water

2 (28 ounce) cans chopped tomatoes

2 (16 ounce) packages frozen okra

1 pound fish (halibut, cod, or haddock), diced

1 pound cooked sea scallops (if scallops are large, cut in half)

1 cup cooked long grain white rice

1 cup white wine

1 cup sherry

2 pounds (21-25 count) shrimp, peeled and deveined, tails removed

In a 6-quart stockpot, sauté bacon. Add onion, celery, bell pepper, garlic, basil and oregano. Cook 10 minutes on medium heat, stirring frequently. Add clam juice, water, tomatoes and okra. Cook for 15 minutes more. Stir in fish, scallops, rice, wine and sherry. Simmer for 35 minutes. Add shrimp and cook on low for 10 minutes more. Ladle soup into bowls and serve with crackers.

Vickie Skelton
(Representative B.R. Skelton)

The wild turkey is the Official State Wild Game Bird.

The Okra Strut Festival began in 1973 as a garage sale to raise funds to build a library in Irmo. It attracted 240 people. Today 50,000 people attend the September weekend festivities that include carnival rides, a parade, food vendors, a street dance, and the ever-so-proper okra eating contest.

Chicken Chili Stew

This is my sister Susan's recipe. Great for an easy and delicious dinner on a cold night.

SERVES 4-6

1 tablespoon vegetable oil	1 (14½ ounce) can diced tomatoes, undrained
1½ pounds boneless, skinless chicken breasts, cubed	1 tablespoon chili powder
1 small onion, chopped	1 teaspoon ground cumin
2 garlic cloves, minced	1 teaspoon dried oregano
1 medium bell pepper, chopped	1 teaspoon sugar
½ cup chicken broth	¼ cup chopped flat leaf parsley
1 (14 ounce) can red kidney beans, undrained	

Heat oil in an 8-quart stockpot. Sauté chicken, onion, garlic and bell pepper. Add broth, beans, tomatoes, chili powder, cumin, oregano, sugar and parsley. Bring to boil over medium high heat. Reduce heat and simmer for 20-30 minutes.

Ruth Rice
(Representative Rex F. Rice)

Calhoun County's first golf course was located in a cow pasture and its clubhouse was a former police station.

White Chicken Chili

SERVES 12

1	pound dried navy beans	1	teaspoon white pepper
2	large onions, chopped	4	(4 ounce) cans chopped green chilies, drained
1	cup unsalted butter	5	pounds chicken, cooked and diced
½	cups all-purpose flour		
1½	cups chicken broth	1	(12 ounce) package shredded Monterey Jack cheese
4	cups half and half		
2	teaspoons Tabasco sauce	1	cup sour cream
3	teaspoons chili powder	½	cup chopped cilantro
3	teaspoons ground cumin		
1	teaspoon salt		

Cover beans in cold water by 2 inches. Soak overnight. Drain beans and place in stockpot covered by about 4 inches of water. Simmer beans about 1 hour until tender. Drain in colander and set aside.

In a large stockpot, melt butter and lightly sauté onions for about 2 minutes. Whisk in flour until smooth. Gradually add broth and half and half, whisking constantly. Bring to boil. Reduce heat and simmer, stirring occasionally, for 5 minutes or until thickened. Stir in Tabasco, chili powder, cumin, salt and pepper. Add beans, chilies, chicken and Jack cheese. Simmer for 15 minutes. Stir in sour cream. Garnish with cilantro and serve.

Executive Chef Michael Deevey
South Carolina Governor's Mansion

Submitted by Jenny Sanford
(Governor Marshall C. Sanford, Jr.)

Clarendon County was named for Edward Hyde, Earl of Clarendon, one of the eight Lords Proprietors. His granddaughters, Mary and Anne, became Queens of England.

Tomato Mushroom Soup

Great on a cold day with a grilled ham and cheese sandwich.

SERVES 6-8

1   medium onion, chopped

1   (8 ounce) package fresh white mushrooms, chopped

1   (5½ ounce) can spicy tomato-vegetable juice cocktail

1   (14½ ounce) can diced tomatoes

1   (10¾ ounce) can cream of mushroom soup

1   (10½ ounce) can beef broth or consommé

½   cup heavy cream or half and half

In a large saucepan, sauté onions and mushrooms in oil until tender. Add juice cocktail, tomatoes, soup and broth. Heat thoroughly. Just before serving, stir in cream.

Susan Wilkins
(Former House Speaker, US Ambassador David H. Wilkins)

The "Richardson Waltz" became the Official State Waltz in 2000. It was maintained by the Richardson family for generations and finally transcribed in 1986 by Mary Richardson Briggs of Summerton.

Watterspiel (Potato Soup)

SERVES 4-6

4	chicken or beef bouillon cubes		3	large potatoes, thinly sliced
4	cups hot water		2	egg yolks, beaten
4	slices lean bacon, diced		1	cup sour cream
6	leeks, thinly sliced		1	tablespoon minced fresh parsley
¼	cup chopped onion		1	tablespoon minced fresh chervil
2	tablespoons all-purpose flour			

Place bouillon cubes and water in a small bowl to dissolve. Sauté bacon in a large saucepan. Add leeks and onion and sauté for 5 minutes. Stir in flour. Slowly stir in bouillon. Add potatoes and cook for 1 hour. Combine egg yolks and sour cream. Whisk into soup. Simmer for 10 minutes, stirring constantly. Add parsley and chervil and serve.

Lisa Courson
(Senator John E. Courson)

Elizabeth Peyre Richardson Manning was related to six South Carolina Governors as wife, sister, niece, mother, aunt, and grandmother.

Vidalia Onion and Lobo Apple Cider Soup

This recipe is from the chefs at the US Ambassador's residence in Ottawa, Canada. Lobo apples are a Canadian variety. Our McIntosh apple is very similar to the Lobo and can be used as a substitute. For testing purposes, we used the apple cider available in the local grocery store. The recipe also calls for Oka cheese, a Canadian cheese. Gruyere or Swiss cheese is a good substitute.

SERVES 8-10

4 cups (Lobo) apple cider	Salt and Pepper to taste
3 Vidalia onions, chopped	Slices of toasted French bread
1 tablespoon vegetable oil	
8 cups chicken broth	Grated (Oka) cheese or Gruyere or Swiss cheese
Sprig of thyme	
2 bay leaves	

Heat apple cider in a small saucepan over medium high until reduced by half. Sauté onions in oil. Add broth, thyme, bay leaves, salt, pepper and cider to onions. Bring to boil. Reduce heat and simmer for 20 minutes. Ladle soup into bowls. Top with a bread slice and sprinkle with cheese. Broil until lightly browned. Serve immediately.

Chef Dino Ovcaric

Chef Dana Gosso
U.S. Ambassador's Residence
Ottawa, Canada

Submitted by Susan Wilkins
(Former House Speaker, US Ambassador David H. Wilkins)

Charleston is home to Spoleto Festival USA, one of the world's major art festivals that features innovative works and an international mix of distinguished artists and emerging talent.

Pumpkin Soup

This recipe was given to me by Executive Chef Bruce Sacino who was the chef at the South Carolina Governor's Mansion when my husband was Governor.

SERVES 8-10

1	tablespoon butter	⅔	cup honey
1	cup chopped onion	¼	teaspoon ground nutmeg
1	cup chopped celery		Salt and pepper to taste
2	pounds pumpkin pulp	1	quart heavy cream
2	pounds hubbard squash pulp		Sour cream or crème fraiche or roasted, chopped chestnuts or splash of rum for garnish
3	quarts chicken broth		

Melt butter in a heavy stockpot. Add onion and celery and cook until translucent. Add pumpkin and squash pulp. Cook over medium heat until squash softens, do not let brown. Add broth, honey, nutmeg, salt and pepper. Bring to boil. Reduce heat and simmer until squash is completely cooked. Puree soup in a food processor or blender. Return to stockpot and add cream. Bring back to a simmer over low heat. Serve immediately with garnish of choice.

Rachel Hodges
(Former Governor James H. Hodges)

James H. Hodges served as State Representative before being elected Governor in 1998. He served in that office until 2003.

Summer Squash Soup

This is a yummy cold soup. Great served with a salad for lunch or a light supper.

SERVES 6-8

2 tablespoons unsalted butter	2 cups chicken broth or more if needed
2 large shallots, minced	Plain yogurt and chives for garnish
1 garlic clove, minced	
1¼ pounds yellow crookneck squash, diced	

Melt butter in large saucepan over medium low heat. Sauté shallots and garlic about 2 minutes. Add squash. Cover and cook about 10 minutes or until squash is tender. Stir occasionally. Add broth. Cover and simmer another 10 minutes. Working in batches, puree soup in a processor or blender. If soup is too thick, add more chicken broth. Cover and refrigerate until ready to serve. May be made a day ahead. Serve with a dollop of yogurt and 2 chives placed perpendicular across the yogurt as a garnish.

Vickie Skelton
(Representative B.R. Skelton)

New Orleans has its gumbo, but South Carolina has its bog. Chicken bog is a stew with chicken, sausage and rice. So taken with this delicious dish, that Loris decided to build a festival around the bog. In late October, The Great Loris Bog-Off Festival gets under way. The highlight of which, of course, is a chicken bog cooking contest.

Spicy Gazpacho with Crabmeat

4	large ripe tomatoes, peeled and seeded		1	teaspoon rice wine vinegar
½	English cucumber, peeled and cut into chunks		3	tablespoons olive oil
½	Vidalia onion, quartered		⅛	teaspoon cayenne pepper
1	bell pepper, seeded and quartered		1	teaspoon salt
				White pepper to taste
1	large garlic clove, peeled and crushed		½	pound jumbo lump crabmeat
				Basil, cut into julienne strips

Combine tomatoes, cucumber, onion, bell pepper and garlic in food processor. Pulse until coarsely chopped. Add vinegar, oil, cayenne, salt and white pepper. Puree until mixture is chunky soup consistency. Refrigerate until ready to serve. Ladle soup in pre-chilled shallow soup bowls. Place 2-3 large crabmeat pieces in center. Sprinkle basil strips on top.

Cookbook Committee

Charles Towne Landing was the site of the first permanent English settlement in South Carolina. The park, which is located at the actual site, contains a 1670 fort, 1600 era ship and an early village. Charles Towne later became Charleston.

Spinach Salad with Cranberry Orange Dressing

SERVES 8

CRANBERRY ORANGE DRESSING

½   teaspoon dry mustard

⅓   cup orange juice or cranberry juice

2   tablespoons cider or wine vinegar

3   tablespoons olive oil

Whisk together mustard, orange juice, vinegar and oil.

SALAD

8   cups spinach, washed and trimmed

1   small red onion, sliced in rings

2   naval oranges (can use any large, juicy orange variety)

½   cup dried cranberries

Toasted pine nuts, sunflower seeds, toasted pecans, Gorgonzola or other blue cheese, crumbled for garnish

Arrange spinach in a large bowl. Separate onion slices into rings and place on top of spinach. Peel oranges and remove pith. Cut oranges into bite size pieces over spinach so juice goes into the bowl. Sprinkle with dried cranberries. Pour dressing over salad and toss to coat. Garnish with toasted pine nuts, sunflower seeds, toasted pecans or blue cheese.

Marie Land
(Senator John C. Land, III)

Campbell's Covered Bridge, which spans the Beaverdam Creek in Greenville County, was built in 1909. It is the only covered bridge still remaining in South Carolina. It has been restored, but is no longer in use.

Mixed Baby Green Salad with Goat Cheese Croutons

This is my daughter Susan's recipe. It is a delicious salad to make for a luncheon or serve as a salad course for a special dinner.

SERVES 6-8

VINAIGRETTE

1	cup olive oil	2	tablespoons sugar
½	cup raspberry vinegar	2	tablespoons Dijon mustard
¼	cup balsamic vinegar		Salt and pepper to taste

Combine oil, raspberry vinegar, balsamic vinegar, sugar, mustard, salt and pepper in a food processor or blender. Process until smooth.

SALAD

8	cups mixed baby greens	½	cup walnuts, lightly toasted
4-6	tomatoes, quartered	½	cup thinly sliced red onion
1	English cucumber, peeled and sliced	3	celery stalks, sliced
2	(10 ounce) cans Mandarin oranges, drained		

Combine baby greens, tomatoes, cucumber, oranges, walnuts, onion and celery in a large bowl. Drizzle on vinaigrette and toss well. Divide salad among serving plates. Arrange 2-3 croutons (see sidebar) at an angle over top of greens.

Jane Spratt
(US Congressman John M. Spratt, Jr.)

Railroad passenger service began in the United States in 1830 when the first steam locomotive left Charleston.

CROUTONS

1 French baguette, cut into ½ inch slices

½ cup olive oil

¼ cup chopped garlic

1 (6 ounce) package goat cheese

Preheat oven to 350 degrees. Mix oil and garlic. Brush on bread slices. Place on baking sheet. Toast in oven until lightly browned. Spread goat cheese on toast.

Mansion Blueberry Salad

SERVES 6

BLUEBERRY DRESSING

2	cups orange juice	1	tablespoon sugar
1	cup fresh blueberries	2	teaspoon Dijon mustard
1	tablespoon honey	1	cup canola oil
1	tablespoon fresh lemon juice		Salt and pepper to taste

Heat orange juice in a medium saucepan until reduced to ¼ cup. The juice reduction will be syrupy. Combine reduced orange juice, blueberries, honey, lemon juice, sugar and mustard in a blender. Blend until smooth. With blender on medium speed, slowly drizzle in oil until thickened. Refrigerate until ready to use. Shake well.

SALAD

1	(12 ounce) package baby spinach or arugula	2	large Granny Smith apples, thinly sliced
2	cups thinly sliced celery	1	cup fresh blueberries
1	cup slivered almonds, toasted	1	(4 ounce) package goat cheese, crumbled

Combine spinach, celery, almonds, apple and blueberries. Top with goat cheese. Drizzle with blueberry dressing.

Executive Chef Michael Deevey
South Carolina Governor's Mansion

Submitted by Jenny Sanford
(Governor Marshall C. Sanford, Jr.)

Marshall C. Sanford, Jr. served previously as U.S. Congressman. He was elected Governor in 2002 and re-elected in 2006.

World of Energy is a visitors center located next to Duke Energy's Oconee Nuclear Station. It is open to the public and offers tours of various exhibits which show how electricity works using water, coal and uranium.

Strawberry Salad with Poppy Seed Dressing

SERVES 10-12

POPPY SEED DRESSING

¾ cup sugar

⅓ cup white wine vinegar

1 cup vegetable oil

1 teaspoon salt

1 teaspoon dry mustard

1 teaspoon grated onion

1 tablespoon poppy seeds

Combine sugar, vinegar, oil, salt, mustard and onion in a blender. Process until well blended. Stir in poppy seeds. Refrigerate about 1 hour before serving.

SALAD

3 hearts romaine lettuce, torn

1 pound fresh strawberries, sliced

1 cup chopped walnuts, toasted

Combine romaine, strawberries and walnuts. Pour on dressing and toss to coat.

Emilie Theodore
(Former Lt. Governor Nick Theodore)

The gardens at Middleton Place are thought to be the oldest formal gardens in the United States. The detailed landscape design began in the1740s and took many years to complete.

Country Greek Salad

SERVES 6

3-4	tomatoes
2	medium cucumbers, peeled and thinly sliced
1	head lettuce of your choice, thinly sliced
1	onion, thinly sliced
1	bell pepper, thinly sliced
1	(5 ounce) can black olives, drained
2	tablespoons capers (optional)
2-3	tablespoons red wine vinegar
3-4	tablespoons olive oil
1	teaspoon dried oregano
	Salt to taste
7	ounces feta cheese, crumbled

Slice tomatoes into thin wedges. Add cucumbers, lettuce, onion, bell pepper, olives and capers. Blend vinegar, oil, oregano and salt. Pour dressing over salad and toss to coat. Sprinkle with feta cheese.

Anne Elliott
(Senator Dick Elliott)

Bob Jones University Museum and Gallery, located in Greenville, houses one of the most prestigious religious art collections in the United States. The collection includes works by Rembrandt, Rubens & Van Dyck.

Tomato Salad with Tangy Dressing

SERVES 4

DRESSING

3	tablespoons balsamic vinegar	1½	teaspoons green peppercorn mustard
3	tablespoons canola oil		Salt and pepper to taste
¼	cup olive oil		

Blend vinegar, canola oil, olive oil, mustard, salt and pepper until smooth.

SALAD

4	large tomatoes, sliced thick	5	green onions, chopped
2	tablespoons chopped fresh basil	6	ounces feta cheese, crumbled
2	tablespoons chopped fresh flat leaf parsley		

Arrange tomato slices on serving plates. Sprinkle with basil, parsley, onions and feta cheese. Drizzle dressing over tomatoes and serve.

Vickie Skelton
(Representative B.R. Skelton)

The USS Yorktown, an almost 900 foot Naval aircraft carrier, is docked at Patriot's Point Maritime Museum in Charleston. It is the only ship of its kind open to the public.

Ribbon Salad

SERVES 6-8

VINAIGRETTE

¼	cup red wine vinegar	1	teaspoon salt
2	small garlic cloves, minced	¾	cup canola oil
4	teaspoons sugar		Freshly ground pepper to taste

Blend vinegar, garlic, sugar and salt in a small bowl. Slowly whisk in oil and add pepper.

SALAD

1	large head romaine lettuce or 2 (5 ounce) packages torn romaine	1	medium Vidalia onion, chopped
2	large ripe tomatoes, seeded and chopped	½	pound bacon, cooked and crumbled
2	ripe Haas avocados, diced	6	ounces blue cheese, crumbled

Arrange lettuce on the bottom of a shallow bowl or deep platter. Place tomatoes, avocados, onion, bacon and blue cheese in rows on top of lettuce. The colorful rows will look like ribbons. When ready to serve, drizzle vinaigrette over salad and toss to coat.

Cookbook Committee

Poinsett Bridge, located in northern Greenville County, is said to be the oldest bridge in South Carolina. It was completed in 1820 as part of a road connecting Charleston to the Blue Ridge Mountains. It was named after Greenville resident Joel Poinsett.

Sweet Tea Salon's Famous Apple Salad

SERVES 6-8

DRESSING

⅓ cup olive oil

2 tablespoons cider vinegar

1½ tablespoons Dijon mustard

½ tablespoon dried tarragon

Salt to taste

Whisk together oil, vinegar, mustard, tarragon and salt until smooth.

SALAD

3 tart apples, unpeeled and diced (mix red and green for color)

1 cup diced celery

½ cup walnut pieces

½ cup diced dates or dried cranberries

4 ounces shredded sharp Cheddar cheese

1 head Boston lettuce, torn

Combine apples, celery, walnuts, dates, Cheddar cheese and lettuce. Pour on dressing and toss to coat.

Jean Littlejohn
(Representative Lanny F. Littlejohn)

Charleston is called the "Holy City" because of the numerous churches located in the city. Many of these buildings have historical and architectural significance.

Chopped Broccoli Salad

SERVES 6-8

1	large bunch of broccoli	¼	cup sugar
1	small red onion, thinly sliced	2	tablespoons white wine vinegar
¼	cup dark raisins	4-5	slices bacon, cooked and crumbled
¾	cup mayonnaise		

Wash and chop broccoli. Add onion and raisins. Mix well. Whisk together mayonnaise, sugar and vinegar. When ready to serve, add bacon and dressing. Toss to coat.

Emilie Theodore
(Former Lt. Governor Nick Theodore)

Marinated Green Pea Salad

SERVES 8-10

2	(15 ounce) cans green peas, drained	1	medium sweet onion, thinly sliced
1	(4 ounce) and 1 (2 ounce) jar diced pimiento, drained	¾	cup vegetable oil
1	cup small diced celery	½	cup packed light brown sugar
		¾	cup apple cider vinegar

In a medium bowl, combine peas, pimiento, celery and onion. In another bowl, whisk together oil, brown sugar and vinegar. Pour marinade over vegetables and toss well. Refrigerate until ready to serve. Best made the day before.

Dot Spears
(Adjutant General Stan S. Spears)

Those of you involved in committee work will appreciate the efforts of General Henry M. Robert, a native of Jasper County. Robert gave us Robert's Rules of Order published in 1876.

Chilled Asparagus Salad

This is a recipe from my brother-in-law, B.J. Skelton. He loves to have his Sunday School class and other groups over to his house for dinners. This is one of my favorite dishes he serves.

SERVES 6-8

2	(15 ounce) cans asparagus spears, drained, reserve ½ cup of liquid
1	cup white wine vinegar
½	cup sugar
1	teaspoon salt
2	cinnamon sticks
6	whole cloves
½	teaspoon celery seeds
	Bibb lettuce leaves
1	(4 ounce) jar diced pimiento

Arrange asparagus spears in single layer in a 13x9x2-inch baking dish. Combine asparagus liquid, vinegar, sugar, salt, cinnamon sticks, cloves and celery seeds in a medium saucepan. Bring to boil. Cook for 2 minutes. Pour marinade over asparagus. Refrigerate at least 3 hours. Serve asparagus chilled over lettuce leaves and sprinkle pimiento over top.

Vickie Skelton
(Representative B.R. Skelton)

Pendleton Historic District, covering Anderson and Pickens Counties, is one of the largest historical districts in the United States.

Overnight Coleslaw

SERVES 15

DRESSING

1 cup sugar	1 teaspoon dry mustard
1 cup cider vinegar	1 teaspoon celery seed
¾ cup canola oil	1 tablespoon salt

Combine sugar, vinegar, oil, mustard, celery seed and salt in a medium saucepan. Bring to boil. Remove from heat.

COLESLAW

1 large head cabbage, shredded	1 bell pepper, chopped
2 Vidalia onions, chopped	1 sweet red pepper, chopped

Combine cabbage, onion, bell pepper and red pepper in a large bowl. Pour dressing over cabbage mixture. Mix well. Refrigerate overnight. Store in refrigerator for several days.

Linda Witherspoon
(Representative William D. Witherspoon)

Brookgreen Gardens was created in 1931 by sculptor, Anna Hyatt Huntington and her husband, Archer. It covers 30 acres and is best known for its sculptures as well as the gardens.

Rice and Black Bean Salad

SERVES 6

DRESSING

½	cup olive oil	1	teaspoon ground cumin
¼	cup apple cider vinegar	1	teaspoon minced garlic
1	tablespoon Dijon mustard		Salt and pepper to taste

Whisk together oil, vinegar, mustard, cumin and garlic until smooth. Add salt and pepper.

SALAD

1	(15 ounce) can black beans, drained and rinsed	¾	cup chopped green onions
¾	cup chopped sweet red pepper	2½	cups cooked long-grain white rice (1 cup raw), cooled
¾	cup chopped yellow pepper		

Combine black beans, red pepper, yellow pepper, green onions and rice. Pour dressing over rice mixture and mix well. Cover and refrigerate until ready to serve. May be made 6 hours prior to serving.

Anne Perry
(Representative Robert S. "Skipper" Perry, Jr.)

Charleston native Robert Mills was appointed by President Thomas Jefferson to be the first federal architect. He designed many of the buildings in Washington, DC as well as Columbia.

Wild Rice Salad with Vegetables

This salad was served at a Palmetto Cabinet luncheon at the University of South Carolina President's Home hosted by Mrs. Andrew (Donna) Sorenson. It is a wonderful side dish!

SERVES 6-8

1	(6 ounce) package long-grain and wild rice mix	⅔	cup vinaigrette dressing (any brand you like)
½	cup finely chopped onions	½	cup toasted chopped pecans
½	cup finely chopped carrots	6	ounces blue cheese, crumbled
½	cup finely chopped asparagus		

Cook rice with seasoning packet according to package directions. Sauté onions, carrots and asparagus in small amount oil until tender. Combine rice and vegetables. Pour about ½ cup dressing over rice mixture and mix well. Pour more dressing if needed. Refrigerate overnight. Garnish with toasted pecans and blue cheese.

Sue Kirsh
(Representative Herb Kirsh)

The University of South Carolina, or South Carolina College as it was originally known, was chartered in 1801 and opened for classes with 5 students in 1805. It was one of the first colleges in the United States fully supported by state funds. There are now approximately 25,000 students at the Columbia campus.

New Potato Salad

SERVES 10-12

4	pounds new potatoes, peeled	6	green onions, sliced
¼	cup red wine vinegar	½	cup sweet salad cubes
1	teaspoon salt	1	cup mayonnaise
¾	teaspoon freshly ground pepper	4	tablespoons Dijon mustard
6	hard-cooked eggs, chopped	½	cup chopped fresh parsley

Cover potatoes with water in a large stockpot. Bring to boil over medium high heat. Reduce heat, cover and simmer for about 20 minutes or until done. Check frequently to not overcook. Remove potatoes and cut into 1 inch cubes. Place potatoes in a large bowl. Sprinkle evenly with vinegar, salt and pepper. Set aside.

Combine eggs, green onions, salad cubes, mayonnaise, mustard and parsley in another bowl. Fold egg mixture into potatoes. Refrigerate until ready to serve. Always better the next day.

Vickie Skelton
(Representative B.R. Skelton)

Thomas Green Clemson, son-in-law of John C. Calhoun, left his estate to South Carolina to establish an agricultural college. In 1889, Clemson Agricultural College was established and later opened to students in 1893. In 1964, it was renamed Clemson University. Today, it is known for its agriculture, engineering, science and architecture programs.

Classic Southern Potato Salad

Great summertime dish!

SERVES 4-6

4	large baking potatoes	½	cup mayonnaise (more or less as desired)
¼	cup chopped bell pepper		Salt and pepper to taste
¼	cup chopped onion		
¼	cup chopped celery		

Boil potatoes in skin until done. Drain, peel and dice potatoes. In a large mixing bowl, combine potatoes, bell pepper, onion, celery, mayonnaise, salt and pepper. Refrigerate until ready to serve.

Dotty Edwards
(Former Representative T.W. Edwards, Jr.)

Mediterranean Pasta Salad

SERVES 8

4	cups chopped tomatoes	½	teaspoon salt
2	tablespoons chopped fresh basil	⅛	teaspoon crushed red pepper
3	tablespoons sliced ripe olives	1	garlic clove, minced
1	tablespoon olive oil	4	cups cooked angel hair pasta
1	tablespoon red wine vinegar	¼	cup crumbled feta cheese

Combine tomatoes, basil, olives, oil, vinegar, salt, red pepper and garlic. Marinate for 10 minutes. Add angel hair pasta and toss to coat. Sprinkle with feta cheese. Refrigerate until ready to serve.

Robin Stilwell
(Former Representative Sam Stilwell)

South Carolina is blessed with many beautiful public gardens such as the Edisto Memorial Garden in Orangeburg, Brookgreen Gardens in Myrtle Beach, Cypress Gardens in Moncks Corner, Swan Lake Iris Gardens in Sumter, Riverbanks Botanical Gardens in Columbia and the South Carolina Botanical Gardens in Clemson.

Beach Food

I often make this on Friday afternoon at the beach and feed it to family and friends as they arrive for the weekend. Any leftovers make a great lunch.

SERVES 8

2   pounds South Carolina shrimp

1   (12 ounce) can beer (any brand you like)

    Old Bay seasoning to taste

1   (16 ounce) package rotini pasta (may use low carb)

1   (16 ounce) can artichoke hearts, drained and quartered

1   (2¼ ounce) can sliced ripe olives, drained

3   celery stalks, diced

1   large onion, diced

1   bell pepper (any color you prefer), chopped

6   ounces feta cheese, crumbled

1   (16 ounce) bottle Greek salad dressing

1   pint cherry or grape tomatoes

    Greek seasoning to taste (Cavender's)

    Salt and Pepper to taste

Cook shrimp in beer and Old Bay seasoning in a covered stock pot. Drain and peel shrimp. Set aside. Cook pasta according to the package directions. Drain well. Add shrimp, artichoke hearts, olives, celery, onion, bell pepper, feta cheese, dressing, tomatoes, Greek seasoning, salt and pepper. Mix well. May garnish with additional tomatoes and peppers. Refrigerate at least 2-4 hours or overnight.

Amelia Cotty
(Representative William F. Cotty)

The oldest building in Oconee County is Oconee Station, located in Walhalla. It was built in 1792 and was used to house troops at one time. The Richards House, located next door, is thought to be the first brick house built in northwestern South Carolina around 1800.

Seashells at the Seashore Salad

Bet you can't say that three times real fast!! This makes a great summer pasta salad. Perfect for the beach, but also good for a picnic in the foothills.

SERVES 6-8

2	tablespoons fresh lemon juice	¼	cup chopped green onions
1	tablespoon olive oil	1	cup diced celery
1	(8 ounce) package shell pasta, cooked al dente	½	cup chopped parsley
¼	cup mayonnaise	½	cup sliced pimiento stuffed green olives
¼	cup sour cream	¼	cup diced bell pepper
1	tablespoon white wine vinegar	2	hard-cooked eggs, chopped
1	teaspoon salt	2	tablespoons sunflower seeds
½	teaspoon freshly ground pepper		

Blend lemon juice and oil in a large bowl. Add pasta and toss to coat. Refrigerate for at least 1 hour. Blend mayonnaise, sour cream, vinegar, salt and pepper in a small bowl. Add green onions, celery, parsley, olives, bell pepper, eggs and sunflower seeds to pasta. Stir in mayonnaise mixture and mix well. Refrigerate until ready to serve.

Vickie Skelton
(Representative B.R. Skelton)

Astronaut Charles M. Duke, Jr., a former Lancaster resident, piloted Apollo 16 Lunar Mission in 1972. He was the tenth man to walk on the moon.

Tably

This is a Lebanese cracked wheat salad, very similar to Tabbouleh. This recipe comes from my husband's grandmother, Lucile Sheheen. This dish is best served the same day, but will keep up to one day in the refrigerator.

SERVES 6-8

2 cups cracked wheat (not wheat germ), sold in health food stores and some grocery stores	2 cucumbers, chopped
1¼ cups chopped fresh parsley	4 green onions, chopped
	Juice from 2 lemons
1½ tablespoons chopped fresh mint	½ cup vegetable oil
	½ teaspoon salt
4 large ripe tomatoes, chopped	⅛ teaspoon pepper
	6 dashes of ground cinnamon

Cover wheat with water and let stand 15 to 20 minutes until softened. Drain well (squeeze between hands). Combine parsley, mint, tomatoes, cucumbers and onions in a large bowl. Mix in drained wheat. Add lemon juice, oil, salt, pepper and cinnamon. Stir until well blended. Serve on a bed of lettuce.

Amy Sheheen
(Senator Vincent A. Sheheen)

The Angel Oak, located on John's Island, is believed to be about 1,400 years old. It has a circumference of about 25 feet.

Fruited Chicken Salad

My grandmother, Beth Green, was a wonderful cook. This is her chicken salad recipe. She always had something new for us to try as well as old favorites each time we visited her. She was a lady who always looked out for others and did so much for her family, church and community.

SERVES 6-8

2½-3	pounds chicken, cooked and shredded	1	teaspoon curry powder
1	(8 ounce) can water chestnuts, drained	1	tablespoon soy sauce
2	cups chopped celery	2	tablespoons fresh lemon juice
1	pound seedless grapes		Salt and pepper to taste
2-3	cups toasted slivered almonds, reserve ½ cup for garnish	1	head lettuce, Boston or Bibb
2	cups mayonnaise (or more if needed)	1	(20 ounce) can pineapple chunks, drained

Combine chicken, water chestnuts, celery, grapes and almonds in a large bowl. Blend mayonnaise, curry, soy sauce, lemon juice, salt and pepper. Add to chicken mixture. Toss well. Refrigerate for several hours. When ready to serve, place a few lettuce leaves on individual plates. Top with a scoop of chicken salad. Sprinkle with some pineapple chunks and remaining ½ cup almonds.

Amy Wright
(Former Representative David Wright)

Did you know that South Carolina has a UFO Welcome Center? No one can dispute that South Carolinians are a friendly bunch.

The South Carolina Cotton Museum in Bishopville is a great place to find out more about "King Cotton".

107

Hot Chicken Salad

SERVES 6-8

3	pounds chicken, cooked about 4 cups	3	cups chopped celery
1	(10 ¾ ounce) can cream of mushroom soup	3	teaspoons fresh lemon juice
1	(10 ¾ ounce) can cream of chicken soup	1	cup mayonnaise
1	medium onion, chopped	1	teaspoon salt
8	hard-cooked eggs, chopped	2	cups crushed potato chips
		1	cup slivered almonds

Preheat oven to 400 degrees. Chop chicken into 1-inch pieces. Combine mushroom soup, chicken soup, onion, eggs, celery lemon juice, mayonnaise and salt. Add chicken. Pour chicken salad into a greased 2½-quart casserole dish. Top with crushed chips and almonds. Bake for 10 minutes or until bubbly. Salad can also be served in individual pastry party shells.

Jolene Lander
(Former Senator Jim Lander)

David Neilson
(Representative Denny W. Neilson)

The South Carolina State Fair held in Columbia in October attracts about 600,000 people each year.

South Carolina Shrimp Salad

SERVES 8

2	pounds South Carolina shrimp, boiled	½	teaspoon salt
4	hard-cooked eggs	1½	teaspoons finely ground black pepper
2	cups chopped celery		Tomato slices, Blue cheese, crumbled, cold asparagus spears for garnish
1	tablespoon minced onion		
1½	cups mayonnaise		
1	tablespoon fresh lemon juice		

Process eggs in a food processor until finely chopped. Combine eggs, celery, onion, mayonnaise, lemon juice, salt and pepper. Cover and refrigerate overnight. About 30 minutes before serving, pour dressing over shrimp and toss well. Place about ¾ cup shrimp salad on a lettuce leaf for each serving. Serve salad with sliced tomato, blue cheese crumbles, asparagus, and crackers.

Jeanette Gardner
(Former Representative John Gardner)

BMW Zentrum is a state of the art visitor's center that promotes the Company's engineering achievements. The Zentrum is located at the plant site along Interstate 85 between Greenville and Spartanburg. This plant was built in 1994 and is the first BMW plant outside of Europe.

Darlington is home to the Joe Weatherly Stock Car Museum and the National Motorsports Press Association Hall of Fame.

The University of South Carolina is a mecca for history lovers because it is home to the valuable Movietone Newsreels. Many of the reels are quite fragile and are being restored.

Sister Salad

SERVES 8-10

1	(3 ounce) package lime flavored gelatin	1	(8 ounce) container small curd cottage cheese
½	cup pineapple juice or orange juice	½	cup crushed pineapple, drained
1	cup miniature marshmallows	½	cup chopped pecans
1	cup heavy cream, whipped		

Cook gelatin and juice for 7 minutes on medium low heat. Stir in marshmallows and cool. Add marshmallow mixture to whipped cream. Fold in cottage cheese, pineapple and pecans. Pour mixture into a greased, chilled 10x6-inch casserole dish. Refrigerate until firm.

Jean Littlejohn
(Representative Lanny F. Littlejohn)

Citrus Congealed Salad

SERVES 10-12

1	(3 ounce) package lime flavored gelatin	1	(8 ounce) can crushed pineapple, undrained
1	(3 ounce) package lemon flavored gelatin	½	cup pecans
1½	cups hot water	1	cup small curd cottage cheese
1½	cups cold water	2	tablespoons mayonnaise

Dissolve lime and lemon gelatins in hot water. Add cold water and pineapple with juice. Refrigerate until almost set. Stir in pecans. Blend cottage cheese and mayonnaise. Using a fork, mash cottage cheese until very fine. Add cottage cheese mixture to gelatin. Mix well. Pour mixture into a 9x9-inch square dish. Refrigerate until well congealed.

David Neilson
(Representative Denny W. Neilson)

Spoleto Festival is a 17-day celebration of the arts with operas, gallery exhibits, plays, ballets, concerts, etc. The festival kicks off in May each year.

Icebox Strawberry Banana Salad

SERVES 12

1 **(8 ounce) package cream cheese, softened**

¾ **cup sugar**

1 **(20 ounce) can crushed pineapple, drained**

1 **(10 ounce) package frozen strawberries, thawed**

2 **bananas, diced**

½ **cup pecans**

1 **(12 ounce) frozen whipped topping, thawed**

In a small bowl, blend cream cheese and sugar. Set aside. Combine pineapple, strawberries, bananas, pecans and whipped topping. Fold in cream cheese mixture. Pour into a 11x8x2-inch baking dish. Freeze until ready to serve.

Linda Witherspoon
(Representative William D. Witherspoon)

David Neilson
(Representative Denny W. Neilson)

Greenville County Museum of Art has one of the best Andrew Wyeth collections in the world. Many of his later works are in this collection.

Frozen Cranberry Salad

This recipe is Linda's famous frozen salad. It is so good and easy. Makes a great frozen salad for the holidays.

SERVES 12-14

1   (16 ounce) can whole cranberry sauce

1   (8 ounce) container frozen whipped topping, thawed

1   (14 ounce) can sweetened condensed milk

½   cup chopped pecans, slightly toasted

1   (20 ounce) can crushed pineapple, drained

⅓   cup fresh lemon juice (2-3 lemons)

1   teaspoon lemon zest

In a large bowl, combine cranberry sauce and whipped topping until well blended. Pour in milk, pecans and pineapple. Add lemon juice and zest and mix well. Pour mixture into a 13x9x2-inch baking dish. Freeze until ready to serve. Remove from freezer about 15 minutes before serving. Cut into squares and serve on bed of lettuce leaves.

Jane Spratt
(US Congressman John M. Spratt, Jr.)

The Olde English District, which covers York, Chester, Chesterfield, Fairfield, Kershaw, Union and Lancaster Counties, provides visitors a glimpse into our military history and South Carolina's significance in the Revolutionary and Civil Wars.

Quick Cherry Salad

SERVES 8

1   (21 ounce) can cherry pie filling

1   (8 ounce) container frozen whipped topping, thawed

1   (20 ounce) can crushed pineapple, drained

1   (14 ounce) can sweetened condensed milk

½   cup chopped pecans

Combine filling, whipped topping, pineapple, milk and pecans. Mix well. Pour mixture into an 11x8x2-inch baking dish. Refrigerate until ready to serve.

Norma Jean Barfield
(Representative Liston D. Barfield)

The Chatooga River which runs along the Georgia border in Oconee County is one of the longest mountain rivers in the southeastern US. It drops 49.3 feet per mile and is a top whitewater rafting destination. The movie Deliverance was filmed here.

Watergate Salad

SERVES 10-12

1   (8 ounce) container frozen whipped topping, thawed

1   (3 ounce) package instant pistachio pudding mix

½   cup chopped pecans

1   (8 ounce) can crushed pineapple, undrained

1   cup miniature marshmallows

Combine whipped topping and pudding mix. Fold in pecans and pineapple with juice. Add marshmallows and mix well. Pour mixture into a 9x9x2-inch square dish. Refrigerate until ready to serve.

Jolene Lander
(Former Senator Jim Lander)

Autumn Apple Salad

SERVES 10-12

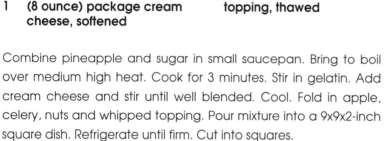

1	(20 ounce) can crushed pineapple, undrained	
⅔	cup sugar	
1	(3 ounce) package lemon flavored gelatin	
1	(8 ounce) package cream cheese, softened	

1	cup chopped unpeeled apple
1	cup chopped celery
¾	cup chopped nuts
1	cup frozen whipped topping, thawed

Combine pineapple and sugar in small saucepan. Bring to boil over medium high heat. Cook for 3 minutes. Stir in gelatin. Add cream cheese and stir until well blended. Cool. Fold in apple, celery, nuts and whipped topping. Pour mixture into a 9x9x2-inch square dish. Refrigerate until firm. Cut into squares.

Representative Vida O. Miller

Molded Ambrosia

This recipe is wonderful as a salad or as a dessert.

SERVES 6-8

1 (6 ounce) package orange flavored gelatin

2 cups boiling water

1 (8 ounce) can crushed pineapple, reserve juices

⅓ cup sugar

1 (10 ounce) can Mandarin oranges, drained

1 (6 ounce) package frozen coconut

½ cup chopped pecans

1 (8 ounce) container sour cream

Dissolve gelatin in boiling water. Add juice from pineapple and sugar. Mix well and cool. Stir in oranges, coconut, pecans and sour cream. Pour mixture into individual molds, muffin pan or an 8x8x2-inch glass baking dish. Refrigerate until ready to serve. Looks pretty served on a bed of lettuce or with a slice of pound cake as a dessert.

Marie Land
(Senator John C. Land, III)

The South Carolina National Heritage Corridor stretches 240 miles across the state from Oconee County to Charleston. This area highlights the state's history, culture and natural resources.

Strawberry Fluff

My aunt Diane serves this delicious dish at family get togethers. It is a great side dish for any meal.

SERVES 8-10

1 cup small curd cottage cheese	1 (8 ounce) can crushed pineapple, drained
1 (3 ounce) package strawberry flavored gelatin	1 (8 ounce) container frozen whipped topping, thawed
	1 cup chopped pecans

In a medium bowl, combine cottage cheese and gelatin. Stir in pineapple. Fold in whipped topping and pecans. Pour mixture into an 8x8x2-inch baking dish. Refrigerate until firm.

Kelly Talley
(Representative Scott F. Talley)

The Middleton Oak, located near Charleston, is thought to be over 900 years old. The diameter of this tree is 12 feet.

Three Layer Pretzel Salad

SERVES 8-10

3   tablespoons plus 1 cup plus ¼ cup sugar, divided

1½ sticks butter or margarine, melted

2   cups pretzels, crushed

1   (8 ounce) package cream cheese, softened

1   teaspoon vanilla

1   (12 ounce) container frozen whipped topping, thawed

1   (6 ounce) package strawberry flavored gelatin

2   cups boiling water

2   (10 ounce) packages frozen strawberries, thawed

1   (16 ounce) container sour cream

Preheat oven to 350 degrees. Combine butter with 3 tablespoons sugar. Add crushed pretzels and mix well. Press mixture into the bottom of a 13x9x2-inch baking dish. Bake for 10 minutes. Cool completely. Beat cream cheese and 1 cup sugar until well blended. Add vanilla and mix well. Fold in whipped topping. Spread over pretzel crust. In a large bowl, dissolve gelatin in boiling water. Add strawberries. Stir to separate berries. Refrigerate until slightly thickened. Spread over cream cheese layer. Refrigerate overnight or until set. Blend sour cream and remaining ¼ cup sugar. Spread over gelatin and serve.

Martha Walker
(Representative Robert E. Walker)

Caesar's Head, located in northwestern Greenville County near the North Carolina border, rises to an elevation of 3,266 feet. There is a large rock outcropping which serves as an overlook and is said to resemble Julius Caesar's head. The overlook provides a spectacular view of the Blue Ridge Mountains.

Layered Fruit Salad with Citrus Sauce

SERVE 12-14

CITRUS SAUCE

½	teaspoon orange zest		⅓	cup fresh lemon juice
½	teaspoon lemon zest		1	cinnamon stick
⅔	cup fresh orange juice		⅓	cup packed brown sugar

Combine orange zest, lemon zest, orange juice, lemon juice, cinnamon stick and brown sugar in a medium saucepan. Bring to boil over medium heat. Reduce heat and simmer for 5 minutes. Cool. Remove cinnamon stick and refrigerate.

SALAD

2	cups diced fresh pineapple		2	oranges, sectioned
3	medium bananas, sliced		2	kiwis, peeled and sliced
2	pints fresh strawberries, sliced		1	cup seedless red grapes

In a glass bowl, layer pineapple, bananas, strawberries, oranges, kiwi and grapes. Pour on sauce. Refrigerate until ready to serve.

Rachel Hodges
(Former Governor James H. Hodges)

South Carolinians are also called "Sandlappers." During Revolutionary War battles, the SC militia would lay flat on the ground when under fire. The British considered this to be cowardly and taunted the militia with the name "sandlapper" saying they looked like they were lapping the sand. Because of the militia's success against the British, it became a badge of honor for South Carolinians.

Summer Grape Salad

Lovely side dish for a summer luncheon.

SERVES 8-10

1 (8 ounce) package cream cheese, softened

½ cup sugar

1 (8 ounce) container sour cream

1 tablespoon vanilla

1 pound red seedless grapes

1 pound green seedless grapes

1 cup packed light brown sugar

¾ cup powdered sugar

Combine cream cheese, sugar, sour cream and vanilla. Add red grapes and green grapes. Toss until well coated. Spoon in a large glass bowl. Blend brown sugar and powdered sugar. Sprinkle over grape mixture. Cover and refrigerate overnight. Before serving, toss again.

Susan Wilkins
(Former House Speaker, US Ambassador David H. Wilkins)

South Carolina State University was founded in 1896.

Edgefield County is home to almost 1 million peach trees. During blooming season, a drive through the back roads is breathtaking.

Heavenly Hash

(Liz Patterson is the daughter of the late Olin D. Johnston, former governor of South Carolina.) This is an old recipe from my mother, Gladys Atkinson Johnston. You can add different fruits, if you prefer.

SERVES 4-6

1¼ tablespoons unflavored gelatin	4 ounces maraschino cherries
1 cup boiling water	4 ounces blanched, sliced or slivered almonds
1 cup sugar	1 pint heavy cream
6 large marshmallows or 2 cups miniature	
6 macaroons, slightly crushed	

Dissolve gelatin in water. Add sugar and mix well. Cool. Stir in marshmallows, macaroons, cherries and almonds. Whip cream until stiff peaks form. Gently fold cream into marshmallow mixture. Spoon into a large mold or several individual molds. Refrigerate until ready to serve. Serve with additional whipped cream.

Former State Senator and US Congresswoman Liz Patterson

Dijon Vinaigrette

MAKES ABOUT 1 CUP

¼ cup white wine vinegar	⅛ teaspoon freshly ground black pepper
1 tablespoon Dijon mustard	Pinch of sugar
¼ teaspoon kosher salt	¾ cup extra virgin olive oil

Combine vinegar, mustard, salt, pepper and sugar in a food processor. Gradually pour in oil while machine is running. Adjust salt and pepper.

Cookbook Committee

Old Pickens Presbyterian Church listed on the National Register of Historic Places was a church and meeting place. It is the only building left at the site where the town of Pickens Courthouse was established in 1828.

Red Wine Vinaigrette

½	cup red wine vinegar	½	teaspoon paprika
¾	cup sugar or ½ cup sugar substitute	½	teaspoon salt
		½	teaspoon ground pepper
2	garlic cloves, minced	1	cup vegetable oil

Combine vinegar, sugar, garlic, paprika, salt and pepper. Slowly whisk in oil until well blended. May also combine in blender or food processor. Serve over your favorite salad.

Reba Stille
(Former Representative Harry Stille)

Honey Mustard Dressing

Rainbow Row is the term for the brightly painted houses along East Bay Street. These buildings are some of the most well known images of Charleston.

½	cup honey	2	tablespoons Dijon mustard
¼	cup cider or white wine vinegar	1	(1-inch thick) slice onion
		1	teaspoon poppy seeds
1	tablespoon fresh lemon juice	¼	teaspoon salt
		1	cup vegetable oil

Combine honey, vinegar, lemon juice, mustard, onion, poppy seeds and salt in a food processor or blender. Process until smooth. With machine running, gradually add oil. Blend well. Refrigerate until ready to use.

Sue Kirsh
(Representative Herb Kirsh)

W.J. Breas' Blue Cheese Dressing

My husband and I owned a restaurant in Clemson named W.J. Breas. The restaurant was opened in 1979 and remained in business until it was sold in 1995. Former customers tell us that this is the best blue cheese dressing they ever had. I hope you'll agree.

MAKES 3½ CUPS

2 cups mayonnaise	6 ounces Clemson blue cheese, crumbled
¾ cups ranch dressing (any brand you prefer)	1½ teaspoons Worcestershire sauce
1 tablespoon fresh lemon juice	¼ cup beer (any brand you prefer)
½ teaspoon garlic powder	Salt and pepper to taste

Whisk together mayonnaise, ranch dressing, lemon juice, garlic powder, blue cheese, Worcestershire sauce, beer, salt and pepper. Refrigerate at least one day before serving.

Vickie Skelton
(Representative B.R. Skelton)

Reedy River Falls Historic Park is located in downtown Greenville and has recently undergone some renovations. A pedestrian bridge which provides a better view of the falls was erected and many new restaurants, hotels and shops have located in this area.

Dicksie Cribb's Ginger Dressing

This is my mother's delicious recipe for ginger dressing. It is great over a fresh fruit salad.

MAKES ABOUT 2 CUPS

1 (8 ounce) container frozen whipped topping, thawed

1¾-2 cups mayonnaise

1 tablespoon honey

3 ounces crystallized ginger, chopped

Sugar, if needed

Blend whipped topping and mayonnaise. Add honey. Stir in ginger. Some ginger is hotter than others so if the ginger does not have a good sugar coating, add a little sugar. Mix well.

Evelyn Ritchie
(Senator James H. Ritchie, Jr.)

Gullah refers to the African-Americans who live in the Lowcountry of South Carolina and are believed to be descendants of slaves brought to South Carolina from West Africa. They have maintained the Gullah language that is a combination of their native language and English.

Vegetables & Sides

Vegetables & Sides

Swan Lake located in Sumter County

Skillet Sesame Asparagus

This recipe comes from my good friend and golfing partner, Marilyn Rogers. This dish is a Hayes family favorite.

SERVES 4

1	**pound fresh asparagus, rinsed and ends trimmed**
¾	**cup olive oil**

Kosher salt to taste

Sesame seeds, toasted (optional)

Preheat oven to 450 degrees. Dry asparagus thoroughly. Cover bottom of a 10-inch iron skillet with oil. Place skillet in oven for 15 minutes until oil is very hot. Remove from oven and place asparagus in skillet. Be careful, oil will splatter. Sprinkle with salt and sesame seeds. Bake for 5 minutes.

Sally Hayes
(Senator Robert W. "Wes" Hayes, Jr.)

Roasted Asparagus

SERVES 6

1½	**pounds fresh asparagus, rinsed and ends trimmed**
2	**tablespoons (or less) olive oil**

Garlic salt to taste

Morton's Nature's Seasoning to taste

Preheat oven to 400 degrees. Dry asparagus thoroughly. Arrange asparagus in a single layer on a foil-lined baking sheet. Drizzle with oil. Sprinkle with garlic salt and seasoning. Bake for 10-15 minutes.

Marie Land
(Senator John C. Land, III)

The York Bailey Museum housed in the first school for freed slaves on St. Helena Island hopes to preserve the unique language of the Gullah people and their traditions.

Quick and Easy Asparagus Casserole

SERVES 8

4	pounds fresh asparagus, ends trimmed and cut into 1-inch pieces
¾	cup milk
4	ounces goat cheese
4	ounces cream cheese

Salt and ground white pepper to taste

| 1 | cup soft bread crumbs |
| 3 | tablespoons unsalted butter, melted |

Preheat oven to 325 degrees. Steam asparagus until tender. In a medium saucepan, whisk together milk, goat cheese and cream cheese on medium-low heat until cheese melts. Stir in salt and pepper. Arrange asparagus in a greased 13x9x2-inch baking dish. Pour cheese mixture over asparagus. Combine bread crumbs and butter and mix well. Sprinkle crumbs over top. Bake for 25-30 minutes. Serve hot.

Cookbook Committee

Sweetgrass basket making is a Gullah tradition. To celebrate this art form, a Sweetgrass Festival is held each June in Mt. Pleasant.

Big Jamie's Baked Beans

This is a great dish to take to a covered dish supper. Best baked beans ever!

SERVES 20

2	(31 ounce) cans pork and beans	1	tablespoon prepared mustard
6	slices bacon	1	tablespoon Worcestershire sauce
1	tablespoon liquid smoke	¾	cup packed light brown sugar
3	cups chopped onion		
1	cup chopped celery	1	teaspoon ground black pepper
1	cup chopped bell pepper		
2	tablespoons minced garlic	¼	teaspoon salt
2	(14 ounce) cans diced tomatoes with chilies, drained	2	cups ketchup

Preheat oven to 300 degrees. Cook bacon in a skillet until almost done. Do not cook until crisp. Chop bacon into small pieces. Transfer drippings to a Dutch oven or large casserole dish. Add bacon, pork and beans, liquid smoke, onion, celery, bell pepper, garlic, tomatoes, mustard, Worcestershire sauce, brown sugar, pepper, salt and ketchup. Mix well. Bake uncovered for 3 hours.

Marie Land
(Senator John C. Land, III)

The Cowpens Depot is a one hundred year old depot that features a museum. The museum houses relics and memorabilia from the USS Cowpens, a World War II aircraft carrier.

Beet Napoleons

SERVES 6 (18 NAPOLEONS)

CHIVE PURÉE

¾ **cup chopped fresh chives**

¾ **cup extra virgin olive oil**

Salt and pepper to taste

Combine chives and oil in a food processor. Purée until smooth. Add salt and pepper. Refrigerate until ready to serve.

NAPOLEONS

1½ **pounds small beets (can use red, golden, or both)**

6 **ounces soft goat cheese**

1 **tablespoon sour cream**

¼ **cup minced fresh chives**

Salt to taste

Freshly ground black pepper to taste

Preheat oven to 400 degrees. Wrap beets tightly in groups of 4 in foil. Roast for 1 hour or until soft. Cool 5-10 minutes. Peel beets and cut into ¼-inch slices. Cool. Blend goat cheese, sour cream and chives until smooth. Add salt and pepper.

May cook beets and prepare goat cheese mixture and chive purée a day in advance and refrigerate. Bring all ingredients to room temperature. To assemble, spread ½ teaspoon goat cheese mixture on top beet slice. Cover with another beet slice and dollop of goat cheese. Repeat to give 3 beet slices and 3 layers goat cheese. Drizzle 1 to 3 tablespoons chive purée on individual serving plates. Arrange about 2 to 3 napoleons in center of each plate and serve.

Rachel Hodges
(Former Governor James H. Hodges)

Pretty Place also known as Symmes Chapel is located near Caesar's Head and is an outdoor chapel with spectacular mountain views. The chapel is a very popular place for weddings.

Broccoli Rice Casserole

SERVES 8-10

2	(10 ounce) packages frozen broccoli florets, thawed	½	teaspoon plus ½ teaspoon salt, divided
2	tablespoons plus 6 tablespoons unsalted butter, divided	¼	teaspoon cayenne pepper
1	cup finely chopped onion	1	(8 ounce) package shredded sharp Cheddar cheese, divided
6	tablespoons all-purpose flour	2	eggs
3	cups milk	1½	cups cooked long-grain white rice
		1	(4 ounce) jar diced pimiento

Preheat oven to 350 degrees. Cook broccoli according to package directions. Drain well. Melt 2 tablespoons butter in a large skillet. Sauté onions until tender. Set aside. Melt remaining 6 tablespoons butter in a large saucepan. Whisk in flour until smooth. Gradually stir in milk, ½ teaspoon salt and cayenne. While whisking constantly, bring to boil over medium-high heat. Boil for 1-2 minutes until thickened. Remove from heat. Add 1 cup Cheddar cheese and stir until cheese melts. Whisk eggs until light yellow in color and thickened. Ladle some hot cheese mixture into eggs while vigorously whisking. Once eggs are tempered, slowly add egg mixture into hot cheese mixture, whisking constantly. Add broccoli, onion, ½ teaspoon salt, rice and pimiento. Mix well. Spoon broccoli mixture into a greased 13x9x2-inch baking dish. Sprinkle remaining 1 cup Cheddar cheese over top. Bake for 20-25 minutes or until bubbly.

Vickie Skelton
(Representative B.R. Skelton)

October means chilly temps, red and golden leaves, and Fall for Greenville. Held each October, Fall for Greenville is a celebration of restaurants in the area featuring samplings from the participating restaurants and activities involving the staff of these establishments. There is a waiter's race, bartender's mix-off, chili cook-off and more.

Cheesy Broccoli Casserole

SERVES 8

2	(10 ounce) packages frozen chopped broccoli, thawed or 2 fresh bunches	1	(8 ounce) package shredded sharp Cheddar cheese
2	eggs, beaten	1	medium onion, finely chopped
1	(10 ¾ ounce) can cream of mushroom soup	1	cup mayonnaise
		1	cup crushed round buttery crackers

Preheat oven to 350 degrees. Cook broccoli according to package directions. If using fresh, steam and chop. Drain and transfer broccoli to a large bowl. Add eggs, soup, Cheddar cheese, onion and mayonnaise. Mix well. Pour mixture into a greased 13x9x2-inch baking dish. Sprinkle cracker crumbs on top. Bake for 30-40 minutes or until bubbly.

Jean Littlejohn
(Representative Lanny F. Littlejohn)

Susan Wilkins
(Former House Speaker, US Ambassador David H. Wilkins)

Tamassee DAR School located in Oconee County was founded in 1919 by the South Carolina Chapter of the Daughters of the American Revolution to provide a place for children to learn patriotism and citizenship. The school is still in operation today.

Brussels Sprouts Casserole

SERVES 6

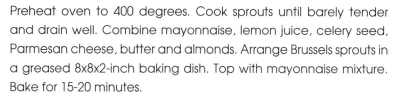

2	(10 ounce) packages frozen Brussels sprouts, thawed	1	teaspoon celery seed
1	cup reduced fat mayonnaise	1	cup grated Parmesan cheese
2	teaspoons fresh lemon juice	¼	cup butter or margarine, melted
		½	cup sliced almonds

Preheat oven to 400 degrees. Cook sprouts until barely tender and drain well. Combine mayonnaise, lemon juice, celery seed, Parmesan cheese, butter and almonds. Arrange Brussels sprouts in a greased 8x8x2-inch baking dish. Top with mayonnaise mixture. Bake for 15-20 minutes.

Floride Carter
(Former House Speaker Rex L. Carter)

Roper Mountain Science Center in Greenville contains the largest planetarium in South Carolina and one of the largest telescopes in the United States. The Center also contains the Living History Farm which is a reconstructed rural town typical of the area in the 1800s. It is open to the public on a limited schedule.

Favorite Butter Bean Casserole

This casserole is one of Governor Sanford's favorites. It is best made with fresh butter beans and tomatoes.

SERVES 8

2 (16 ounce) packages frozen lima beans, thawed (or fresh, cooked)

1 (28 ounce) can diced tomatoes (or 3 cups fresh diced)

1 small onion, chopped

1 bell pepper, chopped

½ cup plus ½ cup grated sharp Cheddar cheese, divided

Preheat oven to 350 degrees. Combine butter beans, tomatoes, onion, bell pepper and ½ cup Cheddar cheese. Pour mixture into a greased 11x8x2-inch baking dish. Top with remaining ½ cup Cheddar cheese. Bake for about 25-30 minutes or until bubbly.

Jenny Sanford
(Governor Marshall C. Sanford, Jr.)

Nana's Yummy Carrots

SERVES 4

1 pound carrots (about 6-8 medium)

2 tablespoons butter

¼ cup packed light brown sugar

2 tablespoons cold water

1½ teaspoons cornstarch

Rinse and cut carrots into ½ inch diagonal slices. Combine carrots, butter and brown sugar in a 1-quart casserole dish. Cover and microwave on high for 9-11 minutes. Stir after 5 minutes. Whisk together water and cornstarch until smooth. Stir into carrot mixture. Cover and microwave on high for 2-4 minutes until thickened. Stir before serving.

Cathy Harrell
(House Speaker Robert W. Harrell, Jr.)

Southwestern Corn Casserole

SERVES 8-10

1   **(15 ounce) can whole kernel corn**

1   **(15 ounce) can cream-style corn**

2   **eggs, beaten**

1   **(8 ounce) container sour cream**

½   **cup yellow cornmeal**

1   **(8 ounce) package shredded sharp Cheddar cheese, divided**

1   **(4 ounce) can chopped green chilies**

½   **teaspoon salt**

¼   **teaspoon freshly ground black pepper**

Preheat oven to 350 degrees. Combine kernel corn, cream-style corn and eggs. Stir in sour cream and cornmeal. Mix well. Add 1 cup Cheddar cheese and chilies. Stir in salt and pepper. Pour mixture into a greased 2½-quart casserole dish. Bake for 25 minutes. Remove from oven, stir and top with remaining 1 cup Cheddar cheese. Bake for 20 minutes more or until bubbly.

Cookbook Committee

Issaqueena Falls, located near the Stumphouse Mountain Tunnel has a drop of about 200 feet. It is said to be named after a young Indian maiden who jumped to her death from the falls.

Hoppin' John

This is a recipe from Zoe D. Sanders, wife of former College of Charleston President, Alex Sanders. This dish can be made a day ahead and refrigerated overnight. Remove from refrigerator about 1 hour before reheating at 350 degrees for 30 minutes or until hot.

SERVES 8-10

1	cup dry cow or field peas	1	slice thick-sliced bacon
6	cups water	1	(12 ounce) ham hock
2	teaspoons plus 1 teaspoon salt, divided	2	cups chopped jumbo yellow onion
¼	teaspoon black pepper	1	cup long-grain white rice

Combine peas, water, 2 teaspoons salt, pepper and ham hock in a 3-quart saucepan. Bring to boil. Reduce heat, partially cover and cook peas for 45 minutes or until soft, but not mushy. Set aside. Cook bacon in large skillet until all fat is rendered. Makes about 3 tablespoons of fat. Discard bacon and reserve drippings. Pull skin and all membrane from ham hock. Reserve meat. Combine skin and membrane in the skillet and fry on low until all fat is rendered. Discard skin and membrane. Combine bacon drippings with ham drippings. Add onions and simmer for 15 minutes or until onions are soft. Set aside. Combine 2 cups broth from peas, remaining 1 teaspoon salt and rice in 1½-quart saucepan. Bring to boil. Reduce heat and simmer for 25-30 minutes or until all liquid is absorbed. Fluff with fork.

Preheat oven to 350 degrees. Peas should have soaked up remaining broth. Shred ham hock meat. Mix with reserved onions and fat. Combine with rice in 3-quart baking dish. Cover and bake for 15-20 minutes or until hot.

Marie Land
(Senator John C. Land, III)

Hoppin' John is a classic South Carolina dish that is believed to have been introduced to our state by West African slaves. The dish is traditionally served on New Year's Day for good luck.

Green Bean and Corn Casserole

SERVES 6-8

1 **(15 ounce) can French-style green beans, drained**	½ **cup grated sharp Cheddar cheese**
1 **(10 ounce) can shoe peg corn, drained**	½ **cup sour cream**
1 **(10¾ ounce) can cream of celery soup**	½ **cup butter or margarine, melted**
½ **cup chopped onion**	1½ **cups crushed round buttery crackers**
	½ **cup slivered almonds**

Preheat oven to 350 degrees. Combine green bean, corn, soup, onion, Cheddar cheese and sour cream. Pour mixture into a greased 13x9x2-inch baking dish. Stir butter, cracker crumbs and almonds together. Sprinkle over casserole. Bake for 45 minutes.

Emilie Theodore
(Former Lt. Governor Nick Theodore)

Melody Duncan
(Representative Jeffrey D. Duncan

Shoeless Joe Jackson, the former Chicago White Sox outfielder, started his baseball career in 1903 in Greenville. He played in the early textile league.

Mixed Vegetable Casserole

SERVES 6-8

1	(10 ounce) package frozen lima beans, cooked and drained	1	small onion, chopped
		1½	cups mayonnaise
1	(10 ounce) package frozen cut green beans, cooked and drained	1	teaspoon prepared mustard
		1	teaspoon Worcestershire sauce
1	(17 ounce) can green peas, drained	½	teaspoon fresh lemon juice
1	(5 ounce) can sliced water chestnuts, drained	½	cup crushed round buttery crackers

Preheat oven to 350 degrees. Combine lima beans, green beans, peas, water chestnuts and onion. In a separate bowl, blend mayonnaise, mustard, Worcestershire sauce and lemon juice until smooth. Fold mayonnaise mixture into vegetables and mix well. Pour mixture into an ungreased 2-quart casserole dish. Sprinkle cracker crumbs on top. Bake for 45 minutes.

Alinda Mahaffey
(Representative Joseph G. Mahaffey)

Sue Kirsh
(Representative Herb Kirsh)

Hatcher Garden and Woodland Preserve in Spartanburg is a wildlife and bird center as well as a beautiful garden housing more than 10,000 plants.

Herb Stuffed Tomatoes

SERVES 6

6	medium ripe tomatoes	½	teaspoon minced fresh oregano
1¾	cups soft bread crumbs		Salt and freshly ground pepper to taste
⅔	cup chopped green onions		Extra virgin olive oil
¼	cup chopped fresh basil	1	cup grated low moisture, part-skim mozzarella cheese
2	tablespoons chopped fresh parsley		
2	garlic cloves, minced		

Preheat oven to 400 degrees. Remove stem of tomato. Squeeze tomato to remove seeds. Scoop out any remaining seeds. Turn upside down on a paper towel to drain. Combine bread crumbs, green onions, basil, parsley, garlic, oregano, and salt. Sprinkle inside of tomato with salt and pepper. Arrange tomato in a casserole dish. Fill tomato cavity with bread crumb mixture. Mound mixture on top. Drizzle with oil. Bake for 14-15 minutes or until soft. Remove from oven. Sprinkle with mozzarella cheese. Bake for 2-3 minutes more or until cheese melts.

Cookbook Committee

Whitewater Falls is located near Salem in Oconee County. It is a set of two falls which plunge almost 700 feet in over a half mile into Lake Jocassee. It is said to be one of the highest falls in eastern United States.

Tomato Onion Pie

Delicious! A nice alternative to a stuffed tomato side dish.

SERVES 6-8

1	large Vidalia onion, very thinly sliced
1	(9-inch) deep dish pie shell, baked
1	large ripe tomato, peeled and sliced
1/8	teaspoon dried oregano
1/8	teaspoon dried basil
1/8	teaspoon ground black pepper
1	(8 ounce) package shredded low fat mozzarella cheese
1/2	cup mayonnaise

Preheat oven to 350 degrees. Separate onion slices into ringlets. Place in microwave safe bowl. Cook in microwave on high for 2-3 minutes or until tender. Cool and drain well on a paper towel. Layer cooled onion in pie crust. Top with tomato slices. Sprinkle with oregano, basil and pepper. Mix together mozzarella cheese and mayonnaise. Spread cheese mixture over tomato. Bake for 30 minutes.

Susan Martin
(Senator Larry A. Martin)

Hollywild Animal Park is a 100 acre animal park located in Inman. It is home to hundreds of exotic animals and is open to the public. The park's Christmas Lights Safari is a special treat during the holidays.

Summer Squash Soufflé

SERVES 10-12

4-5	pounds yellow squash, sliced	6	eggs, well beaten (may substitute a cholesterol-free egg product)
3	large onions, chopped	3	cups plus 1 cup grated sharp Cheddar cheese, divided
1½	teaspoons salt		
1	cup water		Salt and pepper to taste

Preheat oven to 350 degrees. Cook squash, onions and salt in water until tender. Drain well and mash. Combine squash mixture, eggs, 3 cups Cheddar cheese, salt and pepper. Pour mixture into a greased 13x9x2-inch baking dish. Top with remaining 1 cup Cheddar cheese. Bake for 50-60 minutes or until knife inserted in center comes out clean. Serve hot.

Floride Carter
(Former House Speaker Rex L. Carter)

Yellow Squash Casserole

SERVES 6-8

2	pounds yellow squash, sliced	½	cup butter or margarine, melted
1	small onion, chopped	1	carrot, grated
½	cup water		Salt and pepper to taste
1	(10¾ ounce) can cream of chicken soup	1	cup sour cream
			Seasoned bread crumbs or cheese of choice

Preheat oven to 350 degrees. Cook squash and onion in water until tender. Drain well and mash. Place squash in a large bowl. Add soup, butter, carrot, salt, pepper and sour cream. Mix well. Pour mixture into a greased 2-quart casserole dish. Top with bread crumbs. Bake for 20-25 minutes.

Jolene Lander
(Former Senator Jim Lander)

South Carolina celebrates its apple harvest the week after Labor Day each year with the annual South Carolina Apple Festival. The festival is held in Westminster, the state's largest apple producing region, and features many fun activities including a parade, World Championship Rodeo, arts and crafts shows and whitewater rafting on the Chatooga River.

Lois' Famous Squash Praline

Delicious side dish!

SERVES 8-10

PRALINE SAUCE

1   cup butter

1   (16 ounce) package light
     brown sugar

¼   cup heavy cream

Melt butter in a saucepan over low heat. Gradually whisk in brown sugar until mixture looks like caramel. Whisk in cream until thickened. Keep warm.

SQUASH

2   acorn squash

2   tablespoons all-purpose
     flour

½   cup butter

Pinch of salt

2   eggs

4   cups chopped pecans

Duncan Park in Spartanburg is the oldest minor league stadium in current use in the United States.

Preheat oven to 375 degrees. Cut squash in half lengthwise. Remove seeds. Place squash cut side down in a baking dish. Add enough hot water to ½-inch depth. Bake uncovered for 35 minutes or until tender. Reduce heat to 350 degrees. Remove squash peel. Mash squash pulp. Add flour, butter, salt and eggs. Mix well. Pour mixture into a greased 13x9x2-inch baking dish. Bake for 20-30 minutes or until lightly browned. Spread pecans over cooked squash. Pour sauce over pecans. Serve hot.

Former Representative Joyce C. Hearn

Spinach Artichoke Casserole

SERVES 10

½	cup butter	2	cups sour cream
1½	cups finely chopped onion	1	teaspoon ground black pepper
3	(10 ounce) packages frozen chopped spinach, thawed and squeezed dry	½	teaspoon salt
		½	teaspoon Morton's Nature's seasoning blend
1	(8½ ounce) can artichokes, drained and mashed	½	cup plus ¼ cup grated Parmesan cheese, divided

Preheat oven to 350 degrees. Melt butter in a heavy skillet and sauté onion. Combine spinach, onion, artichoke, sour cream, pepper, salt, seasoning and ½ cup Parmesan cheese in a large bowl. Mix well. Pour mixture into a greased 13x9x2-inch baking dish. Top with remaining ¼ cup Parmesan cheese. Bake for 20-30 minutes or until bubbly.

Marie Land
(Senator John C. Land, III)

Spinach Casserole

SERVES 8

3	(10 ounce) packages frozen chopped spinach, thawed	1	(1 ounce) envelope dried onion soup mix
1	cup sliced mushrooms	1	(8 ounce) can water chestnuts, drained
2	cups sour cream	2	eggs, beaten

Preheat oven to 350 degrees. Cook spinach according to package directions and drain well. Sauté mushrooms in a non-stick skillet until tender. Combine spinach, mushrooms, sour cream, soup mix, water chestnuts and eggs. Mix well. Pour mixture into a greased 2½-quart casserole dish. Bake for 25-35 minutes.

Sue Kirsh
(Representative Herb Kirsh)

Beauty queens from South Carolina:

1954-Miriam Stevenson from Winnsboro – Miss Universe

1957-Marian McKnight from Manning – Miss America

1980-Shawn Weatherly from Sumter – Miss Universe

1993-Kimberly Aiken from Columbia – Miss America (also the first African-American Miss SC)

141

Spinach Squares

MAKES 6 LARGE SQUARES OR 12 SMALL SQUARES

2	(10 ounce) packages frozen chopped spinach, thawed and squeezed dry
1	cup cooked rice
2	green onions, sliced
1	cup shredded Swiss cheese
1	(10¾ ounce) can cream of mushroom soup
3	eggs, lightly beaten
⅛	teaspoon salt
⅛	teaspoon pepper
½	teaspoon fresh basil or ¼ teaspoon dried basil
¼	cup soft bread crumbs
1	tablespoon butter, melted
2	tablespoons grated Parmesan cheese

Preheat oven to 325 degrees. Combine spinach, rice, green onions and Swiss cheese. Mix well. In a separate bowl, combine soup, eggs, salt, pepper and basil. Add soup mixture to spinach. Stir until well blended. Spoon mixture into a greased 8x8x2-inch square baking dish. Combine bread crumbs, butter and Parmesan cheese. Sprinkle over spinach mixture. Bake for 30 minutes or until lightly browned. Cool for 10 minutes before serving. Cut into squares.

Marie Land
(Senator John C. Land, III)

The State Dance, the shag, is a 4-step shuffle similar to the Jitterbug or Lindy Hop.

Sweet Potato Coconut Casserole

SERVES 6

3	cups cooked, mashed sweet potato	1	cup flaked coconut
1	cup sugar	1	cup chopped pecans
¼	cup milk	1	cup packed light brown sugar
2	eggs	½	cup butter or margarine, softened
1	teaspoon vanilla	⅓	cup all-purpose flour
½	cup butter or margarine, melted		

Preheat oven to 325 degrees. Combine sweet potatoes, sugar, milk, eggs, vanilla, butter and coconut. Pour mixture into a greased 2½-quart casserole dish. Mix together pecans, brown sugar, butter and flour until well blended. Sprinkle over sweet potatoes. Bake for 20-25 minutes.

Emilie Theodore
(Former Lt. Governor Nick Theodore)

Nanny's Candied Yams

This is my grandmother's recipe. She was a great cook. She always made this for Thanksgiving and Christmas dinners.

SERVES 6-8

6	sweet potatoes	¼	cup butter
1	cup sugar	1	teaspoon vanilla
1	cup water		

Preheat oven to 350 degrees. Boil and peel sweet potatoes. Cut lengthwise and place cut side up in a greased 13x9x2-inch baking dish. Boil sugar and water until sugar dissolves. Remove from heat. Stir in butter and vanilla until smooth. Pour sauce over potatoes. Bake for 30-40 minutes or until the syrup thickens. Serve hot.

Kelly Talley
(Representative Scott F. Talley)

Cowpens National Battlefield is the site of the historic January 17, 1781 Revolutionary War victory for the Patriot soldiers. The Battle of Cowpens was a major defeat for the British and led to their surrender a few months later. The anniversary of the Battle is marked by special events held each January at the battlefield site.

Pineapple Au Gratin

SERVES 6-8

2 (20 ounce) cans crushed pineapple, drained

1 cup pineapple juice

½ cup sugar

¼ cup butter

3 tablespoons all-purpose flour

1 cup crushed round buttery crackers

¼ cup butter, melted

Preheat oven to 350 degrees. Combine pineapple, pineapple juice, sugar, butter and flour. Pour mixture into a greased 2½-quart casserole dish. Mix together cracker crumbs and butter. Sprinkle over casserole. Bake for 30 minutes. Serve hot.

Norma Jean Barfield
(Representative Liston D. Barfield)

Kathy Koon
Former Representative Larry Koon)

Sue Kirsh
(Representative Herb Kirsh)

Blacksmith Phillip Simmons is responsible for much of the ornamental ironwork seen around Charleston's historic districts. Simmons was named a National Heritage Fellow by the National Endowment of the Arts. He was commissioned to create a gate for display in the South Carolina State Museum.

Boursin Potato Gratin

SERVES 6

2	cups heavy cream
1	(1½ ounce) package Boursin cheese
1	garlic clove, minced
2½-3	pounds red potatoes, cut into ¼-inch slices

Salt and pepper to taste

2 tablespoons snipped chives

2 tablespoons snipped parsley

Preheat oven to 400 degrees. Heat cream, Boursin cheese, and garlic over medium heat in a heavy saucepan. Stir until cheese melts. Arrange one-half potato slices in slightly overlapping rows in a buttered 13x9x2-inch baking dish. Sprinkle with salt, pepper and chives. Top with half cheese mixture. Repeat layers. Sprinkle with parsley. Bake for about 1 hour or until golden browned.

Sally Hayes
(Senator Robert W. "Wes" Hayes, Jr.)

Palmetto Pigeon Plant in Sumter is the largest supplier of squabs in the country.

Most major comprehensive art collections contain the work of Sumter's Jasper Johns. He is considered a major figure in the evolution of twentieth century art.

Garlic Mashed Potatoes

Who doesn't love mashed potatoes? A great variation of this recipe is to make roasted garlic mashed potatoes. Place a head of garlic that has been broken apart in the center of a large sheet of foil. Drizzle with olive oil and wrap up in foil. Place in a 425 degree oven for 15 minutes or until garlic is softened. Remove and cool. Squeeze roasted garlic out of skins and mash. Use as much roasted garlic as desired. Add to potatoes and stir in cream and butter.

SERVES 4

3 large baking potatoes, peeled and diced	4 tablespoons butter
2 large garlic cloves, chopped	1 cup heavy cream (more or less)
½-1 teaspoon salt	Salt and pepper to taste

Combine potatoes, garlic and salt in a large, heavy saucepan. Add enough water to cover the potatoes. Cook until potatoes are tender, but not mushy. Drain potatoes for 2-3 minutes. Melt butter in the saucepan. Remove from heat. Add drained potatoes and mash. Stir in cream until reached desired consistency. Add salt and pepper and serve.

Dotty Edwards
(Former Representative T.W. Edwards, Jr.)

The Thoroughbred Hall of Fame attracts many equestrians to Aiken. Some of the most famous thoroughbreds have trained in Aiken. The primary season for the major stables is November through March.

Party Potatoes

SERVES 8

2	cups heavy cream	2-3	pounds russet potatoes, peeled and sliced ⅛-inch thick
2	cups milk		
1	garlic clove, minced	1	cup shredded Gruyere cheese (or Swiss cheese)
¾-1	teaspoon salt		
¼	teaspoon freshly ground black pepper	3	tablespoons unsalted butter, cut into pieces

Preheat oven to 350 degrees. Combine cream, milk, garlic, salt and pepper in a large heavy saucepan. Bring to simmer. Cook, stirring constantly, until thickened. Remove from heat. Arrange a layer of potato slices in a buttered 13x9x2-inch baking dish. Pour half cream mixture over potatoes. Arrange another layer of potatoes. Repeat layering with remaining potatoes. Pour remaining cream mixture over top. Cover with foil and bake for 30 minutes. Remove cover and cook for about 30 minutes more. Remove from oven. Sprinkle Gruyere cheese on top. Dot with butter pieces. Bake for 20 minutes more. Remove from oven. Cool for 10-15 minutes before serving.

Vickie Skelton
(Representative B.R. Skelton)

The Colonial Cup horse race takes place in Camden in November and is one of the nation's richest steeplechase races. Many festivities are held the week prior to the event.

Hash Brown Casserole

SERVES 8-10

1   (32 ounce) package shredded hash brown potatoes, thawed

1   (8 ounce) container sour cream

1   (8 ounce) package shredded Cheddar cheese

1   (10¾ ounce) can cream of mushroom soup

1   small onion, finely chopped

1   teaspoon salt

    Pepper to taste

Preheat oven to 350 degrees. In a large bowl, combine potatoes, sour cream, Cheddar cheese, soup, onion, salt and pepper. Mix well. Pour mixture into a greased 13x9x2-inch baking dish. Sprinkle extra cheese on top, if desired. Bake for 50-60 minutes.

Mary Margaret Bannister
(Representative Bruce W. Bannister)

Kelly Talley
(Representative Scott F. Talley)

Martha Walker
(Representative Robert E. Walker)

The Carolina Cup held in March in Camden is one of the state's largest outdoor cocktail parties/fashion shows/horse races.

Wild Rice Casserole

This is a wonderful side dish for almost anything-chicken, fish, beef or pork.

SERVES 10

2	tablespoons unsalted butter
2	(6 ounce) packages long-grain and wild rice mix
4	cups chicken broth

5-6	green onions, chopped
10	medium white mushrooms, sliced
1½	cup chopped pecans, toasted

Preheat oven to 350 degrees. Melt butter in a Dutch oven. Add rice and cook over medium heat until lightly browned, stirring constantly. Stir in seasoning package from rice mix, broth, green onions and mushrooms. Bring to boil. Remove from heat and pour into a greased 13x9x2-inch baking dish. Cover with foil. Bake for 30 minutes. Remove cover and bake an additional 15 minutes. Stir in pecans. Cook for an additional 15 minutes or until all liquid is absorbed. Serve hot.

Cookbook Committee

A water tank called "The Peachoid" was built in 1981 in Gaffney. It serves as a symbol of one of the area's most profitable crops. The Peachoid looks like a giant peach and is easily seen from Interstate 85. It is said to be used by many as a landmark for giving directions.

Saffron Risotto

This is a classic recipe for risotto. May add almost any cooked vegetable or seafood for a heartier dish.

SERVES 6

6	tablespoons plus 2 tablespoons unsalted butter, divided	1	teaspoon salt
		⅛	teaspoon white pepper
1	small onion, finely chopped	1	teaspoon saffron threads
1	cup dry white wine	6	cups low sodium chicken broth
2	cups Arborio rice	½	cup freshly grated Parmesan cheese

Melt 6 tablespoons butter in a large saucepan over medium-high heat. Sauté onion until just transparent. Add white wine and cook until almost all liquid has evaporated. Add rice, salt, pepper and saffron. Stir until well mixed, about 1 minute. Add 1 cup of broth and stir well. When broth has evaporated, add another 1 cup broth and reduce heat to medium-low and simmer. Stir frequently. Continue to add 1 cup broth and let evaporate for about 25 minutes until rice is creamy and al dente. When rice is done, remove from heat. Add 2 tablespoons butter and Parmesan cheese. Stir until well blended. Serve immediately.

Representative B.R. Skelton

Cheraw is home to jazz great, Dizzy Gillespie. What better city to play host to the SC Jazz Festival in October.

Spicy Mac and Cheese

SERVES 6

1 (8 ounce) package elbow macaroni

1 (12 ounce) can evaporated milk

2 eggs

¾ cup milk

1 (8 ounce) package shredded sharp Cheddar cheese

1 (8 ounce) package shredded pepper Jack cheese

¼ cup butter or margarine, softened

Salt and pepper to taste

Preheat oven to 350 degrees. Cook macaroni according to package directions and drain. Whisk together evaporated milk, eggs and milk. Stir in macaroni, Cheddar cheese, Jack cheese and butter. Sprinkle with salt and pepper. Pour mixture into a greased 2½-quart casserole dish. Bake for about 30 minutes or until bubbly.

Judy Frye
(Representative Marion B. Frye)

Suber's Mill built in 1908 is located in Greer. The mill still grinds corn using water power.

Three Cheese Macaroni Casserole

Yummy on a cool night. My family loves this dish. The grandchildren like to help with the cooking. The very best comfort food.

SERVES 6

1	(8 ounce) package elbow macaroni		Freshly ground black pepper
1	small yellow onion, minced		Freshly ground nutmeg
3	tablespoons plus 1½ tablespoons unsalted butter, divided	1	teaspoon hot chili powder
2	tablespoons all-purpose flour	2½	cups grated cheese (I use equal parts white cheddar, Gorgonzola and Parmesan)
2	cups whole milk	2	tablespoons fresh bread crumbs
2	teaspoons salt		

Preheat oven to 350 degrees. Cook macaroni according to package directions and drain. Heat 3 tablespoons butter in a large saucepan. Sauté onion until tender. Add flour and cook for about 3 minutes, stirring constantly. Add milk, salt and pepper. Cook and stir on medium-low until bubbly. Simmer for 1-2 minutes. Remove from heat. Add nutmeg, chili powder and 2 cups cheese. Mix well. Add macaroni and stir until well blended. Pour mixture into a greased 8x8x2-inch square baking dish. Sprinkle remaining ½ cup cheese on top. Dot with remaining 1½ tablespoons butter. Bake for 20-25 minutes or until golden browned.

Betty Ryberg
(Senator W. Greg Ryberg)

Kings Mountain National Military Park in Blacksburg is the site of an October 7, 1780 battle in which the Patriots defeated the British. There were hundreds of British casualties. This was a real turning point for the Patriot cause.

Creamy Baked Noodles

This dish is great with any beef entree.

SERVES 10-12

1	**(8 ounce) package fine egg noodles**
2	**cups sour cream**
1	**cup ricotta cheese**
1	**cup small curd cottage cheese**
	Dash of Tabasco sauce

2	**tablespoons Worcestershire sauce**
¼	**cup finely chopped shallot**
2	**garlic cloves, minced**
1	**teaspoon salt**
	Black pepper to taste
½	**cup grated Parmesan cheese**

Preheat oven to 350 degrees. Cook egg noodles according to package directions. Drain and set aside. Combine sour cream, ricotta cheese, cottage cheese, Tabasco, Worcestershire sauce, shallot, garlic, salt and pepper. Fold in egg noodles and mix well. Pour mixture into a greased 13x9x2-inch baking dish. Sprinkle Parmesan cheese on top. Bake for 30 minutes or until bubbly.

Vickie Skelton
(Representative B.R. Skelton)

Clemson Blue Cheese is a product of the University's dairy science program. In addition to blue cheese, the University makes blue cheese dressing. These delicious products are sold in various retail outlets as well as through the University.

Sesame Noodles

This is a great side dish, but the noodles are also good tossed with cooked, shredded chicken for an easy main dish.

SERVES 8-10

½ cup dark sesame oil

½ cup soy sauce

2 garlic cloves, minced

2 teaspoons hot chili oil

Salt and fresh black pepper to taste

1 (16 ounce) package linguini or spaghetti, cooked al dente

½ cup carrot, julienne

½ cup sweet red pepper, julienne

½ cup bell pepper, julienne

¼ cup chopped green onion

½ cup chopped roasted peanuts (optional)

Whisk together oil, soy sauce, garlic, chili oil, salt and pepper. Add pasta and toss to coat. Refrigerate. Best made a day ahead. When ready to serve, add carrot, red pepper, bell pepper and green onion and toss well. Sprinkle peanuts over top. Serve cold or at room temperature.

Cookbook Committee

The Rocky Shoals Spider Lilies bloom in Landsford Canal State Park located between Great Falls and Lancaster in late May – early June. This is one of only three places in America to see these beautiful and endangered flowers.

Entrées

Entrées

Night view of the State House from Main Street in Columbia, SC

Bistro Steak

This recipe is very similar to the French dish, Steak au Poivre, which is served in most French cafes or bistros. Great served with French fries.

SERVES 4

4	(8 ounce) New York strip steaks, about 1½ inches thick
	Kosher salt to taste
2	tablespoons coarsely cracked mixed peppercorns (red, white, black, green)
4	tablespoons butter, divided
2	tablespoon olive oil
½	cup chopped shallots
1	(15 ounce) can beef broth
½	cup cognac or brandy
¼	teaspoon salt

Place steaks on a plate and sprinkle with salt. Press peppercorns into each side of steak. Heat 2 tablespoons of butter and oil in a large skillet over medium-high heat until butter almost smokes. Want a good sear on the steaks. Sear steaks for 1 minute. Turn and sear other side. Reduce heat to medium and cook for 4 minutes per side for medium rare. Transfer steaks to a plate and cover tightly with foil. Pour all but 1 tablespoon of oil from the skillet. Sauté shallots for 1-2 minutes on medium-low heat. Add beef broth and increase heat to high. Deglaze the pan by scraping bits from the bottom of skillet. Cook and stir about 5 minutes or until reduced by half. Add cognac and cook for 2 more minutes. Add remaining 2 tablespoons butter and salt. Pour sauce over steaks and serve immediately.

Representative B.R. Skelton

Blenheim Ginger Ale was first introduced to South Carolina in the early 1900s. Though this ginger ale is not widely known, it has a cult following and comes in several flavors.

Châteaubriand with Horseradish Sauce

This is the perfect recipe to prepare for that special dinner party. The sauce can be made a day or two in advance and all that is left is roasting the beef. Serve with a potato gratin and stuffed tomato for a meal that is sure to bring compliments.

SERVE 8

HORSERADISH SAUCE

2	cups mayonnaise	2½	tablespoons Dijon mustard
½	cup sour cream	1	tablespoon Country Dijon mustard
1½	tablespoons prepared horseradish	¼	teaspoon kosher salt

Blend mayonnaise, sour cream, horseradish, mustards and salt in a small bowl. Cover and refrigerate until ready to serve with sliced châteaubriand.

TENDERLOIN

2	(2½ pounds each) beef tenderloins, châteaubriand cut and trimmed	2	tablespoons plus 1 tablespoon olive oil, divided
4	garlic cloves, slivered		

Preheat oven to 450 degrees. Make sure oven is clean because there will be a lot of smoke. Cut small slits all over the tenderloins. Place garlic sliver in each slit. Rub tenderloin with about 2 tablespoons of oil. Heat remaining 1 tablespoon oil in a large skillet. Brown meat on all sides. Place on a rack in a roasting pan. Bake for about 45 minutes for medium rare. Use thermometer to check desired degree of doneness. Transfer meat to a cutting board and cover loosely. Let rest for about 10 minutes. Slice meat into ¼-inch slices and serve with sauce.

Vickie Skelton
(Representative B.R. Skelton)

Bomb Island in Lake Murray attracts thousands of Purple Martins. The area has been declared a sanctuary and is a great place for bird watching.

Filet with Easy Blue Cheese Sauce

SERVES 6

6	(6 ounce) filet mignons, about 1¼-inch thick	6	ounces blue cheese, crumbled
	Salt and pepper to taste	½	teaspoon kosher salt
2	cups heavy cream	¼	teaspoon ground white pepper

Sprinkle salt and pepper over filets. Let rest for about 30 minutes at room temperature. Preheat grill to medium-high heat. Pour cream into a medium-sized saucepan. Bring to boil on medium-high heat. Reduce to low heat. Simmer uncovered about 20 minutes until cream is reduced and thickened. Watch carefully during first 10 minutes so cream does not boil over. Whisk frequently. When sauce is very thick, remove from heat and add blue cheese, salt and pepper. Grill filets to desired degree of doneness. For medium rare, grill filets about 3-4 minutes per side. Serve warm sauce over filets.

Cookbook Committee

The Carolina parakeet, now extinct, was reportedly last seen in the Santee River swamp in 1938. At one time, the small bird was found in abundance along the east coast. An image of the parakeet is included in Audubon's <u>Birds of America.</u>

London Broil

This is another recipe from my mother, Gladys Atkinson Johnston. The recipe calls for cooking sherry because my parents would never have real alcohol in the house.

SERVES 4-6

1	(1½-2 pound) flank steak	1	garlic clove, minced
½	cup soy sauce		Dash of Tabasco sauce
⅓	cup cooking sherry		Salt and pepper to taste
⅓	cup vegetable oil		

Place steak in pan with a cover or a large plastic bag. Blend soy sauce, sherry, oil, garlic, Tabasco, salt and pepper. Pour marinade over steak. Marinate for 8 hours or overnight. Drain marinade into a small saucepan and heat. Grill or broil steak to desired degree of doneness. Thinly slice steak across the grain. May pour warm marinade over meat.

Former State Senator and US Congresswoman Liz Patterson

The gardenia was brought to South Carolina by Charleston resident, Dr. Alexander Garden. The shrub is a native plant of China and was originally known as Cape Jasmine.

Favorite Flank Steak

This is a recipe from my friend, Becky. This is simple yet so delicious!

SERVES 6

1	(1½-2 pound) flank steak	¼	cup honey
6	green onions, finely chopped	2	tablespoons white wine vinegar
¾	cup good quality extra virgin olive oil	1-2	large garlic cloves, minced
¼	cup soy sauce		

Score flank steak and sprinkle onions on top. Whisk together oil, soy sauce, honey, vinegar and garlic. Pour over steak. Marinate for several hours turning frequently. Drain marinade into a small saucepan and heat on medium-low heat. Preheat grill to medium-high. Grill steak to desired degree of doneness. Slice across the grain and serve with warm marinade.

Betty Ryberg
(Senator W. Greg Ryberg)

*John C. Calhoun,
born in 1782 in what was
called Abbeville district,
served as State Legislator,
US Congressman, US Senator,
and Vice President
of the US.*

Sunday Brisket Roast

SERVES 12

3-4 pounds flat brisket
1   large garlic clove, minced
1   teaspoon seasoning salt
½   teaspoon paprika

1   (1 ounce) package onion soup mix
2   cups beef broth

Preheat oven to 400 degrees. Rub brisket with garlic. Sprinkle both sides of meat with seasoning salt and paprika. Place roast flat in a greased roasting pan. Sprinkle soup mix on top of meat. Pour on broth. Cover and seal tightly with foil. Bake for 30 minutes. Reduce heat to 300 degrees. Cook for another 2 hours, 30 minutes. Remove from oven and let rest for 10 minutes. Thinly slice across the grain and serve.

Ann Edwards
(Former Governor James B. Edwards)

South Carolina was the first government in America to declare its independence on March 28, 1776.

Three weekends in March feature the Aiken Triple Crown when Aiken trained Thoroughbreds race for the first time. Events azaleas include the Trials, the Steeplechase, and Polo—all accompanied by tailgating from casual to extravagant.

Marinated Pot Roast

SERVES 8-10

1	(3-5 pound) roast (can use sirloin tip or chuck)	⅓	cup vegetable oil
1	small onion, sliced	1	or more cups strong coffee
¾	cup apple cider vinegar	1	teaspoon salt
		½	teaspoon pepper

Place roast in a large glass container. Cut slits in roast and insert onion pieces in slits. Pour vinegar over beef and cover. Refrigerate overnight, turning several times. Heat oil in a large Dutch oven on medium-high heat. Sear all sides of roast. Add coffee and enough water to cover roast. Season to taste with salt and pepper. Cover and cook on medium-low for 2 hours, 30 minutes to 3 hours or until tender. May add any chopped vegetables of your choice during the last hour of cooking time.

Jean Littlejohn
(Representative Lanny F. Littlejohn)

Think you know what a knob is – no, not a door handle – it's a first year cadet at the Citadel. The Citadel first became a military school in 1842.

Company Beef Stew

This is similar to the classic Beef Bourguignon. The stew takes some time to make, but is well worth the effort. Best made a day or two in advance. I like to serve with noodles and a great loaf of French bread. This dish freezes well.

SERVES 10-12

4½-5	pounds chuck roast, cut into 1-inch pieces (I sometimes use beef tenderloin)
1	cup all-purpose flour
2	teaspoons salt
	Freshly ground pepper
½	cup plus ¼ cup plus ¼ cup unsalted butter, divided
¼	cup olive oil
⅓	cup cognac or brandy
½	pound bacon, diced
2	large garlic cloves, minced
6	carrots, chopped
2	leeks, washed carefully and chopped
2	large onions, chopped
1	tablespoon plus ¼ cup chopped fresh flat leaf parsley, divided
2	tablespoons tomato paste
1	teaspoon chopped fresh thyme
1	bay leaf
3½	cups good quality dry red wine
3-4	cups beef broth
	Salt and pepper to taste
40	small pearl onions, fresh or frozen
1	tablespoon sugar
¼	cup water
12	ounces small white mushrooms

Preheat oven to 350 degrees. Combine flour, salt and pepper in a bowl. Add meat and toss to coat. In a large skillet, heat the ½ cup butter and oil on high heat. Brown meat on all sides. May have to do this in several batches. Add more oil and butter, if needed. Transfer beef to a large roasting pan or extra large casserole dish. Pour cognac into skillet to deglaze and ignite. Scrape the pan to loosen any browned bits of meat. Pour cognac over beef. Sauté bacon, garlic, carrots, leeks, onions and 1 tablespoon parsley

(continued)

Lake Murray Dam is the second largest earthen dam in the country.

Company Beef Stew, continued

on medium-low heat until tender. Add tomato paste and thyme and stir well. Add bay leaf and spoon vegetables over beef. Pour wine and enough broth to cover the meat and mix well. Add salt and pepper. Cover roasting pan tightly and bake for 2 hours. Stir meat occasionally and add more broth if needed. Blanch pearl onions in boiling water for 1 minute. Cut off the ends and remove the outer skin. Sauté onions in ¼ cup butter and sugar. Be sure to caramelize evenly. Pour water over onion and simmer for 10 minutes. Transfer onions to a bowl and wipe the skillet. Melt remaining ¼ cup of butter in the skillet. Sauté mushrooms until tender. Sprinkle with remaining ¼ cup parsley. Transfer mushrooms and onions to beef. Stir until well mixed. Bake for 1 hour. Remove bay leaf before serving.

Vickie Skelton
(Representative B.R. Skelton)

The Sword of State remains in a rack on the South Carolina Senate Rostrum during the legislative session or is carried by the Senate Sergeant at Arms on official occasions such as a joint session of the House and Senate. The Sword contains the State Flower and State Seal.

Mousaka Soufflé

SERVES 6-8

2	**pounds eggplant, peeled and diced**
1	**pound ground beef**
1	**cup chopped onion**
2	**tablespoons butter**
1½	**teaspoons salt**
	Pepper to taste
⅛	**teaspoon ground nutmeg**

1	**teaspoon fresh chopped parsley**
½	**cup tomato sauce**
½	**cup water**
1½	**cups plus ½ cup soft bread crumbs (4 slices)**
6	**eggs, separated**
½	**cup grated Parmesan cheese**

Preheat oven to 350 degrees. Soak eggplant in a bowl of cold water. Cook beef and onion in butter until browned. Add salt and pepper. Rinse and drain eggplant. Add eggplant to beef. Cook and stir over moderate heat to slightly browned. Stir in nutmeg, parsley, tomato sauce and water. Simmer until eggplant is soft, stirring occasionally. Remove from heat. Stir in 1½ cups bread crumbs. Mix well. Beat egg yolks and add to eggplant. Beat egg whites until stiff peaks form. Fold into eggplant mixture. Pour mixture into a 2-quart baking dish. Combine remaining ½ cup bread crumbs with Parmesan cheese. Sprinkle over top. Bake for 45 minutes or until firm and golden browned. Serve warm.

Emilie Theodore
(Former Lt. Governor Nick Theodore)

The Mace of the House of Representatives was made in London in 1756 and is the emblem of authority for this legislative body. Its panels contain the royal arms of England, the House of Hanover, and the Province of South Carolina. The Mace remains in a rack at the House Rostrum until adjournment or is carried by the House Sergeant of Arms should the body officially leave the Chambers.

Cheeseburger Pie

This dish freezes well.

SERVES 6

1	pound ground London broil or round	2	eggs, well beaten
1	teaspoon olive oil	1	(12 ounce) can evaporated milk (or fat free)
1	large onion, chopped	½	cup mayonnaise (or reduced fat)
3	cups grated sharp Cheddar cheese		**Salt and pepper to taste**
1	(9-inch) frozen deep dish pie shell, thawed and baked		

Preheat oven to 350 degrees. Brown ground beef in oil. Cool and stir in onion. Spoon alternating layers of meat and Cheddar cheese in pie shell ending with cheese. Combine eggs, milk, mayonnaise, salt and pepper. Pour over cheese. Bake for 45 minutes or until knife inserted in center comes out clean. May substitute a cholesterol-free egg product for eggs.

Floride Carter
(Former House Speaker Rex L. Carter)

Death Valley is the nickname for Clemson University Memorial Stadium. A rock from Death Valley, California rests on a base at the top of the east end zone hill. Before each game, players and coaches rub the rock for good luck before running down the hill into the stadium. This is one of the best-known college football traditions.

Easy Enchiladas

SERVES 6

1	cup vegetable oil	1	(10 ounce) package Longhorn cheese, shredded
12	corn tortillas		
1	pound ground beef	1	(10¾ ounce) can cream of chicken soup
1	large onion, chopped		
1	garlic clove, minced	1	cup milk
1	teaspoon pepper		Salt and pepper to taste

Preheat oven to 300 degrees. Heat oil in a large skillet over medium heat. Warm tortillas until soft. Transfer to paper towels to drain. Brown beef, onion, garlic and pepper in skillet. Top each tortilla with a tablespoon of meat mixture. Sprinkle with some cheese. Roll up tortillas tightly and place in a lightly greased 13x9x2-inch baking dish. Heat soup and milk over medium heat until bubbly. Pour soup over enchiladas. Sprinkle with remaining cheese. Bake for 20-30 minutes.

Barbara Dantzler
(Representative Thomas M. Dantzler)

The Order of the Palmetto is an award initiated by Governor John C. West. The award recognizes contributions and friendship to the State. It is the State's highest honor.

Ranch Style Baked Beans

Goes great with burgers or ribs.

SERVES 4-6

1	pound ground beef
1	teaspoon vegetable oil
1	small onion, chopped
1	bell pepper, chopped
3	(15 ounce) cans pork and beans

2	tablespoons prepared mustard
1	tablespoon cider vinegar
¾	cup barbecue sauce

Preheat oven to 325 degrees. Brown beef, onion and pepper in oil in a large skillet until tender. Drain drippings. Add beans, mustard, vinegar and barbecue sauce to meat. Pour mixture into a 13x9x2-inch baking dish. Bake for 30 minutes.

Amy Wright
(Former Representative David Wright)

*South Carolina is called
the "Tastier Peach State."
The soil and weather conditions
help produce sweeter peaches.
The SC Peach Festival takes
place each July in Gaffney.*

Brother's Chili and Beans

This is a recipe from my brother, Jerry Mack. He makes the best chili.

1	pound ground beef	1	(15 ounce) can black beans
1	pound pork sausage	½	(6 ounce) can tomato paste
1	(14½ ounce) can whole tomatoes, chopped	3-5	tablespoons ketchup
1	(5½ ounce) can Bush Magic Chili Starter		Salt and pepper to taste
1	(15½ ounce) can light red kidney beans		

Brown beef and sausage. Drain well. In a large saucepan, combine beef mixture, tomatoes, chili starter, kidney beans and black beans and mix well. Stir in tomato paste and ketchup. Add salt and pepper. Bring to boil. Reduce heat and simmer for 2 hours. A longer cooking time enhances the flavor.

Kathy Koon
(Former Representative Larry Koon)

General Thomas Sumter, a Revolutionary War hero, was called "The Gamecock" in tribute to his aggressive fighting of the British troops. The Town and County of Sumter were named after this hero. The Gamecock is also the team mascot for the University of South Carolina.

Classic Osso Buco

This dish is great served with risotto and good crusty bread.

SERVES 6

1	cup all-purpose flour
2	tablespoons paprika
1	tablespoon lemon zest
1	teaspoon dried thyme
½	teaspoon freshly ground black pepper
¼	cup extra virgin olive oil
	Salt to taste
6	(12 ounce) veal shanks, 1-inch thick
2	medium yellow onions, chopped
¾	cup chopped carrots
½	cup chopped celery
3	large garlic cloves, minced
1	cup dry white wine
2	cups beef broth
2	cups chicken broth
1	cup diced tomatoes with juice
¼	cup chopped fresh flat leaf parsley
1	bay leaf

Combine flour, paprika, zest, thyme and pepper in a shallow bowl. Heat oil in a large stockpot or Dutch oven over medium-high heat. Sprinkle salt over veal. Dredge in flour mixture. Brown shanks about 4 minutes per sides. May need to brown in batches. Do not overcrowd the pot. Transfer shanks to a plate and set aside. Add onions, carrots, celery and garlic to stockpot. Cook until onion is tender. Add wine and bring to boil. Cook until liquid has almost evaporated. Add beef broth, chicken broth, tomatoes, parsley and bay leaf. Stir well. Return veal shanks to stockpot and reduce heat to low. Cover and cook for 1 hour, 45 minutes. Transfer veal to a plate and cover loosely with foil. Increase heat to medium-high and bring to boil. Cook for about 30 minutes or until thickened. Remove bay leaf. Press liquid and vegetables through a strainer and return strained sauce to stockpot. Adjust seasoning and return veal. Simmer for about 10-15 minutes to reheat. Arrange veal on serving platter and pour sauce over top. Serve hot.

Vickie Skelton
(Representative B.R. Skelton)

South of the Border, located off Interstate 95, is a tourist attraction for those who enjoy eccentric souvenirs. Just look for Pedro – you can't miss him.

Grilled Balsamic Sage Veal Chops

SERVES 4

4	(1¼-inch) bone-in veal rib chops	3	tablespoons good quality aged balsamic vinegar
2	garlic cloves, pressed		Salt and pepper to taste
1	teaspoon dried sage	1	(4 ounce) goat cheese, sliced

Rub both sides of chops with garlic and sage. Drizzle both sides with vinegar. Marinate at room temperature for about 1 hour. Preheat grill to high heat with lid down for 15 minutes. Sprinkle chops with salt and pepper. Grill chops for 2 minutes per side. Reduce heat to medium or turn off one burner. Grill with lid down for about 6 more minutes. Use meat thermometer to check desired degree of doneness, 130 degrees for medium rare. Just before removing, place a slice of goat cheese on top of each chop and let melt slightly. Place chops on serving plates and drizzle with a little more vinegar.

Representative B.R. Skelton

The dance craze, the Charleston, began in Charleston in the early 1900s.

Grilled Pork Tenderloin

SERVES 4

2	**pork tenderloins (1-1½ pounds)**
2	**(1½ ounce) packages McCormick Meat Marinade**

½	**cup soy sauce**
½	**cup packed brown sugar**

Place tenderloins in a glass dish or a large zip-top plastic bag. Prepare marinade according to package directions. Blend marinade, soy sauce and brown sugar. Pour over tenderloins, cover and refrigerate overnight, turning at least once. Grill over medium heat with cover closed for 8 minutes. Turn and grill for 8 more minutes. Slice and serve immediately.

Cathy Harrell
(House Speaker Robert W. Harrell, Jr.)

The Society of Stranders began in North Myrtle Beach in 1980 as a reunion of lifeguards and other workers who spent their summers along the Grand Strand. They continue to meet each year for reminiscing and shagging.

Supper Club Pork Chops

This is a favorite recipe for a casual get together or a weeknight treat.

SERVES 4

2 tablespoons canola oil	1 tablespoon clover honey
4 (¾-inch thick) boneless center cut pork loin chops	⅛ teaspoon salt
	⅛ teaspoon pepper
1 medium onion, sliced	½ cup plus ½ cup chicken broth, divided
1 large garlic clove, minced	
½ cup orange juice	2 tablespoons all-purpose flour
1½ tablespoons cider vinegar	
1 teaspoon paprika	Chopped parsley for garnish

Heat oil in a large heavy sauté pan or deep skillet on medium-high heat. Brown pork chops on both sides. Separate onion into rings and place on top of the chops. Add garlic, orange juice, vinegar, paprika, honey, salt, pepper and ½ cup chicken broth. Bring to boil. Cover, reduce heat and simmer for about 1 hour. Transfer pork chops to a plate and keep warm. In a small bowl, slowly whisk remaining ½ cup broth into flour until well blended. Stir mixture into drippings in skillet and cook, stirring constantly, until thickened. Return chops to sauce and serve. Garnish with chopped parsley.

Cookbook Committee

Greenville native Charles Townes won the Nobel Prize in Physics in 1964 for his invention of the LASER which revolutionized our lives in many ways.

Spring Rack of Lamb with Mint Pesto

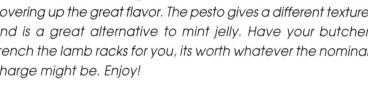

This is a simple dish that always receives rave reviews. The herbs give the lamb just the right amount of enhancement without covering up the great flavor. The pesto gives a different texture and is a great alternative to mint jelly. Have your butcher French the lamb racks for you, its worth whatever the nominal charge might be. Enjoy!

SERVES 4

MINT PESTO (MAKES ABOUT 2 CUPS)

¾	cup loosely packed mint leaves	½	cup grated Parmesan cheese
6	garlic cloves, smashed		Salt and pepper to taste
¾	cup extra virgin olive oil		

Purée mint, garlic, oil and Parmesan cheese in a food processor until smooth. Add salt and pepper. Store in refrigerator but serve at room temperature.

LAMB

¼	cup extra virgin olive oil	2	garlic cloves
1	sprig of rosemary	2	racks of lamb, french cut
1	sprig of thyme		Mint Pesto

Preheat oven to 350 degrees. Cover bottom of large skillet with oil. Heat over medium heat. Carefully add herbs and garlic. Cook gently about 5 minutes so oil takes on the flavor of the herbs. Reduce heat to medium-low and with flat top of lamb rack down, sear the side for 3 minutes. With tongs flip the rack over and sear the loin side for 3 minutes. Bake for 15-20 minutes for medium rare. Serve with the mint pesto and your favorite side dish.

Jenny Sanford
(Governor Marshall C. Sanford, Jr.)

Possum Trot School is a one room schoolhouse originally built in 1880. It has been restored and is located in Gaffney. It is privately owned, but open to the public for tours.

Chicken with Mushroom Sauce

SERVES 6

3	boneless, skinless chicken breasts, split	½	cup sauterne wine
½	teaspoon plus ½ teaspoon salt, divided	1	(6 ounce) jar sliced mushrooms, drained or ½ pound fresh, sliced
3	tablespoons all-purpose flour	½	cup unblanched, sliced almonds
1	cup sour cream		Paprika to taste
1	(10¾ ounce) can cream of mushroom soup		

Preheat oven to 325 degrees. Arrange chicken in the bottom of 11x8x2-inch baking dish. Sprinkle with ½ teaspoon salt. Blend flour and sour cream until smooth. Add remaining ½ teaspoon salt, soup and sauterne. Mix well. Add mushrooms. If using fresh mushrooms, sauté in 1 tablespoon of oil until tender. Pour sour cream mixture over chicken. Sprinkle almonds and a little paprika over top. Bake for 1 hour, 30 minutes.

Joanne Clark
(Former Representative Ken Clark)

The South Carolina Hall of Fame is located in Myrtle Beach.

Spicy Chicken Piazziola

This sauce is also great with veal scaloppine. A great side for this dish is angel hair pasta with some of the sauce.

SERVES 6

½	cup plus 2 tablespoon olive oil, divided
2	large sweet red peppers, seeded and chopped
6	garlic cloves, minced
2	teaspoons fennel seeds
½	teaspoon dried crushed red pepper
2	(28 ounce) cans chopped tomatoes, undrained
2	bunches fresh basil leaves
4	tablespoons tomato paste
1	teaspoon dried oregano
¼	teaspoon ground allspice
	Pinch of ground cloves
	Salt and pepper to taste
6	split chicken breast halves, skinned and boned

Heat ½ cup oil in heavy large saucepan over medium-high heat. Add bell pepper, garlic, fennel seeds and red pepper. Sauté about 2-3 minutes, careful not to burn the garlic. Add tomatoes with juice, basil, tomato paste, oregano, allspice and cloves. Bring to boil. Reduce heat and simmer for about 1 hour. Remove basil and add salt and pepper. Cool. Purée sauce in a food processor or blender. Return to saucepan and keep warm.

Heat remaining 2 tablespoons oil in a large skillet on medium-high heat. Slice chicken horizontally. Sprinkle with salt and pepper. Sauté chicken about 3-4 minutes per side or until done. Pour sauce over chicken. Simmer for about 2-3 minutes until chicken is well coated with sauce. Serve warm.

Vickie Skelton
(Representative B.R. Skelton)

Porgy and Bess, one of the most famous American operas, was officially designated the Opera of the State in 2001. It was written by Charleston native DuBose Heyward and put to music by George Gershwin.

Poached Chicken Breasts in a White Wine Sauce

SERVES 4

4   **(4 ounce) chicken breast halves, skinned and boned**

¾   **cup Chablis or other dry white wine**

2½   **cups sliced fresh mushrooms**

2   **tablespoons chopped fresh parsley**

½   **teaspoon dried whole tarragon**

½   **teaspoon salt**

¼   **teaspoon pepper**

1   **tablespoon cornstarch**

2   **teaspoons water**

Place chicken between 2 sheets of heavy-duty plastic wrap. Using a meat mallet or rolling pin, pound chicken to ¼-inch thickness. Combine Chablis, mushrooms, parsley, tarragon, salt and pepper in a large skillet. Bring to boil over high heat. Arrange chicken in a single layer in skillet. Reduce heat, cover and simmer for 15 minutes or until chicken is tender. Transfer chicken to serving plate and keep warm. Blend cornstarch and water. Stir into skillet. Bring mixture to boil. Cook for 1 minute, stirring constantly. Pour sauce over chicken and serve.

Tunky Riley
(Former Governor Richard W. Riley)

Bob Campbell Geology Museum, located at Clemson University, houses one of the largest faceted gem collections in the southeast.

Chicken Spectacular

SERVES 8-10

3	cups cooked, chopped chicken	1	cup mayonnaise
1	(6 ounce) package long-grain and wild rice mix, cooked	1	(8 ounce) can sliced water chestnuts, drained
1	(10¾ ounce) can cream of celery soup	1	(2 ounce) jar diced pimiento
1	medium onion, chopped	1	(4 ounce) jar sliced mushrooms, drained
2	(15 ounce) cans French style green beans, drained	1½	cups soft bread crumbs
		2	tablespoons butter, melted

Preheat oven to 350 degrees. Combine chicken, rice, soup, onion, green beans, mayonnaise, chestnuts, pimiento and mushrooms. Pour mixture into a 2½-quart casserole dish. Cover and bake for 40 minutes. Mix together bread crumbs and butter. Sprinkle mixture over top. Broil until browned. Serve immediately.

Emilie Theodore
(Former Lt. Governor Nick Theodore)

Pendleton Historic District contains 6,316 acres and more than 40 points of interest. It is listed in the National Register of Historic Places and is one of the most visited historic districts in the country.

Chicken Reuben

SERVES 8

8   chicken breast halves, skinned and boned

½   cup all-purpose flour

2   eggs, beaten

1   cup fine rye bread crumbs

    Salt and pepper to taste

4   tablespoons unsalted butter

¼   cup canola oil

12 tablespoons Thousand Island dressing (any brand)

8   tablespoons sauerkraut, drained

8   slices Swiss cheese

Preheat oven to 350 degrees. Pound chicken between 2 sheets of plastic wrap. Place flour in a shallow dish and bread crumbs in another shallow dish. Pour eggs in a third dish. Dredge chicken in flour. Dip in egg and then bread crumbs. Sprinkle with salt and pepper. Heat butter and oil in large skillet on medium heat. Brown chicken about 3 minutes per side. Add more oil as needed, being careful not to burn. Arrange cooked chicken on a baking sheet. Top each chicken breast with 1½ tablespoons dressing and 1 tablespoon sauerkraut. Top with cheese slice. Bake for 20 minutes or until cheese is bubbly.

Vickie Skelton
(Representative B.R. Skelton)

Clayton "Peg Leg" Bates was a native of Fountain Inn. He lost his leg at an early age but went on to become a famous tap dancer. He made many appearances on the Ed Sullivan Show.

Old-Fashioned Chicken Pot Pie

SERVES 6-8

2½ pounds boneless, skinless chicken breast halves	2 cups chicken broth
⅓ cup butter	1 cup milk
½ cup sliced onion	Salt and pepper to taste
1 cup sliced celery	1 (2 ounce) jar diced pimiento (optional)
1 cup sliced carrots	2-3 hard-cooked eggs, chopped
½ cup chopped potatoes	1 refrigerated pie crust
½ cup all-purpose flour	

Preheat oven to 400 degrees. Boil chicken and chop. Melt butter in a large skillet on medium-high heat. Add onion, celery, carrots and potatoes. Sauté for 10 minutes until tender. Stir in flour until smooth. Gradually add broth and milk. Cook on medium heat until thickened and bubbly, stirring constantly. Stir in chicken, salt, pepper, pimiento and eggs. Spoon mixture into a greased 13x9x2-inch baking dish. Roll out pie crust to fit over baking dish. Place over top of chicken mixture. Seal and crimp the edges. Cut slits in top to vent. Bake for 30 minutes or until golden browned. After 20 minutes, may need to lightly cover to prevent edges from burning. Great served over rice.

Anne Elliott
(Senator Dick Elliott)

Anderson is known as "The Electric City" because of the ingenuity of native son, engineer William Whitner. He realized that hydroelectricity could be transmitted long distances by wire and built a power plant near the city of Anderson. The first cotton gin to be powered by electricity was located in Anderson.

Supreme Chicken Casserole

SERVE 10-12

6	boneless, skinless chicken breasts halves	1	(4 ounce) jar diced pimiento
8	ounces white mushrooms, sliced	1	(6 ounce) package long-grain and wild rice mix, cooked
1	tablespoon olive oil		
1	cup unsalted butter	1	(8 ounce) can water chestnuts, drained
1	cup finely chopped onion		
½	cup all-purpose flour	3	tablespoons chopped parsley
3	cups chicken broth	3	teaspoons salt
3	cups half-and-half	¼	teaspoon freshly ground white pepper

Preheat oven to 350 degrees. Boil chicken until tender. Cool and chop chicken into small pieces. Set aside. In a large, heavy skillet, sauté mushroom in oil until tender. In a large stockpot, melt butter and sauté onion until tender. Whisk in flour until well blended. Cook for about 3 minutes. Slowly add chicken broth, whisking constantly. Stir in half-and-half. Cook until thickened and bubbly, stirring constantly. Add chicken, mushrooms, pimiento, rice mix, water chestnuts, parsley, salt and pepper. Pour mixture into a greased 13x9x2-inch baking dish. Bake for 40 minutes or until bubbly.

Cookbook Committee

Old Stone Church located in Clemson was built in 1797. The original church burned a few years after completion and was replaced by a stone structure that still stands today. Services are held on special occasions and it is a popular place for weddings. Former Governor and Revolutionary War hero Andrew Pickens, Jr. is buried in the cemetery.

Easy Chicken and Noodles

SERVES 6

4   boneless, skinless chicken breast halves

2   (15 ounce) cans chicken broth

3   (10¾ ounce) cans cream of chicken soup

2   cups half-and-half or milk

1   (8 ounce) package wide egg noodles

Salt and pepper to taste

Cook chicken and shred. Combine chicken, broth, soup and milk in a large stockpot. Bring to boil. Add noodles and water if necessary to cover. Simmer until noodles are tender. Let stand 20 minutes or until thickened as desired. Add salt and pepper.

Melody Duncan
(Representative Jeffrey D. Duncan)

Greenville native, Joel Poinsett, was the first ambassador to Mexico from 1825 until 1830. He introduced to the US a plant from Mexico which later became known as the poinsettia. This plant accounts for about 85 percent of the potted plants sold during the Christmas holidays.

Margarita Chicken with Black Bean and Corn Salsa

SERVES 6

CHICKEN

½	cup gold tequila	1	tablespoon minced cilantro
1	cup fresh lime juice	1	teaspoon kosher salt
½	cup fresh orange juice		Freshly ground black pepper
1	tablespoon chili powder		
1	jalapeño pepper, seeded and quartered	6	boneless chicken breast halves
2	garlic cloves, minced		

Blend tequila, lime juice, orange juice, chili powder, jalapeño, garlic, cilantro, salt and pepper in a medium bowl until well mixed. Place chicken in a large glass dish. Pour marinade over chicken. Cover and refrigerate overnight.

SALSA

6	tablespoons fresh lime juice	1½	teaspoons ground cumin
6	tablespoons canola oil	2	(15 ounce) cans black beans, rinsed and drained
½	cup chopped cilantro	1	(15 ounce) can whole kernel corn, drained
¼	cup finely chopped sweet onion		Salt and pepper to taste
¼	cup chopped green onion	2	ripe tomatoes, seeded and chopped

In a large bowl, blend lime juice, oil, cilantro, onions and cumin. Add black beans and corn. Stir until well blended. Add salt and pepper. Refrigerate until ready to serve. Remove from refrigerator and add tomatoes. Adjust seasonings.

Heat grill to medium-high heat. Remove chicken from marinade. Grill, skin side down, for about 4 minutes. Turn over and cook for about 10 minutes with lid down. Serve with the salsa.

Vickie Skelton
(Representative B.R. Skelton)

Sassafras Mountain, located in northern Pickens County, is 3,560 feet in elevation and is the highest point in South Carolina. Four states can be viewed from the top: South Carolina, Tennessee, North Carolina and Georgia.

Easy Chicken Cacciatore

SERVES 4

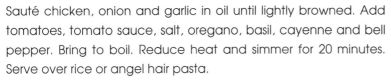

1	pound boneless chicken tenders	1	(8 ounce) can tomato sauce
½	cup chopped onion	1	teaspoon salt
1	garlic clove, minced	½	teaspoon dried oregano
2	tablespoons olive oil	½	teaspoon dried basil
1	(28 ounce) can tomatoes, chopped	⅛	teaspoon cayenne pepper
		1	cup chopped bell pepper

Sauté chicken, onion and garlic in oil until lightly browned. Add tomatoes, tomato sauce, salt, oregano, basil, cayenne and bell pepper. Bring to boil. Reduce heat and simmer for 20 minutes. Serve over rice or angel hair pasta.

Amy Wright
(Former Representative David Wright)

Farmers Society Hall, built in 1828, is located on the site of a former courthouse on the town square in Pendleton. It is the oldest farmer's hall in continuous use in the United States.

Chicken Parmesan

SERVES 6

MARINARA SAUCE

¼ cup extra virgin olive oil

2 garlic cloves, minced

2 (28 ounce) cans crushed tomatoes

1 teaspoon dried basil

1 teaspoon dried oregano

¼ teaspoon sugar

½ teaspoon salt

¼ teaspoon freshly ground pepper

Heat oil in large heavy saucepan over medium heat. Sauté garlic for about 1 minute. Do not burn. Add tomatoes, basil, oregano, sugar, salt and pepper. Reduce heat and simmer for about 20 minutes or until sauce thickens. Keep warm.

CHICKEN

2 large eggs, beaten

1½ cups fine dry bread crumbs

1 teaspoon salt

¼ teaspoon pepper

6 boneless, skinless chicken breast halves, rinsed and trimmed

½ cup extra virgin olive oil

1 (8 ounce) package part skim sliced mozzarella cheese, sliced into 12 slices

¾ cup freshly grated Parmesan cheese

1 pound angel hair pasta, cooked al dente

Beat eggs in a large shallow dish. Set aside. Combine bread crumbs, salt and pepper in another shallow dish. Pat dry chicken and slice each breast in half horizontally. Lightly pound each piece. Dredge in egg and then in bread crumbs. Heat oil in large skillet on medium heat. Sauté chicken about 4 minutes per side, working in batches. Do not overcrowd and be careful not to burn. Add more oil as needed. Transfer cooked chicken to a wire rack set on a baking sheet. This keeps chicken from getting soggy. Place a cheese slice on each chicken piece. Sprinkle with Parmesan cheese. Broil until cheese melts. Pour some marinara sauce on pasta and toss to coat. Place pasta on serving plates. Top with chicken and spoon a little sauce over chicken.

Cookbook Committee

Carmel Church located in Liberty was founded in the mid-1700s and is believed to be the oldest church in the Upstate.

Jean Chesno's Famous Greek Chicken

This recipe comes from my dear friend, Jean Chesno. Jean is the legislative aide for the Pickens County delegation and just celebrated her 20th year with the House of Representatives in 2006. This is one of my husband's favorite recipes that Jean was kind enough to share. I am sure you will also enjoy.

SERVES 4

2 medium ripe tomatoes, peeled and chopped	⅓ cup dry white wine
¼ cup all-purpose flour	⅓ cup chicken broth
1 tablespoon dried oregano	3 tablespoons sliced ripe olives
4 boneless, skinless chicken breast halves	2 tablespoons capers
3 tablespoons olive oil	2 tablespoons crumbled feta cheese

Blanch tomatoes in boiling water for 1 minute. Remove tomatoes and place in ice water for 1 minute to stop cooking process. Peel tomatoes and chop. Set aside. Combine flour and oregano in a shallow dish. Dredge chicken in flour. Heat oil in a large skillet over medium heat. Cook chicken for about 10 minutes, turning once. Add wine and broth and simmer for 10-15 minutes. Stir in tomatoes, olives and capers. Cook until thoroughly heated. Spoon onto serving dish and sprinkle with feta cheese.

Vickie Skelton
(Representative B.R. Skelton)

The Fran Hanson Discovery Center at Clemson University is one of four discovery centers in the SC National Heritage Corridor. This center focuses on the mountain and lakes area of the Corridor.

Barbecued Turkey

SERVES 8-10

10-12 pound turkey

SAUCE

1	quart vinegar	3	tablespoons cayenne pepper
¼	cup salt	3	tablespoons black pepper
¼	cup sugar		Tabasco sauce to taste
6	tablespoons crushed red pepper	2	drops liquid smoke

Preheat oven to 325 degrees. Wash and salt turkey. Cook turkey in a roaster half full of water for 1 hour, 30 minutes-2 hours or until meat thermometer registers 180 degrees. Pour off stock for gravy or dressing. Remove turkey from bone and place in baking dish. Blend vinegar, salt, sugar, red pepper, cayenne, black pepper, Tabasco and liquid smoke. Pour sauce over turkey, tossing to coat. Reduce heat to 275 degrees. Bake for approximately 30 minutes. May be served immediately, but even better the next day. May adjust seasoning to make sauce less spicy.

Judy Frye
(Representative Marion B. Frye)

Greenville's Greek Festival celebrated each May showcases this wonderful heritage with food, folk dance and music.

Quail in Wine Sauce

SERVES 4

6-8	quails	¼	cup all-purpose flour
	Salt and pepper to taste	1 ½	cups chicken broth
¼	cup butter	½	cup white wine
1	onion, finely chopped		

Preheat oven to 275 degrees. Wash and dry quail. Sprinkle with salt and pepper. Lightly brown in butter in heavy skillet. Transfer quail to a 13x9x2-inch baking dish. Sauté onion in pan drippings. Add flour and stir for about 2 minutes. Slowly stir in chicken broth and wine. Pour sauce over quail. Bake for 1 hour, 15 minutes.

Mary Wood Beasley
(Former Governor David M. Beasley)

*David M. Beasley
was a State Representative
and later served as Governor
from 1995-1999.*

187

Shrimp with Tomatoes and Feta Cheese

SERVES 6

1	teaspoon olive oil
2	onions, finely chopped
2-3	ripe tomatoes, finely diced
2	garlic cloves, minced
1	bay leaf
2	teaspoons sugar

	Salt and pepper to taste
½	cup water
2¼	pounds medium shrimp, peeled and deveined
7	ounces feta cheese, crumbled

Preheat oven to 375 degrees. In a large saucepan, sauté onions in oil. Add tomatoes, garlic, bay leaf, sugar, salt and pepper. Add water and simmer for 30 minutes on medium-low heat. Add shrimp and cook for another 4 minutes. Remove from heat and Transfer mixture to a 13x9x2-inch baking dish. Sprinkle feta on top. Bake for 10 minutes. Serve immediately.

Anne Elliott
(Senator Dick Elliott)

The Pickens County Museum is housed in a former county jail built in 1902.

Dotty's Shrimp and Rice Casserole

SERVES 6

1	(10¾ ounce) can cream of mushroom soup	4-5	dashes Tabasco sauce
½	cup mayonnaise	1	cup sliced water chestnuts
1	cup milk	1½	pounds cooked medium shrimp, peeled and deveined
1	cup chopped onion		
1	cup chopped celery	2	cups cooked rice
½	teaspoon chopped parsley	1½	cups soft bread crumbs
		2	tablespoons butter, melted

Preheat oven to 350 degrees. Combine soup, mayonnaise, milk, onion, celery, parsley and Tabasco until well blended. Stir in water chestnuts. Add shrimp and rice. Mix well. Pour mixture into a lightly greased 2½-quart casserole dish. Combine bread crumbs and butter. Sprinkle over top. Bake for 40-45 minutes.

E.V. Leventis
(Senator Phil P. Leventis)

Abbeville was a stopover for theater companies traveling by rail between New York and Florida during the early 1900s. The Abbeville Opera House was built in 1908 and played host to many of the stars of vaudeville. The Opera House was renovated in 1968 and is still in use today.

Welcome Neighbor Shrimp Casserole

This recipe is Michael's famous shrimp casserole. The perfect dish to welcome newcomers.

SERVES 4

2	cups cooked rice
1	(10¾ ounce) can cream of mushroom soup
¾	pound raw, shelled and deveined medium shrimp
½	cup cubed sharp Cheddar cheese
2	tablespoons melted butter
2	tablespoons chopped bell pepper
2	tablespoons chopped onion
1	tablespoon fresh lemon juice
½	teaspoon Worcestershire sauce
¼	teaspoon pepper
½	teaspoon dry mustard
½	cup cashews

Preheat oven to 375 degrees. Combine rice, soup, shrimp, Cheddar cheese, butter, bell pepper, onion, lemon juice, Worcestershire sauce, pepper, mustard and cashews. Mix well. Pour mixture into a greased 1½-quart casserole dish. Bake uncovered for 40 minutes.

Susan Wilkins
(Former House Speaker, US Ambassador David H. Wilkins)

McCormick County is the smallest county in South Carolina at 360 square miles.

Waccamaw Shrimp Casserole

SERVES 8-10

2	pounds boiled shrimp, peeled and deveined	1	(8 ounce) can sliced water chestnuts, drained
4	hard-cooked eggs, chopped	3	dashes of Tabasco sauce
1	cup chopped onion	3	dashes of Worcestershire sauce
½	cup chopped bell pepper		Salt and pepper to taste
1	cup chopped celery	1½	cups crushed round buttery crackers
1	(2 ounce) jar diced pimiento	2	tablespoons butter, melted
1	(10¾ ounce) can cream of mushroom soup		

Preheat oven to 350 degrees. Combine shrimp, eggs, onion, bell pepper, celery, pimiento, soup, water chestnuts, Tabasco, Worcestershire sauce, salt and pepper. Pour mixture into a greased 13x9x2-inch baking dish. Mix cracker crumbs and butter. Sprinkle over top. Bake for 30 minutes or until bubbly.

Linda Witherspoon
(Representative William D. Witherspoon)

The Treaty Oak Marker, located in Clemson, is the site where the first treaty between the United States and the Cherokee Indian Nation was signed.

Shrimp and Asparagus over Pasta

This recipe is from my friend, Gale Kennedy. Gale's father, Bobby Rigby, is a former Sergeant at Arms for the Senate. Gale started working in the House of Representatives in 1976 and has been in the Senate for 12 years. In 1993 and 2003, she wrote 2 cookbooks. She also helped the Palmetto Cabinet with its first cookbook in 1983. Her granddaughters Rigby, Maddy and Nettie love to help her cook using five generations of family recipes.

SERVES 4

16	fresh asparagus spears	1	tablespoon tomato paste
32	fresh medium shrimp	¼	cup brandy
1	tablespoon plus 1 tablespoon oil, divided	¼	cup white wine
1	tablespoon plus 1 tablespoon butter, divided	¼	cup water
1	carrot, chopped	1	cup heavy cream
2	shallots, minced		Salt and pepper to taste
1	stalk celery, chopped		Angel hair pasta, cooked al dente

Denver Downs, a family owned farm in Anderson, cuts a maze in its cornfield each year for visitors to enjoy. The maze pattern changes from year to year. One year it featured a pattern to acknowledge the football rivalry between USC and Clemson University.

Cook asparagus in boiling salted water for 2-3 minutes. Drain and plunge into a bowl of iced water and set aside. Peel and devein raw shrimp and save the shells. In a saucepan, heat 1 tablespoon each oil and butter. Sauté carrot, shallots and celery for 2-3 minutes until soft. Add shrimp shells and tomato paste. Mix well. Remove from heat. Stir in brandy. Add white wine and water. Return to heat and simmer on low for 10 minutes. Strain broth into a small pot and discard shells and vegetables. Add cream, salt and pepper to broth and simmer on medium heat for 20 minutes. Do not boil. In a skillet, heat remaining 1 tablespoon oil and butter. Cut each asparagus spear into thirds and sauté for 1 minute. Add shrimp and sauté until pink and done. Combine shrimp and asparagus with the sauce. Serve over angel hair pasta.

Betty Ryberg
(Senator W. Greg Ryberg)

Carolina Crab Au Gratin

SERVES 4-6

- ¾ cup shredded white Cheddar cheese
- 3 green onions, finely chopped
- ½ cup mayonnaise
- 2 cups jumbo lump crabmeat
- ½ cup heavy cream
- ⅓ cup Parmesan cheese
- ⅓ cup soft breadcrumbs
- ¼ cup chopped parsley

Preheat oven to 375 degrees. In a medium bowl, combine Cheddar cheese, onions and mayonnaise. Fold in crabmeat. Spoon mixture into a greased casserole dish. Pour cream over top. In a small bowl, combine Parmesan cheese, bread crumbs and parsley. Sprinkle bread crumbs over the top. Bake for 15-20 minutes or until bubbly.

Cookbook Committee

Park Seed Company, one of the largest family owned seed companies, is known for its beautiful gardens and is the focal point of the annual South Carolina Festival of Flowers held in Greenwood each June.

Blue Crab Cakes with Avocado Corn Salsa

SERVES 6

AVOCADO CORN SALSA

1	cup whole kernel corn	¼	cup diced sweet red, yellow and bell pepper
1	cup diced avocado	1	teaspoon fresh lemon juice
1	tablespoon chopped cilantro	½	diced jalapeño pepper
1	cup diced Roma tomatoes (about 3)	2	tablespoons cider vinegar
1	teaspoon diced shallot		Salt and pepper to taste

Combine corn, avocado, cilantro, tomatoes, shallot, bell pepper, lemon juice, jalapeño, vinegar, salt and pepper. Mix well. Marinate for at least 2 hours.

CRAB CAKES

1	pound lump crabmeat	¼	cup mayonnaise
¼	cup diced onion	1	tablespoon Dijon mustard
¼	cup diced sweet red and bell pepper	¾	cup panko breadcrumbs
2	tablespoons capers, diced		Juice of ½ lemon
2	eggs, beaten		Salt and pepper to taste
2	tablespoons Cajun seasoning	½	cup all-purpose flour
		½	cup vegetable oil

Lightly combine crabmeat, onion, bell pepper, capers, eggs, seasoning, mayonnaise, mustard, bread crumbs, lemon juice, salt and pepper. Shape mixture into small cakes and place on a baking sheet. Refrigerate until ready to fry. Dredge cakes in flour and shallow fry the cakes in heated oil. Serve atop the avocado corn salsa.

Executive Chef Michael Deevey
SC Governor's Mansion

Submitted by Jenny Sanford
(Governor Marshall C. Sanford, Jr.)

The Town and County of Laurens is named for Henry Laurens of Charleston who was President of the Continental Congress during the Revolutionary War.

Moncks Corner Seafood Casserole

SERVES 6-8

2-3 celery stalks, chopped	Dash of Tabasco sauce
1 medium onion, chopped	1 pound fresh or canned white crabmeat
1 bell pepper, chopped	1½ pounds medium shrimp, peeled and deveined
1¼ cups mayonnaise	Salt and pepper to taste (small amount of salt)
¼ cup flavored sandwich and salad sauce (I use Durkee's)	2 tablespoons unsalted butter, cut into small pieces
1 tablespoon fresh lemon juice	2-3 bread slices
Dash of Worcestershire sauce	

Preheat oven to 400 degrees. Combine celery, onion, bell pepper, mayonnaise, salad sauce, lemon juice, Worcestershire sauce and Tabasco. Mix well. Fold in crabmeat and shrimp. Add salt and pepper. Pour mixture into a greased casserole dish. Bake for 30 minutes, uncovered. Spread butter over bread. Cut into cubes. Toast under broiler. Top casserole with toasted bread cubes and serve.

Vera W. Helmly
(Former Representative Robert L. Helmly)

Hanover House, built in 1716 in St. John's Berkeley Parish, was dismantled and moved to the campus of Clemson University when the area was about to be flooded by the Santee Cooper hydroelectric project.

Bay Scallops with Spinach and Garlic

SERVES 4

1 teaspoon plus 1 teaspoon olive oil, divided	1 teaspoon plus ½ teaspoon kosher salt, divided
3 large garlic cloves, minced	Freshly ground pepper to taste
1 teaspoon lemon zest	1 pound bay scallops
2 pounds fresh spinach, stemmed and washed, but not dried	2 tablespoons fresh lemon juice
	¼ cup white wine

Richard W. Riley served as State Representative and as State Senator. He was elected Governor in 1978 and served until 1987. He was appointed U.S. Secretary of Education (1992-2001) by President Bill Clinton.

Heat 1 teaspoon oil in a large pot over medium heat. Sauté garlic and lemon zest, stirring constantly, for 20 seconds. Add spinach and toss frequently until wilted. Drain off liquid. Sprinkle with 1 teaspoon of salt and pepper. Keep warm.

In a large nonstick skillet, heat remaining 1 teaspoon oil on medium-high heat. Sauté scallops about 1 minute until just cooked through. Transfer scallops to a plate and keep warm. Add lemon juice and wine to skillet. Cook, scraping the bottom of pan, for 15 seconds. Remove from heat and return scallops. Add remaining salt and pepper. Spoon a mound of spinach in the center of 4 plates. Surround with scallops. Serve immediately.

Tunky Riley
(Former Governor Richard W. Riley)

Oyster Pie

SERVES 6-8

- 1 pint South Carolina oysters
  Salt and pepper to taste
- 2 tablespoons plus 1 tablespoon butter, divided
- 1 cup oyster crackers, crushed (can use any buttery crackers as substitute)
- 2 (10¾ ounce) cans cream of mushroom soup
- ½ cup milk

Preheat oven to 350 degrees. Arrange a layer of half oysters in a greased casserole dish. Sprinkle with salt and pepper. Top with 2 tablespoons butter pieces. Add a layer of cracker crumbs. Cover with 1 can of soup. Repeat layers. Pour milk over top and dot with remaining 1 tablespoon butter. Bake for 30 minutes. Serve immediately. Can be made a day ahead and refrigerated until ready to bake.

Josephine McNair
(Former Governor Robert E. McNair)

Oysters are found in such abundance along the South Carolina coast that there are several festivals held to celebrate. The party starts in Mt. Pleasant in January, proceeds to Moncks Corner in March and ends in Columbia in April with the South Carolina Oyster Festival.

197

Oyster Spinach Casserole

Dish pairs well with sliced tomatoes and hot bread.

SERVES 6-8

1	cup sliced mushrooms	¼	teaspoon ground nutmeg
¼	cup minced green onions		Dash of white pepper
1	garlic clove, minced	2	(12 ounce) containers Select oysters, drained and rinsed
2	(10 ounce) packages frozen chopped spinach		
1	tablespoon butter or margarine	¼	cup grated Parmesan cheese
2	tablespoons all-purpose flour	2	tablespoons fine dry bread crumbs
1	cup skim milk		Pimiento strips for garnish (optional)
1	teaspoon lemon juice		

Preheat oven to 350 degrees. Sauté mushrooms, green onions and garlic until tender in a greased skillet. Drain and set aside. Cook spinach according to package directions, omitting salt. Drain spinach well and set aside. Melt butter in a medium saucepan over low heat. Whisk in flour until smooth. Cook 1 minute, stirring constantly. Gradually whisk in milk and cook over medium heat until thickened and bubbly. Stir in lemon juice, nutmeg and white pepper. Remove sauce from heat. Add reserved vegetables and spinach, stirring well. Spoon mixture into a greased 10x6x2-inch baking dish. Arrange oysters over spinach mixture. Sprinkle with Parmesan cheese and bread crumbs. Bake uncovered for 20 minutes or until oyster edges curl. Garnish with pimiento strips. Serve hot.

Tunky Riley
(Former Governor Richard W. Riley)

The 17th US President, Andrew Johnson, ran a tailor shop on the Laurens Town Square when he resided there in the 1820s.

Scalloped Oysters

SERVES 6-8

1	pint oysters	¾	cup heavy cream
4	cups saltine crackers, broken (not fine crumbs)	2	eggs, beaten
½	cup butter, melted	¼	cup oyster liquor
½	teaspoon salt	¼	teaspoon Worcestershire sauce
	Dash of pepper		

Preheat oven to 350 degrees. Drain oysters, save liquor. Combine cracker crumbs, butter, salt and pepper. Spread one half crumb mixture in bottom of greased 2-3 quart casserole dish. Cover with oysters. Combine cream, eggs, liquor and Worcestershire sauce. Pour one half sauce over oysters. Spread remaining cracker crumbs over top. Cover with remaining sauce. Place dish in a baking pan with enough water to one half depth of the casserole dish. This prevents casserole from drying out during baking. Bake for 40 minutes. Serve hot.

Mary Wood Beasley
(Former Governor David M. Beasley)

William B. Dorn mined one of the richest gold veins in South Carolina in McCormick during the 1840-50s. There are about 5 miles of tunnels from those earlier mines beneath the streets of McCormick.

199

Spicy Salmon with Avocado Mayonnaise

SERVES 6

AVOCADO MAYONNAISE

1	ripe Haas avocado	5	tablespoons mayonnaise
2	teaspoon fresh lemon juice		

Cut avocados in half, remove pit and scoop out flesh. Mash avocado with lemon juice. Whisk in mayonnaise until smooth. Cover and refrigerate until ready to serve.

SALMON

1	tablespoon light brown sugar	½	teaspoon chili powder
2	teaspoons paprika	½	teaspoon ground pepper
1½	teaspoon salt	6	salmon fillets, skin on
½	teaspoon ground cumin	2	tablespoons olive oil

Preheat oven to 425 degrees. Combine brown sugar, paprika, salt, cumin, chili powder and pepper. Mix well. Rinse fillets and pat dry. Place salmon fillets skin down on broiler pan. Brush tops with oil. Sprinkle with brown sugar mixture. Bake 5 inches from heat for 12-15 minutes. Serve with a dollop of avocado mayonnaise on top.

Emilie Theodore
(Former Lt. Governor Nick Theodore)

The Ware Shoals Catfish Festival held each May is a highlight for fisherman and catfish connoisseurs alike.

Grilled Salmon with Honey Mustard Glaze

SERVES 4

½	cup dry mustard	2	tablespoons water
½	cup sugar		Freshly ground black pepper to taste
2	tablespoons clover honey		
2	teaspoons soy sauce	4	6-ounce salmon fillets, with or without skin on

In a small bowl, combine mustard and sugar. Stir in honey and soy sauce. Whisk in water until smooth and thickened. If too thick, add more water. Add pepper. Heat grill to medium-high heat. Grill salmon for about 3 minutes per side for medium or to desired degree of doneness. Do not overcook. If skin is on, remove. Preheat broiler to high. Place fillets on broiler pan. Brush some glaze on top. Broil for about 1 minute or until lightly browned. Serve immediately.

Cookbook Committee

The Newberry Opera House was renovated in 1999 and currently attracts nationally recognized performers.

Grilled Tuna with Tomato Olive Relish

SERVES 4

3	tablespoons balsamic vinegar	1	(11 ounce) jar pitted kalamata olives, drained and chopped
2	small garlic cloves, minced	½	cup capers
½	cup good quality extra virgin olive oil		Salt and pepper to taste
6-8	Roma tomatoes, quartered	4	(6-ounce) tuna fillets, about 1-inch thick

Combine vinegar and garlic in large bowl. Whisk in oil. Add tomatoes, olives, capers, salt and pepper. Mix well. Marinate relish for at least 1 hour, stirring occasionally. Sprinkle tuna with salt and pepper. Heat grill on high with lid closed for about 10 minutes. Grill fillets with lid closed for about 2-3 minutes per side for medium rare. Top tuna with tomato relish and serve.

Vickie Skelton
(Representative B.R. Skelton)

Blackstock Battlefield Monument was erected near the Tyger River to memorialize the Patriots' victory at that site on November 20, 1780.

Island Grilled Mahi-Mahi with Melon Salsa

If you do not like Jamaican jerk seasoning, just omit it and sprinkle fish with salt and pepper.

SERVES 4

1   ripe Haas avocado

1   cup diced cantaloupe

½   cup finely chopped red onion

⅓   cup chopped fresh cilantro

3   tablespoons fresh lime juice

4   (6 ounce) mahi-mahi fillets (you can substitute any other firm white fleshed fish)

1   tablespoon olive oil

3   tablespoons Jamaican jerk seasoning

Prepare grill at medium high heat. Cut avocado in half and remove pit. Score the flesh into small chunks and scoop out. Mix the avocado, cantaloupe, onion, cilantro and lime juice in a small bowl. Cover with plastic wrap pressing plastic to surface of salsa. Refrigerate until ready to serve. Brush fillets with oil. Place jerk seasoning in a shallow dish. Dredge fillets in seasoning. Grill for about 3-4 minutes per side. Spoon salsa on top of fillets.

Cookbook Committee

The Town of Greenwood boasts that it has the widest Main Street in the World.

Sea Bass with Olive Tapenade

SERVES 4

TAPENADE

1   **(8 ounce) jar kalamata olives, pitted and drained**

1½   **tablespoons capers, drained**

4   **anchovy fillets, drained**

1   **garlic clove**

1   **tablespoon fresh lemon juice**

1   **teaspoon Dijon mustard**

½   **cup olive oil**

½   **teaspoon fresh chopped thyme**

¼   **cup chopped fresh flat leaf parsley**

     Salt and pepper to taste

SEA BASS

4   **(6 ounce) sea bass fillets**

Combine olives, capers, anchovy, garlic, lemon juice and mustard in a food processor. Pulse until chopped. With machine running, gradually add oil and process until well blended. Stir in thyme, parsley, salt and pepper. Set aside. Preheat grill to medium-high heat. Oil grill rack well. Grill for about 3-4 minutes per side depending on thickness of fish. Do not overcook. Transfer fish to serving plates. Spoon tapenade over top. Drizzle a little olive oil over fish and serve.

Cookbook Committee

Uniquely Union Festival is held each September and features a barbecue cook-off, music and more.

Cakes, Cookies & Dessert Sauces

Cakes, Cookies & Dessert Sauces

Houses along the Battery in Charleston, SC

Peanut Butter Cake with Chocolate Frosting

SERVES 12-15

CAKE

1	(18 ounce) package yellow cake mix	1	cup milk
1	cup packed light brown sugar	½	cup vegetable oil
		4	eggs, beaten
1	cup crunchy peanut butter	1	cup chopped peanuts

Preheat oven to 300 degrees. Combine cake mix, brown sugar, peanut butter, milk, oil and eggs until smooth. Stir in peanuts. Divide batter among three greased and floured 9-inch round cake pans. Bake for 45 minutes. Cool completely on wire racks. Transfer to a serving plate and frost.

CHOCOLATE FROSTING

¾	cup unsalted butter or margarine, softened	¾	cup unsweetened cocoa powder
9	tablespoons milk	1½	packages powdered sugar, sifted

Beat together butter, milk and cocoa. Gradually add powdered sugar. Beat until well blended.

Vera W. Helmly
(Former Representative Robert L. Helmly)

The town square of Abbeville was built around a spring owned by Revolutionary War hero, General Andrew Pickens.

Red Velvet Cake

SERVES 12-15

CAKE

Vegetable oil for pans

2½ cups all-purpose flour

1½ cups sugar

1 teaspoon baking soda

1 teaspoon fine salt

1 teaspoon cocoa powder

1½ cups vegetable oil

1 cup buttermilk, room temperature

2 large eggs, room temperature

2 tablespoons (1 ounce) red food coloring

1 teaspoon white distilled vinegar

1 teaspoon vanilla

Chopped pecans for garnish

Preheat oven to 350 degrees. In a large bowl, sift together flour, sugar, baking soda, salt and cocoa. In another large bowl, whisk together oil, buttermilk, eggs, food coloring, vinegar and vanilla. Beat flour mixture into milk mixture with an electric mixer until just combined and a smooth batter is formed. Divide batter evenly among three lightly oiled and floured 9-inch round cake pans. Place pans in oven evenly spaced apart. Bake about 30 minutes, rotating pans halfway through baking. Bake until cake pulls away from pan and toothpick comes out clean. Remove from oven and run a knife around edges to loosen cake from pans. Cool for 10 minutes. Remove cakes from pans to a cooling rack until completely cooled. Place one cake layer on a serving plate. Top with ¼ to ½-inch layer of frosting. Set another cake layer on top, rounded side down and frost. Top with remaining cake layer. Cover entire cake with remaining frosting. Sprinkle top with pecans.

Collins Ole Towne is a recreated 1930s village located in Central. It contains a general store, barbershop, and schoolhouse.

(continued)

Red Velvet Cake, continued

CREAM CHEESE FROSTING

2 (8 ounce) packages cream cheese, softened	1 cup unsalted butter, softened
4 cups sifted powdered sugar	1 teaspoon vanilla

In a large bowl, beat cream cheese, powdered sugar and butter on low speed until well blended. Increase to high speed and beat about 5 minutes until light and fluffy, scraping sides occasionally. Reduce to low speed and add vanilla. Increase to high speed to mix briefly until fluffy. Store in refrigerator until thickened. May be stored in the refrigerator for 3 days.

Jenny Sanford
(Governor Marshall C. Sanford, Jr.)

*Woodburn Plantation,
built in 1828 by former
Lt. Governor Charles Pinckney,
is located in Pendleton.
Two members of the Pinckney
family were signers of
the US Constitution.*

Three Day Coconut Cake

SERVES 12-15

3	**(6 ounce) packages frozen coconut, thawed, divided**
2	**cups sugar**
1	**(16 ounce) container sour cream**
1	**(18 ounce) package butter cake mix**
1	**(8 ounce) container frozen nondairy whipped topping, thawed**

The day before baking cake, combine 2 packages coconut, sugar and sour cream in a bowl and cover. Refrigerate overnight.

Preheat oven to temperature in cake mix directions. Sift cake mix. Prepare cake mix according to package directions. Pour batter into three greased and floured 9-inch round cake pans. Bake for time stated on cake package. Cool in pan for 10 minutes. Place cake layers on cooling rack. Cool completely. Split layers in half horizontally. (May also bake layers in 6 pans. If using 6 pans, adjust cooking time to about 15 minutes per pan or just until toothpick comes out clean.) Reserve 1 cup of coconut mixture. Spread remaining coconut mixture between cake layers. Do not spread on top of the cake. Fold reserved 1 cup coconut mixture into whipped topping until well blended. Frost top and sides of the cake with whipped topping mixture. Press remaining package of coconut over entire cake. Refrigerate for at least one day, 2-3 days is best. The longer the cake sits, the better.

Kathy Koon
(Former Representative Larry Koon)

David Neilson
(Representative Denny W. Neilson)

The South Carolina Botanical Gardens is a 270-acre public garden located on the campus of Clemson University. The Gardens feature a geology and natural history museum, Hanover House, a discovery center and one of the country's largest camellia and daffodil collections.

Chocolate Marble Cheesecake

SERVES 12-15

1	(6 ounce) package semi-sweet chocolate chips	2	(8 ounce) packages cream cheese, softened
½	cup plus 2 tablespoons plus ¾ cup sugar, divided	½	cup sour cream
1¼	cups graham cracker crumbs	1	teaspoon vanilla
2	tablespoons unsalted butter, melted	4	eggs

Preheat oven to 325 degrees. Combine chocolate chips and ½ cup sugar in small saucepan. Heat on low until chocolate melts, stirring occasionally. May also use a microwave. Remove from heat and set aside. In a small bowl, combine cracker crumbs, 2 tablespoons sugar and butter. Mix well. Press mixture into bottom and 1½-inches up side of a 9-inch springform pan. Set aside. In a large bowl, beat cream cheese until light and fluffy. Gradually beat in remaining ¾ cup sugar. Add sour cream and vanilla and beat well. Add eggs, one at a time, beating well after each addition. Divide batter in half. Stir chocolate mixture into one half of batter. Mix well. Pour chocolate batter over crust. Carefully pour remaining batter over chocolate batter. Gently run a knife through two batters and form a marbleized pattern. Bake for 50 minutes or until cake is set around edges and a 2-3 inch circle in middle shakes. Turn off oven. Carefully run a knife around the edge of cake. Keep cake in oven for 30 minutes with oven door ajar. This will help to prevent cake from cracking. Remove from oven to a wire rack. Cool to room temperature. Cover cake and refrigerate overnight.

Vickie Skelton
(Representative B.R. Skelton)

Duke's Mayonnaise was created by a Greenville resident and has been produced there ever since. Duke's is a staple for most South Carolinians – what would a summer tomato sandwich be without it?

Black Bottom White Chocolate Cheesecake

SERVES 12-15

CHEESECAKE

1 (9 ounce) package chocolate wafer cookies, crushed (about 1¾ cups)

¼ cup plus 2 tablespoons butter or margarine, divided

1 (12 ounce) package white chocolate chips or block, 2 cups chopped into pieces

2 (8 ounce) packages cream cheese, softened

½ cup sugar

3 eggs

1 cup heavy cream

1 teaspoon vanilla

Preheat oven to 325 degrees. Melt ¼ cup butter in small bowl. Add cookie crumbs. Mix well. Press into bottom of 10-inch springform pan. Refrigerate. Place white chocolate chips in a small bowl in microwave until melted. In a large bowl, beat cream cheese until smooth. Gradually add sugar and beat until smooth. Add eggs one at a time, beating well after each addition. Add remaining 2 tablespoons softened butter, white chocolate chips, cream and vanilla. Beat until smooth. Pour filling over crust. Bake for 55-65 minutes or until edges are set and center is soft. Turn off oven and open oven door. Allow cheesecake to sit in oven about 30 minutes. This may help prevent cracking. Remove from oven and cool on a wire rack for 1 hour. Cover and refrigerate overnight. May top with raspberry sauce.

Fort Hill is the plantation home of former Vice President John C. Calhoun. It later became the home of Thomas Green Clemson who married Calhoun's daughter, Anna Maria. The home was left to South Carolina in Clemson's will with the stipulation that it be preserved and open to the public. It is located in the center of Clemson University's campus.

(continued)

Black Bottom White Chocolate Cheesecake, continued

RASPBERRY SAUCE

2	cups fresh or frozen (thawed) raspberries	2	tablespoons sugar
1	cup cranberry juice cocktail	2	teaspoons cornstarch

Combine raspberries and juice cocktail in a food processor or blender. Process until smooth. Press raspberry mixture through a strainer into a medium saucepan. Add sugar and cornstarch. Mix well. Cook over medium heat until mixture boils and thickens, stirring constantly. Remove from heat and cool for at least 1 hour before serving.

Jean Littlejohn
(Representative Lanny F. Littlejohn)

Golden Creek Mill is located in Easley at one of South Carolina's oldest grist mill sites. The mill produces freshly ground cornmeal and grits. Also located in Pickens County is Hagood Mill, a restored 1845 grist mill. It is the only mill in SC which still uses the original wheel components.

Chess Cake

SERVES 10-12

1	(18 ounce) package yellow cake mix	1	(16 ounce) package powdered sugar
½	cup butter, melted	1	cup chopped pecans (optional)
1	egg plus 2 eggs, divided		
1	(8 ounce) package cream cheese, softened		

Preheat oven to 325 degrees. Combine cake mix, butter and 1 egg. Press mixture into bottom of an ungreased 13x9x2-inch baking dish. Beat cream cheese, remaining 2 eggs and powdered sugar. Pour over cake mixture. Bake for 30 minutes. Sprinkle with pecans. Bake for another 10-15 minutes.

Kathy Koon
(Former Representative Larry Koon)

Kelly Talley
(Representative Scott F. Talley)

The Town of Central got its name because it was the mid-point between Atlanta and Charlotte. The town was incorporated and became an important stop along the railroad route.

Vanilla Wafer Cake

SERVES 12-15

1	(12 ounce) package vanilla wafers, crushed	½	cup milk
1¾	cups sugar	1	(7 ounce) package flaked coconut
1	cup butter, melted	1	cup chopped pecans
6	eggs		

Preheat oven to 275 degrees. Combine wafer crumbs, sugar and butter in a large bowl. Add eggs one at a time, beating well after each addition. Add milk and beat well. Fold in coconut and pecans. Pour batter into a greased and floured 9-inch tube pan. Bake for 2 hours.

E.V. Levenitis
(Senator Phil P. Leventis)

Golden Ring Cake

SERVES 10-12

CAKE

2	eggs		1	teaspoon salt

2 eggs
1¼ cups sugar
1 cup canned pumpkin
½ cup vegetable oil
⅓ cup water
1¾ cups sifted all-purpose flour

1 teaspoon salt
¾ teaspoon baking soda
2 teaspoons ground cinnamon
1 teaspoon ground nutmeg
1 cup quick rolled oats, uncooked

Preheat oven to 350 degrees. Beat eggs until frothy. Gradually add sugar. Beat until thickened and light colored. Stir in pumpkin, oil and water. Blend well. Combine flour, salt, baking soda, cinnamon and nutmeg. Gradually add to pumpkin mixture, mixing well. Stir in oats. Pour batter into a well-greased and floured 1½-quart ring mold. Bake for 30-40 minutes or until toothpick comes out clean. Loosen edges with a spatula. Cool for 10 minutes in pan. Invert on a serving plate. Frost with cream cheese frosting.

CREAM CHEESE FROSTING

1 (3 ounce) package cream cheese, softened
½ cup butter, softened

½-1 (16 ounce) package powdered sugar
1 teaspoon vanilla

Beat together cream cheese and butter until creamy. Gradually add powdered sugar to reach good spreading consistency. Add vanilla and beat until well blended.

Sharon Herdklotz
(Former Representative Richard Herdklotz)

Ashtabula Plantation is a restored 1820s home located in Pendleton. It contains many antiques and furnishings that belonged to previous owners.

213

Honey Bun Cake

SERVES 12-15

CAKE

1   (18 ounce) package yellow cake mix

4   eggs, beaten

¾   cup vegetable oil

1   (12 ounce) container sour cream

1   cup packed light brown sugar

3   tablespoons ground cinnamon

Preheat oven to 325 degrees. Combine cake mix, eggs, oil and sour cream. Mix well. Pour half batter into a 13x9x2-inch greased and floured baking dish. Mix brown sugar and cinnamon. Sprinkle half mixture over batter. Pour on remaining batter. Sprinkle remaining brown sugar mixture on top. Bake for 45 minutes. Remove from oven and pour glaze over top of warm cake.

GLAZE

1   (16 ounce) package powdered sugar

½   cup milk

1   teaspoon vanilla

Mix together powdered sugar and milk to reach a good spreading consistency. Add more milk if needed. Stir in vanilla.

Sandra Sandifer
(Representative William E. Sandifer, III)

Carolina Q Cup is held in October in Columbia at the Farmers Market. It is just one of many barbecue festivals that take place in SC each year. The different types of Carolina barbecue sauces are put to the test.

Japanese Fruit Cake

This is my grandmother Clara Twitty's recipe.

SERVES 15

CAKE

1 cup butter or margarine, softened	1 cup chopped nuts
6 egg yolks	½ cup dark raisins
2 cups sugar	1 cup butter or margarine, softened
1 teaspoon ground allspice	6 egg whites
1 teaspoon ground cloves	2 cups sugar
1 teaspoon ground cinnamon	1 tablespoon lemon extract
1 teaspoon vanilla	2 cups self-rising flour
2 cups self-rising flour	½ cup water or milk
½ cup water or milk	1 cup chopped nuts
	½ cup golden raisins

Preheat oven to 350 degrees. For dark layers, cream butter, egg yolks and sugar. Add allspice, cloves, cinnamon and vanilla. Alternately add flour and water. Fold in nuts and raisins. Divide batter between two greased and floured 9-inch round cake pans. For white layers, cream butter, egg whites and sugar. Add lemon extract. Alternately add flour and the water. Fold in nuts and raisins. Divide batter between two greased and floured 9-inch round cake pans. Bake for 30 minutes or until a toothpick comes out clean. Spread icing between four cake layers.

ICING

1 fresh coconut, grated or 2 (6 ounce) packages frozen grated coconut, thawed	2 cups sugar
	2 teaspoons cornstarch mixed with a little water
Juice of 7 oranges (about 1½ cups)	

Combine coconut, orange juice, sugar and cornstarch mixture in a medium saucepan. Boil until thickened.

The Come See Me Festival held in April in Rock Hill is a celebration of Southern Hospitality. A must see – Glencairn Gardens.

Jolene Lander
(Former Senator Jim Lander)

215

Nut Torte

SERVES 12-15

1	cup zwieback crumbs	½	cup sugar
1	cup chopped nuts	1	teaspoon plus 1 teaspoon vanilla, divided
¼	teaspoon ground cinnamon	3	egg whites, stiffly beaten
1	teaspoon baking powder	1	cup cold heavy cream
¼	teaspoon salt	2	tablespoons powdered sugar
3	egg yolks		

Preheat oven to 325 degrees. Combine crumbs, nuts, cinnamon, baking powder and salt. Beat egg yolks and sugar in a separate bowl. Stir in 1 teaspoon vanilla. Add egg yolk mixture to dry ingredients and mix well. Fold in stiff egg whites. Divide batter between two greased and floured 8-inch round cake pans. Bake for 30 minutes. Cool on a wire rack. Whip cream until thickened. Gradually add powdered sugar and remaining 1 teaspoon vanilla. Whip until stiff peaks form. Frost cake layers with whipped cream and serve.

Lisa Courson
(Senator John E. Courson)

Parsons Mountain Park in the Sumter National Forest features a motorcycle trail and a horse trail.

Franklin Nut Cake

This recipe comes from the Rohner family in North Carolina.

SERVES 12-15

1 pound butter, softened	1 teaspoon baking powder
2 cups sugar	1 pound candied cherries, halved
6 eggs, beaten	½ pound candied pineapple, chopped
½ teaspoon vanilla	1 pound (about 2 cups) chopped pecans
4 cups all-purpose flour	
¼ teaspoon salt	

Preheat oven to 250 degrees. Cream butter and sugar until well blended. Add eggs. Stir in vanilla. Sift together flour, salt and baking powder. Add 3 cups flour mixture to creamed mixture. Mix well. Reserve 1 cup flour mixture. Add cherries, pineapple and nuts to flour mixture and toss to coat. Fold into batter. Will be very thick. Pour batter into a greased and floured 9-inch tube pan. Bake for 2 hours, 30 minutes. Cool in pan for 10 minutes. Turn out onto a wire rack and cool completely. Delicious served with a dollop of whipped cream.

Jolene Lander
(Former Senator Jim Lander)

The Family Circle Cup, one of the richest events in women's professional tennis, takes place each April in Charleston.

Mom's Apple Cake

My mother, Margaret Roach, has made this cake for years. My mother is a great cook, but she hates to bake. This is one of the few desserts that she makes, but that's okay because it is one of the best.

SERVES 12-15

CAKE

2	cups sugar	1	teaspoon baking soda
3	large eggs	1	teaspoon ground cinnamon
1¼	cups canola oil		
¼	cup orange juice	3	medium Granny Smith apples, peeled and small diced
1	teaspoon vanilla		
3	cups all-purpose flour	1	cup chopped pecans
½	teaspoon salt		

Preheat oven to 325 degrees. In a large bowl, combine sugar, eggs and oil. Add orange juice and vanilla. Combine flour, salt, baking soda and cinnamon. Add to creamed mixture. Stir in apples and nuts. Spoon mixture into a greased and floured 9-inch tube pan. Bake for 1 hour, 30 minutes. Remove from oven. Immediately pierce holes in top of cake with a toothpick. Gradually pour glaze over top. Cool for at least 1 hour. Remove cake to a serving plate.

GLAZE

½	cup unsalted butter	½	teaspoon baking soda
1	cup sugar	½	cup buttermilk

Melt butter in a medium saucepan. Add sugar, baking soda and buttermilk. Bring to boil. Be careful not to boil over. Pour glaze over cake immediately after it comes out of oven.

Vickie Skelton
(Representative B.R. Skelton)

American College of the Building Arts in Charleston was born from a need brought about by Hurricane Hugo in 1989. The devastating storm destroyed much of the architectural details important to the historical buildings located in Charleston. Artisans had to be brought from Europe to repair the damage. Realizing the need to train future artisans for this type of restoration, a program was created.

Chocolate Chip Cake

SERVES 10-12

CAKE

1	(18 ounce) package yellow cake mix	½	cup vegetable oil
1	(3 ounce) package instant chocolate pudding mix	4	eggs
1	cup sour cream	1	cup milk chocolate chips
		1	cup chopped toasted pecans

Preheat oven to 325 degrees. Beat cake mix, pudding mix, sour cream, oil and eggs with an electric mixer at high speed for 3 minutes. Beat for 3 more minutes at low speed. The mixture will be very thick. Pour half batter into a greased and floured Bundt pan or tube pan. Combine chocolate chips and pecans. Sprinkle half over batter. Pour on remaining batter. Sprinkle with remaining chip mixture. Bake for 55 minutes. Serve with Chocolate Sauce.

CHOCOLATE SAUCE

½	cup butter	1	tablespoon light corn syrup
1	(4 ounce) package German sweet chocolate baking bar	⅛	teaspoon salt
1	cup sugar	1	teaspoon vanilla
1	(5 ounce) can evaporated milk		

Melt butter and chocolate in a saucepan over medium heat. Stir in sugar, milk, corn syrup and salt. Cook over medium heat for 5 minutes or until smooth. Remove from heat and stir in the vanilla. Serve warm.

Kelly Talley
(Representative Scott F. Talley)

Start your engines!
On September 6, 1950,
Darlington Raceway opened
and NASCAR welcomed one
of its toughest race tracks.
The 1.366 mile, oval-shaped
track is considered a challenge
because of the shape. The
track remains a favorite
among NASCAR fans.

Chocolate Upside Down Cake

SERVES 8-10

1 cup self-rising flour	¾ cup milk
¾ cup plus 1 cup sugar, divided	¾ cup chopped nuts (optional)
1½ tablespoons plus ¼ cup unsweetened cocoa powder, divided	1 teaspoon vanilla
2 tablespoons butter	¾-1 cup boiling water

Preheat oven to 350 degrees. Sift together flour, ¾ cup sugar and 1½ tablespoons cocoa in a large bowl and set aside. Melt butter in 10-inch square baking dish. Add milk, nuts and vanilla to cocoa mixture. Pour excess butter from baking dish into cocoa mixture and mix well. Pour batter into buttered baking dish. Combine remaining 1 cup sugar, remaining ¼ cup cocoa and ¾ cup boiling water. If mixture is too thick, add a little more water. Pour over cake batter. Bake for 25-30 minutes. Serve warm.

Linda Witherspoon
(Representative William D. Witherspoon)

Freedom Weekend Aloft began in 1982 in Greenville from a request by a movie company filming in the Greenville area for a festival backdrop. The movie, Hot Heir, never made it to local theaters, but a festival was born. It is one of the largest hot air balloon festivals in the Southeast. Held each Memorial Day Weekend in Anderson until 2006, when it was moved to Simpsonville.

Whipped Cream Pound Cake

SERVES 10-12

This pound cake recipe is from my mother-in-law, Anne Land. She was a home economist and this is one of her signature dishes. It is wonderful. Placing this cake in a cold oven makes a delicious crust on the cake.

1 **cup unsalted butter, softened**	1 **cup heavy whipping cream**
3 **cups sugar**	½ **teaspoon vanilla**
6 **eggs**	½ **teaspoon almond extract**
3 **cups all-purpose or cake flour**	

Do not preheat oven. Beat butter and sugar until smooth. Add eggs one at a time, beating well after each addition. Add flour, cream, vanilla and almond extract. Pour batter into a greased and floured Bundt pan or tube pan. Place in a cold oven. Turn on oven to 300 degrees. Bake for 1 hour, 20 minutes. Cool in pan for 1 hour. Remove to cool on wire rack.

Marie Land
(Senator John C. Land, III)

The Battery refers to the area at the southern tip of Charleston peninsula.

Coconut Cream Cheese Pound Cake

½ cup unsalted butter, softened

½ cup vegetable shortening

1 (8 ounce) package cream cheese, softened

3 cups sugar

6 eggs

3 cups all-purpose flour

¼ teaspoon baking soda

¼ teaspoon salt

1 (6 ounce) package frozen coconut, thawed

1 teaspoon vanilla

1 teaspoon coconut flavoring

Preheat oven to 350 degrees. In a large bowl, cream butter, shortening and cream cheese with an electric mixer. Gradually add sugar, beating at medium speed until well blended. Add eggs one at a time, beating well after each addition. Combine flour, baking soda and salt. Add to creamed mixture, stirring until just blended. Stir in coconut, vanilla and coconut flavoring. Pour batter into a greased and floured tube pan. Bake for 1 hour or until a toothpick comes out clean. Cool in pan for 10 minutes. Remove to cool on wire rack.

Mary Wood Beasley
(Former Governor David M. Beasley)

The Order of the Silver Crescent, first initiated by Governor David Beasley, recognizes South Carolinians aged eighteen or younger for their contributions and achievements in their community.

Frosted Cream Cheese Pound Cake

SERVES 10-12

CAKE

1½ cups unsalted butter, softened

1 (8 ounce) package cream cheese, softened

3 cups sugar

Dash of salt

1½ teaspoons vanilla

6 jumbo eggs

3 cups all-purpose flour

Preheat oven to 325 degrees. Cream butter, cream cheese and sugar until light and fluffy. Add salt and vanilla and mix well. Add eggs one at a time, beating well after each addition. Stir in flour until well blended. Spoon mixture into a greased and floured 10-inch tube pan. Bake for 1 hour, 30 minutes. Cool in pan for 10 minutes. Remove to cool on wire rack. May frost cake or serve without. It is delicious both ways.

CREAM CHEESE FROSTING

¼ cup unsalted butter, softened

½ (8 ounce) package cream cheese, softened

2 cups sifted powdered sugar

½ teaspoon vanilla

Beat butter and cream cheese until well blended. Add powdered sugar and vanilla and mix well.

E.V. Leventis
(Senator Phil P. Leventis)

SC State Bluegrass Festival is held in Myrtle Beach in November.

The world's largest Ginkgo farm is located in Dalzell in Sumter County. Advocates of herbal medicines say Ginkgo biloba improves memory.

Gilda's Down Home Pound Cake

This down home recipe is sure to please the pickiest appetites. Remember, it is not low calorie, so you will need lots of will power to eat only one slice.

SERVES 10-12

2 cups unsalted butter, softened	3 cups all-purpose flour
3½ cups sugar	1 cup half-and-half
8 eggs	3 tablespoons vanilla

Preheat oven to 300 degrees. In a large bowl, beat butter on low with an electric mixer until light and fluffy. Gradually add sugar and beat on low for about 1 minute. Add eggs one at a time, beating well after each addition. Beat until well blended. Stir in flour until well incorporated. Add half-and-half and vanilla. Beat for 1 minute starting out on low for 30 seconds and increasing to medium. Divide batter between two buttered and floured 8½x4-inch loaf pans. Bake for 1 hour, 30-40 minutes or until toothpick comes out with a few crumbs. Cool in the pan for 10 minutes.

Representative Gilda Cobb-Hunter

The Heritage Golf tournament held in Hilton Head Island in April is one of the most distinguished tournaments on the PGA tour.

Lemon Pound Cake

My mother, Ruth Wanda Britts, always made this pound cake for church fund raisers. It is delicious.

SERVES 10-12

1 teaspoon vanilla	5 eggs
1 teaspoon lemon extract	3 cups sifted all-purpose flour
1 cup milk	
½ teaspoon baking powder	1½ cups powdered sugar
1 cup butter, softened	1-2 tablespoons fresh lemon juice
3 cups sugar	

Preheat oven to 350 degrees. Blend vanilla, lemon and milk. Sprinkle baking powder into milk. In large bowl, beat butter and sugar on high speed. Add eggs one at a time, beating after each addition. Decrease speed and add flour and milk mixture alternately, beginning and ending with flour. Mix well. Pour batter into a greased and floured 10-inch tube pan. Bake for 30 minutes. Reduce heat to 325 degrees. Bake an additional 40 minutes or until toothpick comes out clean. Cool in pan for 10 minutes. Run knife around inside of the pan to loosen. Remove cake from pan. Place top side up on a serving plate. In a small bowl, blend powdered sugar and enough lemon juice to reach spreading consistency. Pour glaze over top and allow to drizzle down sides of cake.

Ruth Rice
(Representative Rex F. Rice)

The South Carolina Sweet Potato Festival held in Darlington in October is one of the longest running festivals in the area and features a carnival, music, and those delicious pies!

225

Mama's Chocolate Pound Cake

My Mama, Jean Tankersley Osteen, has been making chocolate pound cakes for years and has developed her own version. This cake cannot cook fast enough for us. Our mouths start watering for this moist cake to come out of the oven the minute Mama starts sifting the flour. Enjoy!

SERVES 10-12

1½	cups butter, softened	½	teaspoon baking soda
3	cups sugar	½	teaspoon salt
5	eggs	1	cup milk
3	cups all-purpose flour	2	teaspoons vanilla
6	tablespoons cocoa powder		

Preheat oven to 325 degrees. Beat butter and sugar with an electric mixer until fluffy. Add eggs one at a time and beat until just blended. Do not over mix. Sift together flour, cocoa, baking soda and salt. Add flour mixture to creamed mixture, alternately with milk, starting and ending with flour mixture. Mix in by hand to avoid over mixing. Stir in vanilla. Pour batter into a greased and floured 9-inch tube pan. Bake for 1 hour, 15 minutes. Cool in pan for 10 minutes. Remove to a cooling rack.

Representative Vida O. Miller

The famous Lobster Races are held each May in Aiken. Live Maine Lobsters racing down the streets of Aiken with the winner dodging the dinner table. Not to be missed!

Decadent Chocolate Pound Cake

SERVES 10-12

CAKE

1 cup butter, softened	½ teaspoon salt
½ cup vegetable shortening	½ cup unsweetened cocoa powder
3 cups sugar	1¼ cups milk
5 eggs	1 teaspoon vanilla
3 cups all-purpose flour	

Do not preheat oven. Beat butter, shortening and sugar with an electric mixer until well blended. Add eggs one at a time, beating well after each addition. Sift together flour, salt and cocoa. Add flour mixture to creamed mixture alternately with milk. Mix well. Stir in vanilla. Pour batter into a greased and floured tube pan. Place in cold oven. Set temperature to 325 degrees. Bake for 1 hour, 15 minutes or until toothpick comes out clean. Cool in pan for about an hour. Place cake on a serving plate. Frost with chocolate frosting.

CHOCOLATE FROSTING

2 (1 ounce) squares unsweetened chocolate	4 egg yolks
½ cup sugar	½ cup butter
¼ cup water	1 teaspoon vanilla
	2 cups powdered sugar

Combine chocolate, sugar and water in a saucepan. Cook over low heat until chocolate melts and mixture is smooth, stirring constantly. Remove from heat. Beat in egg yolks thoroughly. Let cool. In a medium bowl, cream butter, vanilla and powdered sugar. Pour cooled chocolate mixture over butter mixture. Beat until well blended.

E.V. Leventis
(Senator Phil P. Leventis)

South Carolina has 46 parks in its state park system. The SC Dept. of Parks, Recreation and Tourism manages the park system.

Gale's Rum Nut Cake

This is Gale Kennedy's famous rum cake recipe. This recipe appears in her cookbook, Still Catering to Columbia. I know you will enjoy!

SERVES 10-12

CAKE

1 (18 ounce) package yellow cake mix	1 (3 ounce) package instant vanilla pudding mix
½ cup water	4 eggs
½ cup vegetable oil	½ cup rum
	1 cup chopped pecans

Preheat oven to 325 degrees. Combine cake mix, water, oil and pudding mix. Add eggs and rum. Beat with an electric mixer for 2-3 minutes until smooth and well blended. Place pecans in bottom of a greased and floured tube pan. Pour batter over nuts. Bake for 45 minutes. Remove from oven. Pierce holes all over top of cake. Immediately pour boiling hot glaze over cake and allow to sit in the pan for 15-20 minutes to absorb glaze. Remove to a serving plate. Prepare cake at least 1-2 days before serving so flavors blend. Store cake at room temperature. Do not refrigerate.

GLAZE

¾ cup sugar	½ cup rum
½ cup butter	

Combine sugar, butter and rum in a saucepan. Bring to boil until sugar dissolves. Pour over hot cake.

Betty Ryberg
(Senator W. Greg Ryberg)

The Sun Fun Festival takes place in Myrtle Beach each June. Sun worshipers are drawn to the area for sun and fun.

Three Milk Cake

MAKES ONE 9-INCH SINGLE LAYER CAKE

- **6** eggs, separated
- **½** cup plus ½ cup sugar, divided
- **1** cup all-purpose flour, sifted
- **1** cup plus 1 cup heavy cream, divided
- **1** (14 ounce) can sweetened condensed milk
- **1** (12 ounce) can evaporated milk
- **1** teaspoon plus ½ teaspoon vanilla, divided
- **2** tablespoons powdered sugar

Preheat oven to 350 degrees. In medium bowl, beat egg whites with ½ cup sugar until stiff peaks form. In a separate bowl, beat remaining ½ cup sugar and egg yolks until pale yellow and thickened. Add flour to egg yolks and mix well. Fold in egg whites. Pour batter into a greased and floured 9-inch springform pan. Bake for 25-28 minutes or until toothpick comes out clean. Place pan on wire rack and cool for 10 minutes. In a medium bowl, whisk together 1 cup heavy cream, condensed milk, evaporated milk and 1 teaspoon vanilla. With a toothpick or wooden skewer, pierce holes all over top of cake about 1-inch apart. Pour milk mixture over cake. Let stand for 30 minutes to absorb the milk. Refrigerate for at least 1 hour or overnight. When ready to serve, carefully remove sides of springform pan. Place cake on a serving plate. Beat remaining 1 cup heavy cream, ½ teaspoon vanilla and powdered sugar until stiff peaks form. Spread whipped cream over top and sides of cake. Refrigerate 1 hour before serving.

Vickie Skelton
(Representative B.R. Skelton)

It was determined in 1984 that milk should be the Official State Beverage. Got Milk?

Anne Land's Caramel Cake Icing

This is another signature recipe from John's mother, Anne Land. Icing will frost one 3 layer cake.

MAKES ABOUT 2 CUPS

1	(16 ounce) package light brown sugar	¾	cup heavy cream
		½	cup butter

Combine brown sugar, cream and butter in heavy saucepan. Cook over low heat until reaches boiling point. Boil slowly for 5 minutes, stirring occasionally. Remove from heat. Beat with wire whisk until reaches spreading consistency. If icing hardens, add a small amount of hot water.

Marie Land
(Senator John C. Land, III)

South Carolina State Museum is housed in an old textile building in Columbia. The Museum began in 1973 under the guidance of the SC Museum Commission and houses many permanent exhibits as well as traveling exhibits.

Peanut Butter Frosting

This frosting will ice an 8x8-inch square cake or double the recipe for a 13x9x2-inch sheet cake.

MAKES ABOUT 2 CUPS

½	cup smooth peanut butter	½	up evaporated milk
¼	cup butter	2	cups powdered sugar
1	cup sugar	1	teaspoon vanilla

Combine peanut butter, butter, sugar and milk in a saucepan. Boil on medium heat until thickened and sugar dissolves. Remove from heat. Stir in powdered sugar and vanilla until well mixed. Frosting will thicken as it cools.

Kathy Koon
(Former Representative Larry Koon)

Peachy Dessert Sauce

Serve over vanilla ice cream or Angel Food Cake.

MAKES ABOUT ¾ CUP

1	teaspoon cornstarch	1½	teaspoons sugar
¼	cup water	¾	cup sliced fresh South Carolina peaches (May use canned, drained)
2	tablespoons apricot jam or preserves		
½	teaspoon fresh lemon juice		

Blend cornstarch and water in a small saucepan. Add jam, lemon juice and sugar. Bring to boil. Cook for 1-2 minutes, stirring constantly. Reduce heat. Add peaches and heat thoroughly. Serve warm.

David Neilson
(Representative Denny W. Neilson)

Fruit Dipping Chocolate Sauce

Excellent sauce to serve with various fruits on a buffet.

SERVES 10 OR ENOUGH SAUCE FOR 4 LARGE BASKETS OF STRAWBERRIES

2	cups sugar	1	(12 ounce) can evaporated milk
5	tablespoons unsweetened cocoa powder	¼	cup butter
		1	teaspoon vanilla

Blend sugar and cocoa in a saucepan. Add milk and cook until thickened, stirring constantly. Add butter and stir until melted. Remove from heat and add vanilla. Serve at room temperature. Store in refrigerator for days.

Marie Land
(Senator John C. Land, III)

Hunting Island Lighthouse, built in 1875, is located in Beaufort County and offers a wonderful view of the coast.

Stickies

This dish is a classic Southern dessert that can be made with leftover biscuit or pie dough. The contents and spices tend to differ from region to region in the state. The up country stickies do not have cinnamon. The lowcountry stickies do, maybe because spices were harder to find in the up country in those early days. Delicious either way!

SERVES 12

1 cup all-purpose flour	½ cup plus 1 tablespoon butter, softened, divided
¼ teaspoon baking powder	1 cup sugar
⅛ teaspoon baking soda	½ teaspoon ground cinnamon
½ teaspoon salt	½ teaspoon ground nutmeg
2 tablespoons vegetable shortening	½ teaspoon ground allspice
⅓ cup milk	

Preheat oven to 400 degrees. Combine flour, baking powder, baking soda and salt. Using fingers or pastry blender, cut in shortening. Stir in milk to form a dough. Roll dough on a floured surface. Cut into 12 (3-inch) squares. Combine ½ cup butter, sugar, cinnamon, nutmeg and allspice. Place small amount spice filling into center of each square. Pull four corners together and pinch seams to seal. Melt remaining 1 tablespoon butter in the bottom of a 13x9x2-inch baking dish. Place stickies touching close together in dish. Bake for about 15-20 minutes or until lightly browned.

Amelia Cotty
(Representative William F. Cotty)

Drayton Hall, built in the early 1700s, is located near Charleston and is one of the oldest Georgian Palladian style houses in America. The house is open for tours.

Benne Seed Wafers

This recipe is from Fran Hamby of Charleston's Hamby Catering. These are the best!

MAKES 100 OR MORE WAFERS

1 cup Benne seeds (sesame seeds)

¾ cup butter, melted

1⅛ cups packed light brown sugar

2 tablespoons sugar

1 egg, slightly beaten

1 teaspoon vanilla

¾ cup all-purpose flour

¼ teaspoon baking powder

¼ teaspoon salt

Preheat oven to 300 degrees. Place Benne seeds on a baking sheet. Bake until lightly browned. In a medium bowl, combine butter, brown sugar and sugar. Add egg and vanilla. Sift together flour, baking powder and salt. Add to sugar mixture. Mix well. Add toasted Benne seeds and stir until fully incorporated. Refrigerate several hours or overnight. Pinch off small piece, size of your fingertip, and roll into a ball. Place balls on a foil lined baking sheet. Bake for about 6-8 minutes until lightly browned. Cool for 1 minute. Remove from sheet. Store in an airtight container.

Marie Land
(Senator John C. Land, III)

The local name for sesame seeds is benne seeds. This product was introduced to South Carolina by African slaves. There are several recipes for the popular benne seed wafer which is often served at teas and cocktail parties.

Chewy Oatmeal Raisin Cookies

MAKES ABOUT 4 DOZEN COOKIES

2 cups all-purpose flour	⅓ cup light corn syrup
1½ teaspoons ground cinnamon	1 egg
1 teaspoon salt	2 teaspoons vanilla
1 teaspoon baking soda	2 cups old-fashioned oats
1¼ cups packed light brown sugar	1 cup dark raisins
1 cup unsalted butter, softened	1 cup chopped pitted dates
	¾ cup chopped pecans

Preheat oven to 350 degrees. Line baking sheet with parchment paper. Sift together flour, cinnamon, salt and baking soda into medium bowl. Set aside. Beat brown sugar and butter with an electric mixer until well blended. Add corn syrup, egg and vanilla. Mix in flour mixture. Stir in oats, raisins, dates and nuts. Drop dough by tablespoonfuls about 2 inches apart onto baking sheets. Bake about 15 minutes or until lightly browned. Transfer to a wire rack and cool completely. Store in an airtight container.

Vickie Skelton
(Representative B.R. Skelton)

Boone Hall Plantation is one of the most beautiful plantations in the lowcountry. It was used in the making of the miniseries, North and South. Open to the public for tours.

Favorite Chocolate Chip Cookies

MAKES 10 DOZEN COOKIES

1	cup butter, softened	1	teaspoon salt
1	cup vegetable oil	1	teaspoon cream of tartar
1	cup firmly packed light brown sugar	1	cup regular uncooked oats
1	cup sugar	1	cup crisp rice cereal
1	egg	1	(12 ounce) package semi-sweet chocolate chips
2	teaspoons vanilla		
3½	cups all-purpose flour	½	cup chopped pecans (optional)
1	teaspoon baking soda		

Preheat oven to 375 degrees. Cream butter and oil with an electric mixer. Gradually add brown sugar and sugar. Add egg and vanilla. Beat at medium speed until well blended. In a small bowl, combine flour, baking soda, salt and cream of tartar. Gradually add flour mixture to creamed mixture. Mix well. Stir in oats, rice cereal, chocolate chips and pecans. Drop dough by teaspoonfuls onto a greased baking sheet. Bake for 10-12 minutes. Cool on a wire rack.

Lt. Governor Andre Bauer

The Water Festival held in Beaufort in July attracts water lovers from all around. There are, of course, boat races and water skiing, but also parades, air shows and the traditional Blessing of the Fleet.

Better Than Fruitcake Cookies

MAKES 7 DOZEN COOKIES

1	cup unsalted butter, softened	1	(8 ounce) container candied red or green cherries, chopped
1½	cups sugar	1	(8 ounce) container candied pineapple, chopped
2	eggs		
2½	cups all-purpose flour	1	(10 ounce) container chopped pitted dates
1	teaspoon baking soda		
½	teaspoon salt	2½	cups chopped pecans
1	teaspoon ground cinnamon		

Preheat oven to 375 degrees. Beat butter with an electric mixer until light and fluffy. Gradually add sugar until well blended. Add eggs one at a time, beating well after each addition. In a medium bowl, sift together flour, baking soda, salt and cinnamon. Add flour mixture to creamed mixture. Stir until well blended. Add cherries, pineapple, dates and pecans. The batter will be very thick. Drop dough by teaspoonfuls onto parchment paper-lined or lightly greased baking sheets. Bake for 11-12 minutes or until lightly browned. Cool on a wire rack.

Vickie Skelton
(Representative B.R. Skelton)

David Neilson
(Representative Denny W. Neilson)

The Rock House, an old rock building built around 1758 in Newberry County, stands in a large field that resembles a French countryside. So much so that soldiers trained at the site to prepare for battle in France during World War II.

Mom's Melting Moments

MAKES 2 DOZEN

DOUGH

1 cup butter or margarine, softened

2 cups all-purpose flour

½ cup powdered sugar

Preheat oven to 325 degrees. Combine butter, flour and powdered sugar. Refrigerate for 1 hour. Roll dough into small marble sized balls. Place on baking sheets. Bake for 10 minutes. Cool completely.

ICING

3 tablespoons butter or margarine, softened

2 tablespoons evaporated milk

1½ cups powdered sugar

¼ teaspoon almond extract

Blend butter, milk, powdered sugar and almond extract until smooth. Spread icing on cooled cookies. May add a little food coloring to icing for holiday colors or festivities.

Ginny Hammond
(Secretary Of State Mark Hammond)

The Beach Music Awards are held in Myrtle Beach in November.

237

Cot Campbell's Dogwood Stable in Aiken was the original Thoroughbred racing partnership. Founded more than three decades ago, Campbell had the innovative idea of group ownership of racehorses. More than 1,200 people have been introduced to racing through Dogwood. The stable has campaigned 71 stake winners, two Champions (Storm Song and Inlander), won the 1990 Preakness Stakes with Summer Squall, and had six millionaires. Dogwood Stable has competed in 10 Triple Crown races, with the results being a win, a second place, and two thirds.

Lemon Crispies

MAKES ABOUT 4 DOZEN

1 **cup butter or margarine, softened**	1 **egg**
1 **cup sugar**	1½ **teaspoons lemon extract**
	1½ **cups all-purpose flour**

Preheat oven to 375 degrees. Cream butter and sugar with an electric mixer. Beat in egg and lemon extract until fluffy. Beat in flour until smooth. Drop dough by heaping teaspoonfuls about 2 inches apart on an ungreased baking sheet. Bake for 10 minutes or until edges are golden browned. Cool for 2 minutes. Remove from sheet. Place on a wire rack to cool completely.

Sue Kirsh
(Representative Herb Kirsh)

Meringue Cookies

MAKES 4 DOZEN COOKIES

3 **egg whites**	1 **teaspoon vanilla**
¾ **cup sugar**	1 **cup chopped pecans**

Preheat oven to 250 degrees. Beat egg whites until thickened. Slowly beat in sugar, scraping down sides so sugar is incorporated. Continue to beat while adding vanilla. Beat until stiff peaks form. Fold in pecans. Drop dough by teaspoonfuls onto parchment paper-lined baking sheet. Bake for 1 hour. Remove and cool on wire racks. Make these on a day with low humidity. Cookies do not set up properly on a rainy or humid day.

Lisa Courson
(Senator John E. Courson)

Peanut Butter Blossoms

My best friend, Harolyn Baker, gave me this recipe. She used to make these and bring some to me when she came to visit. These are so good!

MAKES 2 DOZEN COOKIES

½ **cup vegetable shortening**	2 **tablespoons milk**
½ **cup creamy peanut butter**	1 **teaspoon vanilla**
½ **cup sugar**	1¾ **cups all-purpose flour**
½ **cup packed light brown sugar**	1 **(14 ounce) package chocolate kisses**
1 **egg**	

Preheat oven to 350 degrees. Cream shortening, peanut butter, sugar and brown sugar. Add egg and beat well. Beat in milk and vanilla until well blended. Stir in flour. Drop dough by spoonfuls onto a lightly greased baking sheet. Bake for 10-12 minutes. Place a kiss in center of each cookie while hot. Cool completely.

Vickie Skelton
(Representative B.R. Skelton)

Construction on the SC State House started in 1854 and was not declared complete until 1903. Many events and interruptions, including the Civil War, delayed the work. The last major renovation was in 1995-98.

Chunky Chocolate Brownies

MAKES 16 SQUARES

½ cup unsalted butter

3 (1 ounce) squares unsweetened chocolate, chopped

1¼ cups sugar

2 eggs

½ cup all-purpose flour

⅔ cup coarsely chopped pecans or walnuts, lightly toasted

2 (1 ounce) squares semi-sweet chocolate, chopped into chunks

2 (1 ounce) squares milk chocolate, chopped into chunks

Preheat oven to 350 degrees. Melt butter and unsweetened chocolate in a small saucepan over low heat, stirring constantly. Remove from heat. Cool slightly. Pour chocolate mixture into large bowl. Whisk in sugar and eggs. Add flour and mix well. Stir in nuts, semi-sweet chocolate and milk chocolate. Pour batter into a greased and floured 9x9x2-inch square baking dish. Bake for 25-30 minutes. Cool slightly in pan. Cut into squares.

Cookbook Committee

William Henry Drayton and Arthur Middleton designed the Official State Seal in 1776.

Fudgey Brownies

These brownies are famous around the Blatt Building (House of Representatives offices) in Columbia. They don't last long! Jean Chesno was kind enough to share this recipe for her delicious brownies with us. These moist brownies are totally addictive!

MAKES 2 DOZEN

BATTER

1	cup sugar	1	teaspoon vanilla
½	cup butter, softened	1	cup all-purpose flour
4	eggs	½	teaspoon salt
1	(16 ounce) can chocolate syrup	1	cup chopped nuts (optional)

Preheat oven to 350 degrees. Cream sugar and butter until light and fluffy. Add eggs one at a time, beating well after each addition. Add chocolate syrup, vanilla, flour, salt and nuts. Beat until well mixed. Pour into a greased 13x9x2-inch baking dish. Bake for 25-30 minutes. Spread frosting over brownies while still warm.

CHOCOLATE FROSTING

1	cup sugar	5	tablespoons milk
6	tablespoons butter	1	(6 ounce) package semi-sweet chocolate chips

Combine sugar, butter and milk in a saucepan. Boil for 1 minute. Remove from heat. Add chocolate chips and beat until smooth.

Vickie Skelton
(Representative B.R. Skelton)

Greenville County's Caesars Head State Park features Raven Cliff Falls, which at 400 feet is one of the state's most spectacular waterfalls. There is also a series of hiking trails stretching across the mountainous terrain.

Seven Layer Bars

MAKES 2 DOZEN BARS

¼ cup butter

1 cup graham cracker crumbs

1 cup flaked coconut

1 (6 ounce) package semi-sweet chocolate chips

1 (6 ounce) package butterscotch chips

1 (15 ounce) can sweetened condensed milk

1 cup chopped pecans

Preheat oven to 325 degrees. Melt butter in 13x9x2-inch baking dish. Sprinkle cracker crumbs over butter. Top in order with layers of coconut, chocolate chips, butterscotch chips, milk and pecans. Bake for 30 minutes. Cool in pan before cutting into small squares.

Alinda Mahaffey
(Representative Joseph G. Mahaffey)

Chocolate Peanut Butter Squares

My Aunt Jan makes these at Christmas for her family, but it is great year round. Serve as a dessert or candy. Great to take to a party for an easy pick up dessert.

MAKES ABOUT 30 SQUARES

1½ cups graham cracker crumbs

1 (16 ounce) package powdered sugar

1 cup creamy peanut butter

1 cup butter or margarine, softened

1 (12 ounce) package semi-sweet chocolate chips

Combine cracker crumbs, powdered sugar, peanut butter and butter. Press into the bottom of a greased 13x9x2-inch baking dish. Melt chocolate chips in a saucepan on low heat or in the microwave. Pour over peanut butter mixture. Cool and cut into squares.

Kelly Talley
(Representative Scott F. Talley)

The Marine Corps training camp at Parris Island was once a plantation owned by Col. Alexander Parris. Marines have been stationed there since 1915.

Erskine Crunch

MAKES ABOUT 1½ DOZEN PIECES

2½ cups sugar

2 cups butter

½ cup and ¾ cup and ¾ cup chopped nuts, divided

2 pounds semi-sweet or milk chocolate chips, melted, divided

Combine sugar and butter in a heavy saucepan. Stir constantly over medium high heat to reach hard ball stage (300-310 degrees). Add ½ cup chopped nuts. Spread onto two baking sheets. Mixture will not fill cookie sheet and will be irregular in shape. When cool, spread half melted chocolate over all. Sprinkle ¾ cup nuts on top. When chocolate has set, turn crunch over and repeat chocolate and nut layers. Allow to harden and crack into pieces. Store in an airtight container.

Reba Stille
(Former Representative Harry Stille)

Erskine College located in Due West is the oldest four-year denominational college in South Carolina.

243

Peanut Butter Balls

This recipe is from Granny Hall who made these every Christmas. It is a family tradition for everyone to get together during the holidays and make these delicious treats.

MAKES ABOUT 4 DOZEN

1 **(18 ounce) jar creamy peanut butter**	1 **(8 ounce) package milk chocolate chips**
1 **(16 ounce) package powdered sugar**	1 **(2 ounce) package paraffin**
½ **cup butter or margarine, softened**	

Combine peanut butter, powdered sugar and butter. Roll mixture into small balls. Refrigerate until well chilled. Melt chocolate chips with paraffin. Using a toothpick, dip balls into chocolate. Place on a parchment paper-lined or wax paper-lined baking sheet. Cool to set.

Kelly Talley
(Representative Scott F. Talley)

There are over 340 golf courses in South Carolina with membership in the South Carolina Golf Association which makes the state a popular winter vacation spot for golf enthusiasts fleeing the cold and snow at home.

Pies & Desserts

Pies & Desserts

The Official State Butterfly — Tiger Swallowtail

Fudge Pecan Pie

SERVES 10 (ONE 9-INCH PIE)

½ cup sugar

⅓ cup unsweetened cocoa powder

⅓ cup all-purpose flour

¼ teaspoon salt

1¼ cups light corn syrup

3 eggs

3 tablespoons butter, melted

1½ teaspoons vanilla

½ cup chopped pecans

1 (9-inch) deep dish pie shell, unbaked

½ cup pecan halves

Preheat oven to 350 degrees. Combine sugar, cocoa, flour, salt, corn syrup, eggs, butter and vanilla in a large bowl. Beat for 30 seconds. Do not over beat. Stir in chopped pecans. Pour filling into pie shell. Arrange pecan halves on top. Bake for 1 hour. Cool on a wire rack.

Joanne Clark
(Former Representative Ken Clark)

South Carolina Pecan Pie

SERVES 16 (TWO 9-INCH PIES)

1 (16 ounce) package light brown sugar

3 eggs, beaten

½ cup milk

1 teaspoon vanilla

¼ cup butter, softened

1 cup chopped pecans

2 (9-inch) pie shells, unbaked

Preheat oven to 325 degrees. Combine brown sugar, eggs, milk, vanilla and butter in a bowl. Stir until well blended. Add pecans and mix well. Divide filling between pie shells. Bake for 35 minutes.

Alinda Mahaffey
(Representative Joseph G. Mahaffey)

A hunter's paradise… Old rice plantations and large farm tracts across South Carolina have been converted into hunt clubs which attract locals and hunters from all over the United States.

Decadent Chocolate Bourbon Pecan Pie with White Chocolate Ice Cream

This recipe was submitted by Susan Wilkins, wife of David H. Wilkins, US Ambassador to Canada. Ambassador Wilkins served in the South Carolina House of Representatives from 1981 to 2005. He was the Speaker of the House from December 1994 until June 2005.

SERVES 10 (ONE 9-INCH PIE)

1	cup semi-sweet chocolate chips	½	cup butter, melted
1	(9-inch) deep dish pie shell, unbaked	1	cup light corn syrup
		1	cup sugar
1	cup chopped pecans	2	tablespoons bourbon
4	eggs	1	teaspoon vanilla

Preheat oven to 350 degrees. Scatter chocolate chips in the bottom of pie shell. Top with pecans. Whisk together eggs, butter, corn syrup, sugar, bourbon and vanilla. Pour mixture into pie shell. Place pie on a baking sheet and place on middle oven rack. Bake for about 35 minutes or until filling is firmly set. Cool and serve with white chocolate ice cream.

Aiken County has been called the Newport of the South. During the late 1800s and early 1900s, Aiken hosted a winter colony of the very wealthy from November to March. There was a variety of horse related activities and lavish entertainment to occupy the winter residents. Many of those activities continue today.

(continued)

Decadent Chocolate Bourbon Pecan Pie, continued

WHITE CHOCOLATE ICE CREAM

MAKES 1½ QUARTS

1	quart half-and-half	12	egg yolks
¾	cup sugar	1	pound white chocolate, finely chopped

In a large saucepan, heat half-and-half to the boiling point. Remove from heat. Whisk together sugar and egg yolks in a large bowl. Whisking constantly, gradually pour hot half-and-half over egg mixture. Pour mixture back into saucepan. Cook over medium heat until thickened slightly and coats back of a spoon. Do not allow to boil. Remove from the heat. Stir in white chocolate until melted. Strain mixture into a stainless steel bowl. Place that bowl in another bowl filled with ice water to chill the mixture quickly. Freeze according to ice cream machine directions.

Chef Dino Ovcaric

Chef Dana Gosso
US Ambassador's Residence
Ottawa, Canada

Submitted by Susan Wilkins
(Former House Speaker, US Ambassador David H. Wilkins)

Turf grass is one of South Carolina's most valuable crops. Anyone for a round of golf?

Pineapple Chiffon Pie

SERVES 8 (ONE 9-INCH PIE)

1   cup sugar
2   cups pineapple juice
2   eggs, well beaten
1   (3 ounce) package lemon flavored gelatin
1   (12 ounce) can evaporated milk, refrigerated

1   (9-inch) graham cracker pie shell
Crushed graham cracker crumbs and toasted coconut for garnish

Combine sugar, pineapple juice and eggs in a small saucepan. Bring just to boiling point. Be careful not to scorch. Place lemon flavored gelatin in a large bowl. Pour hot mixture over gelatin and stir until dissolved. Refrigerate until syrupy. Whip cold milk. Fold whipped milk into gelatin mixture. Pour filling into pie shell. Sprinkle top with graham cracker crumbs or toasted coconut. Refrigerate several hours before serving. May also add 1 (8 ounce) can crushed pineapple, drained, to filling or a ½ teaspoon of fresh lemon juice.

Amy F. Wright
(Former Representative David Wright)

Banana Breeze

SERVES 8 (ONE 9-INCH PIE)

⅓ **cup butter or margarine**

¼ **cup sugar**

1 **cup cornflake cereal**

1 **(8 ounce) package cream cheese, softened**

1 **(14 ounce) can sweetened condensed milk**

⅓ **cup plus 2 tablespoons reconstituted lemon juice, divided**

1 **teaspoon vanilla**

4 **medium bananas, divided**

Melt butter and sugar in a small saucepan. Simmer over low heat, stirring constantly, until bubbles form around the edges of the pan. Remove from heat. Add cornflakes and mix well. Press mixture evenly into bottom of a 9-inch pie plate. Refrigerate. Beat cream cheese until fluffy. Blend in condensed milk. Stir in ⅓ cup lemon juice and vanilla. Stir until thickened. Slice 3 bananas. Line crust with slices. Spoon filling on top bananas. Refrigerate for 2-3 hours or until firm. Do not freeze. Cut remaining banana into thin slices. Dip slices in remaining 2 tablespoons lemon juice. Garnish top of pie with banana slices and serve.

Melody Duncan
(Representative Jeffrey D. Duncan)

Movies filmed in SC:

Forrest Gump

The Great Santini

The Prince of Tides

The Patriot

Days of Thunder

Sleeping With the Enemy

The Big Chill

The Notebook

The Program

Deliverance

Orange Blossom Pie

This delicious pie was served at a luncheon for the Palmetto Cabinet hosted by Mrs. Andrew (Donna) Sorenson at the USC President's home. They were kind enough to share the recipe with us.

SERVES 8 (ONE 9-INCH PIE)

3	eggs	1	(15 ounce) can Mandarin oranges, drained or 1 large orange, peeled and segmented
½	cup sugar		
2	teaspoons orange zest		
¼	cup orange juice	1	(9-inch) vanilla wafer pie shell, refrigerated
4	tablespoons butter		
1	cup heavy cream		Orange segments for garnish

Beat eggs until frothy. Combine eggs, sugar, zest and orange juice in a medium saucepan. Cook over low heat, stirring constantly, about 20-25 minutes or until very thickened. Remove from heat. Stir in butter. Pour into a bowl and refrigerate until cold. Whip cream until soft peaks form. Fold into chilled orange mixture. Arrange a layer of orange sections in cold pie shell. Spoon orange mixture over oranges. Garnish top with orange segments. Refrigerate until ready to serve.

Sue Kirsh
(Representative Herb Kirsh)

S.C. Sports Greats:

Shoeless Joe Jackson

Cale Yarborough

Beth Daniel

Althea Gibson

William "The Refrigerator" Perry

Jim Rice

Joe Frazier

Bobby Richardson

Willie Randolph

Alexander English

Mama's Pumpkin Pie

My mother made a delicious pumpkin pie. After she passed away, my son missed Mama's pie. I came up with this recipe which I think tastes close to my mother's recipe. My son says it isn't the same, but very close.

SERVES 16 (TWO 9-INCH PIES)

MERINGUE

3   egg whites

⅛   teaspoon salt

3   tablespoons sugar

Beat egg whites and salt until soft peaks form. Add sugar and beat until stiff peaks form.

FILLING

2   (15 ounce) cans pumpkin

1½   cups sugar

3   eggs, beaten

1   cup evaporated milk

¼   teaspoon salt

1   teaspoon lemon extract

1   tablespoon self-rising flour

¼   cup butter or margarine, melted

2   (9-inch) pie shells, baked

Preheat oven to 350 degrees. Combine pumpkin, sugar, eggs, milk, salt, lemon extract, flour and butter. Mix well. Divide filling between pie shells. Top with meringue. Bake until golden browned on top.

Norma Jean Barfield
(Representative Liston D. Barfield)

Renowned SC Musicians:

Dizzie Gillespie

Eartha Kitt

Brook Benton

James Brown

Bill Pinkney

Chubby Checker

Edwin McCain

Aaron Tippin

Hootie and the Blowfish

Easy Coconut Pie

SERVES 16 (TWO 9-INCH PIES)

1½ cups sugar	½ cup butter or margarine, melted
3 tablespoons self-rising flour	1½ cups milk
3 eggs, beaten	1 teaspoon vanilla
1 (12 ounce) package frozen coconut, thawed	2 (9-inch) pie shells, unbaked

Preheat oven to 350 degrees. Combine sugar, flour and eggs. Mix well. Add coconut, butter, milk and vanilla. Divide filling between pie shells. Bake for 35 minutes or until lightly browned on top.

Judy Frye
(Representative Marion B. Frye)

Coconut Custard Pie

SERVES 16 (TWO 9-INCH PIES)

½ cup butter	2 cups flaked coconut
¾ cup sugar	2 teaspoons lemon extract
1 (14 ounce) can sweetened condensed milk	2 (9-inch) pie shells, unbaked
6 eggs, beaten	

Preheat oven to 350 degrees. Melt butter in a saucepan. Add sugar, milk, eggs, coconut and lemon extract. Mix well. Divide filling between pie shells. Bake for 30 minutes or until lightly browned.

Lynn Owens
(Representative Phillip D. Owens)

Crustless Coconut Pie

This pie recipe makes its own crust!

SERVES 16 (TWO 9-INCH PIES)

4 **eggs, beaten**	¼ **cup butter or margarine, melted**
1¾ **cups sugar**	1 **(6 ounce) package frozen coconut, thawed**
½ **cup self-rising flour**	
2 **cups milk**	1 **teaspoon vanilla**

Preheat oven to 350 degrees. Combine eggs, sugar, flour, milk, butter, coconut and vanilla. Mix well. Divide filling between two greased 9-inch pie plates or one casserole dish. Bake for 40 minutes or until lightly browned.

Betty Knotts
(Senator John M. "Jake" Knotts, Jr.)

Folks in the midlands wait in anticipation for the Greek Festival held in Columbia each September. Traditional Greek meals and sweets attract tens of thousands. Traditional Greek folk dances, music and costumes are part of the festival but it is the food that ties up downtown traffic for hours as people happily wait for a parking space.

253

Frozen Key Lime Pie

SERVES 8 (ONE 9-INCH PIE)

1	cup graham cracker crumbs		Pinch of salt
3	tablespoons sugar		Pinch of cream of tartar
5	tablespoons butter, melted	1	cup heavy cream
½	cup key lime juice	3	tablespoons powdered sugar
3	eggs	1	teaspoon vanilla
1	(14 ounce) can sweetened condensed milk	1	lime, thinly sliced for garnish

Preheat oven to 325 degrees. Combine cracker crumbs, sugar and butter. Press mixture into a 9-inch pie plate. Bake for 5 minutes. Cool completely. If using bottled key lime juice, measure ½ cup of juice. If using fresh, squeeze lemons and limes to get a ¼ cup of juice from each. Separate 2 eggs, placing 2 egg whites into a mixing bowl. Reserve yolks in another bowl. To the yolks, add one whole egg, ½ cup juice and sweetened condensed milk. Whisk well. With an electric mixer, beat egg whites until stiff, but not dry. Add salt and cream of tartar after about 20 seconds. Fold egg whites into yolk mixture. Pour filling into partially baked crust. Bake for 10-15 minutes or until set. Cool at room temperature. Freeze 4 hours or overnight. Remove pie from freezer and soften slightly. Just before serving, whip cream to form soft peaks. Add powdered sugar and vanilla. Beat until stiff peaks form. Spread whipped cream over pie. Garnish with lime slices, if desired.

Debbie DeMint
(US Senator Jim DeMint)

The Dock Street Theatre in Charleston opened in 1736 and was the first building to be constructed for use only as a theater. Its uses were numerous over the years but in 1937, the building was remodeled and reopened as a theater and is still in use today.

Strawberry and Cream Pie

May also substitute raspberries or blueberries or use a combination of all three.

SERVES 8 (ONE 9-INCH PIE)

1	(15 ounce) package refrigerated pie crust	4	cups (2 pints) fresh whole strawberries
1	(8 ounce) package cream cheese, softened	½	cup semi-sweet chocolate chips
⅓	cup sugar	1	tablespoon vegetable shortening
½	teaspoon almond extract		
1	cup heavy cream, whipped		

Preheat oven to 450 degrees. Line one pastry in a 9-inch pie plate. Bake for 9-11 minutes or until golden browned. Cool completely. In a large bowl, beat cream cheese until fluffy. Add sugar and almond extract. Blend well. Fold in whipped cream. Spoon filling over crust. Arrange berries on top. Refrigerate. In a small saucepan, melt chocolate chips and shortening over low heat until smooth. Drizzle over strawberries and filling. Refrigerate about 1 hour until set.

Jean Littlejohn
(Representative Lanny F. Littlejohn)

*Charleston opened
the first free library in the
United States in 1698.*

255

Chocolate Brownie Pie

This pie is delicious served hot with ice cream or whipped topping.

SERVES 8 (ONE 9-INCH PIE)

½ cup butter or margarine	1 cup sugar
2 (1 ounce) squares unsweetened chocolate	1 tablespoon vanilla
2 eggs	¼ cup sifted all-purpose flour
	¼ teaspoon salt

Preheat oven to 350 degrees. Melt butter and chocolate in a double boiler or heatproof bowl over a pan of simmering water. Set aside to cool slightly. Beat eggs, sugar and vanilla until fluffy. Fold in flour and salt. Stir in chocolate mixture until well blended. Pour mixture into greased and floured 9-inch pie plate. Bake for 25 minutes. Do not over bake.

Anne Elliott
(Senator Dick Elliott)

Famous Derby Pie

SERVES 10 (ONE 9-INCH PIE)

1 cup sugar	1 cup chopped walnuts
½ cup all-purpose flour	1 (6 ounce) package semi-sweet chocolate chips
2 eggs, slightly beaten	1 (9-inch) deep dish pie shell, unbaked
½ cup butter, melted and cooled	
1 teaspoon vanilla	

Preheat oven to 350 degrees. Combine sugar and flour. Add eggs, butter and vanilla. Stir in nuts and chocolate chips. Pour filling into pie shell. Bake for 50 minutes.

Katherine Battle
(Representative James A. Battle, Jr.)

Lynn Owens
(Representative Phillip D. Owens

A shipment of 96 golf clubs and 432 golf balls sent from the Port of Leith, Scotland to Charleston in 1743 first introduced the game of golf to the United States. Scottish merchants founded the South Carolina Golf Club in 1786. The re-chartered club still exists though it is now located in Sea Pines.

Million Dollar Pie

SERVES 16 (TWO 9-INCH PIES)

¼	cup lemon juice	1	(8 ounce) can crushed pineapple, drained
1	(14 ounce) sweetened condensed milk	½	cup chopped pecans
1	(8 ounce) container frozen nondairy whipped topping, thawed	½	cup flaked coconut
		2	(9-inch) pie shells, baked

Pour lemon juice into milk in a large bowl. Fold in whipped topping. Add pineapple, pecans and coconut. Divide filling between pie shells. Refrigerate for several hours or overnight.

David Neilson
(Representative Denny W. Neilson)

Easy Apple Pie

SERVES 6

4-5	Gala apples, thinly sliced	1	cup sugar
1	teaspoon apple pie spice	1	egg, beaten
4	slices white sandwich bread	½	cup butter or margarine, melted

Preheat oven to 350 degrees. Arrange apples in a buttered 8-inch square pan. Sprinkle with pie spice. Cut each bread slice into 4 strips. Arrange 16 bread strips over apples. Combine sugar, egg, and butter. Mix well and pour over bread. Bake for 45-50 minutes. May substitute sliced peaches for apples. When using canned fruit instead of fresh, be sure to drain well. Also, omit the apple pie spice.

Melody Duncan
(Representative Jeffrey D. Duncan)

The H.L. Hunley was the first submarine to sink an enemy ship. Following a successful mission during the Civil War, the Hunley sank in Charleston harbor in 1863 where it rested on the ocean floor until it was raised for preservation in 2000.

The General Assembly declared in 1984 that the peach should be the Official State Fruit.

South Carolina is second in size only to California in peach production. Peaches and the ice creams, pies, drinks and cobblers made from this magnificent fruit are celebrated in festivals in Gilbert on the 4th of July, Johnson in April, Trenton in June, and Gaffney in July. Appearing in the Gilbert parade is mandatory for any serious statewide or local politician.

Disappearing Cranberry Pie

SERVES 8 (ONE 9-INCH PIE)

1	**(8 ounce) package cream cheese, softened**
½	**cup powdered sugar**
½	**(14 ounce) can whole cranberry sauce**
¾	**cup chopped nuts**
1	**(8 ounce) container frozen nondairy whipped topping, thawed**
1	**teaspoon vanilla**
1	**(9-inch) graham cracker pie crust**

Beat cream cheese and sugar together until well blended. Mix in cranberry sauce and nuts. Fold in whipped topping and vanilla. Pour filling into pie crust. Refrigerate for at least 2 hours before serving. May refrigerate overnight.

Sue Kirsh
(Representative Herb Kirsh)

Fruit Cobbler

SERVES 8-10

½	**cup unsalted butter**
1	**cup plus 1 cup sugar, divided**
3-4	**cups fresh South Carolina peaches or apples, sliced**
¾	**cup all-purpose flour**
2	**teaspoons baking powder**
	Pinch of salt
¾	**cup milk**
	Ground cinnamon (optional)

Preheat oven to 350 degrees. Melt butter in a 13x9x2-inch baking dish. Sprinkle 1 cup sugar over peaches and toss to coat. Set aside. Combine remaining 1 cup sugar, flour, milk, baking powder, salt and milk in a bowl. Pour batter over butter. Spoon fruit over batter. Sprinkle with cinnamon. Bake for 45-50 minutes or until golden browned.

Iris Campbell
(The late former Governor Carroll A. Campbell, Jr.)

Palmetto Peach Crisp

SERVES 10-12

12	large fresh South Carolina peaches, peeled and sliced
¼	cup plus 1 cup sugar, divided
½	cup plus ½ cup packed light brown sugar, divided

2	tablespoons plus 1½ cups all-purpose flour, divided
1	tablespoon unsalted butter
1	cup quick cooking oats
½	teaspoon salt
1	cup very cold unsalted butter, cut into small pieces

Preheat oven to 350 degrees. Place peach slices into a large bowl. Add ¼ cup sugar, ½ cup brown sugar and 2 tablespoons flour. Mix together and add more flour if there is too much juice. Let stand for about 15 minutes at room temperature. Pour peaches into a buttered 13x9x2-inch baking dish. Combine remaining 1 cup sugar, ½ cup brown sugar, 1½ cups flour, oats, salt and butter pieces. Stir until well blended. Sprinkle mixture over peaches. Bake for about 1 hour or until top is golden browned and peaches are bubbly. Serve warm with vanilla ice cream or whipped cream.

Vickie Skelton
(Representative B.R. Skelton)

A dance craze in the 1920s, the Big Apple, was created in Columbia. During the 1950s another dance—the Shag—was developed at Ocean Drive Beach. The shag is still popular and has been officially named the State Dance.

The Blueberry Thing

This is a recipe from my fellow church member, Lillian Green. May use any fruit pie filling you prefer.

SERVES 10-12

2	cups graham cracker crumbs
⅓	cup plus ¾ cup sugar, divided
10	tablespoons butter or margarine, melted
12	ounces cream cheese, softened
2	eggs
1	(21 ounce) can blueberry pie filling
1	(8 ounce) container frozen nondairy whipped topping, thawed

Preheat oven to 350 degrees. Combine cracker crumbs, ⅓ cup sugar and butter. Press into a 13x9x2 baking dish. Beat cream cheese, eggs and ¾ cup sugar until creamy and smooth. Pour cream cheese mixture over crust. Bake for 15-20 minutes. Cool thoroughly. Spread pie filling on top. Top with whipped topping.

Joan Scott
(Representative John L. Scott, Jr.)

The Atlantic Ocean once covered most of the Lowcountry and sandy soil from that period is found as far inland as the midlands.

Sugar Cookie Pizza

SERVES 8

1   (20 ounce) package refrigerated sugar cookie dough

1   (8 ounce) plus 1 (3 ounce) package cream cheese, softened

¼   cup sugar

1   tablespoon fresh lemon juice

Zest of 1 lemon

3   fresh fruits (strawberries, blueberries, pineapple, kiwi or bananas)

3   tablespoons orange marmalade

2   tablespoons cherry-flavored brandy (optional)

Preheat oven to 375 degrees. Press cookie dough onto an ungreased 10-inch pizza pan. Bake for 14-16 minutes. Cool. Combine cream cheese, sugar, lemon juice and zest in a food processor. Process until well blended. Spread mixture on cooled cookie crust. Slice strawberries, kiwi and/or bananas. Chop pineapple. Arrange fruit over cream cheese mixture. Using just enough fruit to completely cover in one layer. Combine marmalade and brandy in a small saucepan. Cook on low heat until melted. Brush over fruit. Refrigerate before serving.

Peatsy Hollings
(Former US Senator Ernest F. Hollings)

Ernest F. Hollings served as State Representative, Lieutenant Governor and Governor (1959-1963). Served as U.S. Senator from 1967-2005.

Charlotte Slim

Very diet friendly treat!

SERVES 5

½ cup water
1 envelope unflavored gelatin
1 cup skim milk
1 cup non-fat cottage cheese

1 (1.8 ounce) container Crystal Light Classic orange powder
   Whipped cream (optional)

Heat water in microwave for 20 seconds. Dissolve gelatin in water. Combine milk and cottage cheese in blender. Blend dissolved gelatin into milk and cottage cheese. Add Crystal Light. Blend thoroughly. Pour mixture into 5 individual compotes or serving bowls. Refrigerate for 1 hour. Serve with whipped cream.

Former Representative Elsie Rast Stuart

Triple Chocolate Trifle

SERVES 8-10

1 (18 ounce) package chocolate cake mix
1 (5 ounce) package instant chocolate pudding mix
½ cup coffee-flavored liqueur, divided

1 (12 ounce) container frozen nondairy whipped topping, thawed
4-6 chocolate toffee candy bars, crumbled

Prepare cake mix according to package directions and bake for a two layer cake. Cool. Prepare pudding as directed and refrigerate until set. Break one cake layer into pieces. Place in bottom of trifle bowl or deep glass serving bowl. Drizzle ¼ cup liqueur over cake. Spoon half of pudding over liqueur. Top with half of whipped topping. Sprinkle half of candy crumbs on top. Repeat all layers ending with candy. Refrigerate before serving.

Amy F. Wright
(Former Representative David Wright)

South Carolina was home to more than 25 different Indian tribes. Many rivers, swamps, mountains and other natural features were named for these local tribes.

Molten Chocolate Cakes

MAKES 8 (6 OUNCE) CAKES

½	cup butter	½	cup sugar
1	(8 ounce) semi-sweet chocolate baking bar, chopped	¼	teaspoon salt
		2	tablespoons all-purpose flour
4	eggs		Powdered sugar, whipped cream or ice cream for garnish
1	egg yolk		
1	teaspoon vanilla		

Preheat oven to 400 degrees. Butter and flour 8 (6-ounce) ramekins. Place ramekins in a large baking pan. Melt butter and chocolate in a double boiler or in a heatproof bowl over a pot of simmering water. Stir until thoroughly melted. Remove from heat and cool. In a stand mixer with a whisk attachment, beat eggs, egg yolk, vanilla, sugar and salt about 5 minutes until triples in volume and color is very light. If using a hand mixer, beat for 10 minutes on high. Fold egg mixture into cooled chocolate. Sprinkle flour over top and fold in until well blended. Divide batter among ramekins. Bake for 12 minutes or until puffed up about ¼ inch above the rim of the ramekins. Run a knife around the edge and invert the cakes on a serving plate. May dust with powdered sugar. Serve with sweetened whipped cream or scoop of ice cream.

May prepare 6 hours before serving. Refrigerate until ready to bake. May require another minute or two to cook if just removed from refrigerator.

Vickie Skelton
(Representative B.R. Skelton)

All eight species of swans can be found at Swan Lake in Sumter.

Cold Chocolate Soufflé

This recipe is from my husband's grandmother, Gladys Smith Rice. This is just as good without the second ½ cup sugar in the egg whites and with dark chocolate.

SERVES 10-12

2	envelopes unflavored gelatin	1	(12 ounce) package semi-sweet chocolate chips
2	cups milk (can use skim)	1	teaspoon vanilla
½	cup plus ½ cup sugar, divided	½	teaspoon ground cinnamon (optional)
⅛	teaspoon salt	1	cup heavy cream, whipped
4	eggs, separated		

In a 3-quart saucepan, sprinkle gelatin over cold milk. Combine ½ cup sugar, salt and egg yolks in a bowl. Add to gelatin. Stir into chocolate chips. Cook over low heat, stirring constantly, until gelatin and chocolate melts. Remove from heat and cool, stirring occasionally. Beat egg whites until thickened, gradually adding remaining ½ cup sugar, vanilla and cinnamon. Fold into cooled chocolate mixture. Fold in whipped cream. Pour mixture into a soufflé dish or serving bowl. Refrigerate until firm. Top with additional sweetened whipped cream, if desired.

Ruth Rice
(Representative Rex F. Rice)

Myrtle Beach is a national center for country music. Its venues feature performances by major artists throughout the year.

Strawberry Pudding

This recipe was a favorite of my family. My husband, Joe, had never had strawberry pudding prepared this way before we met. He always says my mother hooked him for her daughter with this pudding. This has become a favorite for him and our son.

SERVES 8-10

1½ cups plus 1 teaspoon sugar, divided

1 tablespoon cornstarch

2 eggs, separated

2 cups milk

1 (12 ounce) package vanilla wafers

1 (12 ounce) package frozen strawberries or 2 cups fresh, sliced and sweetened

1 teaspoon vanilla

Preheat oven to 350 degrees. In a large saucepan, combine 1½ cups sugar, cornstarch and egg yolks. Add small amount of milk. Gradually stir in all milk. Cook filling on low heat until thickened. Set aside and cool. Arrange alternating layers of vanilla wafers and strawberries in an 11x8x2-inch baking dish. Pour filling over top. Beat egg whites until soft peaks form. Add remaining 1 teaspoon sugar and vanilla. Beat until stiff peaks form. Spread topping over filling. Bake until meringue is lightly browned.

Alinda Mahaffey
(Representative Joseph G. Mahaffey)

The blue window and door trim found on some homes and porch ceilings along the coast is said to ward off evil spirits.

Quick and Easy Trifle

Great recipe for when you need a yummy dessert that does not take much time to prepare.

SERVES 8-10

2 (3 ounce) packages instant vanilla pudding mix

1 store bought angel food cake

2 pints (4 cups) sliced strawberries or 2 pints raspberries

1 (12 ounce) container frozen nondairy whipped topping, thawed

½ cup sliced almonds, toasted

Prepare pudding according to package directions. Refrigerate until set. Cut angel food cake in half and tear into pieces. Place half of cake in the bottom of a trifle dish or large glass serving bowl. Spoon half of pudding over cake. Spread half of fruit over pudding. Repeat layers with remaining cake, pudding and fruit. Spread whipped topping over fruit. Sprinkle almonds over top. Refrigerate until ready to serve.

Cookbook Committee

South Carolina was home to both rebels and loyalists during the American Revolution, though now no one would admit to having a loyalist ancestor. South Carolina had the largest number of battles and skirmishes fought on its soil: 137.

From the
Professionals

From The Professionals

View down Church Street in Charleston, SC

Magnolias' Collard Greens

I had never had collard greens until my mother-in-law introduced me to this New Year's Day tradition. I found that cooking them long and slow in chicken broth made them better flavored and silkier in texture. The smoked ham hock or neck bones add a subtle smoky flavor and the acidity of the vinegar and Tabasco gives them a nice tart, yet spicy, flavor.

SERVES 4

2 tablespoons light olive oil	12 cups washed, stemmed and roughly chopped collard greens 2 large or 3 small bunches)
1 cup diced yellow onion, cut in ¼-inch dice	
1 tablespoon minced garlic	9 cups chicken broth
1 smoked ham hock or 2 smoked pork neck bones	2 teaspoons Tabasco sauce or to taste
3 tablespoons cider vinegar	Salt and freshly ground black pepper to taste

Heat olive oil in a large heavy-bottomed stockpot over medium heat. Add onion and garlic and sauté for 2 to 3 minutes, stirring or until onions are translucent. Add ham hock or neck bones and vinegar. Gradually add collard greens. Cook the greens over medium heat, stirring occasionally, until all wilted. As greens wilt down, there will be enough room to get them all into the pot. Add chicken broth and 1 teaspoon Tabasco. Bring to boil and simmer for 1 hour, 45 minutes to 2 hours, adding more water if necessary, 1 cup at a time, until greens have a good flavor and are silky in texture. Add remaining teaspoon Tabasco and season with salt and pepper.

Chef Donald Barickman
Magnolias Restaurant
185 East Bay Street
Charleston, South Carolina

One of the South's most notable culinary figures, Barickman has been a guest chef and instructor at numerous culinary programs across the United States including the prestigious Cakebread Cellars American Harvest Workshop, La Varenne at the Greenbrier resort, Star Canyon in Dallas and The Inn at Blackberry Farm. He was a featured chef in the Great Chefs of the South cookbook and television series.

Elwood's Ham Chowder

This chowder has become quite popular over the years. I stumbled upon its main ingredient while trying to figure out what to fix on a rainy winter day. When I came across these Carolina ham trimmings in the grocery store, I knew that they offered a world of opportunity. I made my way back to the produce section and assembled the components that I thought would best complement this newly found ingredient. My father, Elwood, was in town and he helped me put together the first batch. Since its creation, it has been featured by Martha Stewart Magazine, The Best American Recipes 2003-2004 cookbook, and by Turner South Network on Blue Ribbon. This is a unique dish that melds all of the flavors of the South into chowder like none other.

It's much easier to dice up the ham if you freeze it. It's already sliced, so you can just cut it into strips and then into small cubes.

MAKES 12 (10-OUNCE) SERVINGS

1	tablespoon vegetable oil
1	pound Carolina Ham Trimmings, coarsely ground or minced
3	cups medium-diced onion
2	tablespoons sliced garlic
12	cups stemmed and diced fresh collards
1½	tablespoons chopped fresh thyme
2	tablespoons chopped fresh parsley
1	(28-ounce) can whole tomatoes with juice
7	cups chicken broth
1	pint beef stock, homemade or good quality store-bought
6	cups diced red potatoes, cut in ¼-inch dice
1½	teaspoons freshly ground black pepper
1½	teaspoons Tabasco sauce
	Salt to taste

(continued)

Elwood's Ham Chowder, continued

Heat vegetable oil in a heavy pot. Add ham and render the fat from the ham by cooking it slowly over medium heat, stirring frequently to keep it from browning. Add onions and garlic. Continue to cook over low heat, stirring occasionally, until onions and garlic are soft. A little more oil may be needed if the ham doesn't have enough fat. Slowly add collards and allow them to wilt. This should be done in 2 batches, as collards are very bulky raw, but wilt down like any greens. Add thyme, parsley, tomatoes with juice, chicken broth, beef stock and red potatoes. Slowly bring mixture up to a simmer and continue to cook 20 to 30 minutes, or until the potatoes are cooked through. Skim the chowder of any foam or oil that may appear during the cooking process. Add black pepper and Tabasco. Season with salt and more Tabasco if desired.

Chef Donald Barickman
Magnolias Restaurant
185 East Bay Street
Charleston, South Carolina

Donald Barickman graduated from the Culinary Institute of America in 1985, and took his career to the lowcountry of South Carolina, opening Magnolias in 1990. He has become widely recognized as a pioneer in lowcountry cuisine, bringing "uptown" flare to familiar southern staples. Over the past decade, Barickman and his partner at Hospitality Management Group, Inc., Thomas Parsell, have also opened Blossom restaurant and Magnolias Upper Level, a group dining facility. The company's newest venture, Cypress Lowcountry Grille, debuted in the spring of 2001, continuing Barickman's reputation for excellence.

Baked Blue Cheese and Macaroni

For those of you who love blue cheese, and macaroni and cheese, as I do, this is a great recipe to have both at once. It makes for an excellent side dish.

SERVES 8-10, FAMILY-STYLE

1 gallon water	1 pound grated Monterey Jack cheese
2 tablespoons salt	
16 ounces dried macaroni	1 cup milk
3 tablespoons butter	1 teaspoon fine sea salt
3 tablespoons all-purpose flour	½ teaspoon freshly ground black pepper
3 cups half-and-half, room temperature	¼ teaspoon cayenne pepper
	6 ounces blue cheese, crumbled

Bring water to boil in a large stockpot. Add salt just before macaroni and cook for 12 minutes or until cooked but still firm. Remember, the noodles are going to cook again. Strain and rinse in cold water with a few ice cubes until cooled. Drain and cover loosely. I do not recommend oiling the macaroni noodles.

Preheat oven to 400 degrees.

Melt butter in a heavy-bottomed saucepan. Whisk in flour. Cook over low heat for 1-2 minutes. Add ½ of the half-and-half and whisk vigorously as it thickens to a smooth paste. Use a spatula to release the mixture that may be stuck in the corners of the pan. Whisk again until smooth and thickened. Add remaining half-and-half and whisk constantly, slowly bringing the sauce up to a simmer. Cook for 1-2 minutes to cook out some of the starchy flavor of the flour.

(continued)

Baked Blue Cheese and Macaroni, continued

Add ¾-pound of Monterey Jack cheese to the thickened half-and-half. When cheese melts, add milk, salt, black pepper and cayenne pepper. Stir in 5 ounces of blue cheese and allow it to melt slightly. Place the macaroni in a large bowl and pour cheese sauce over it. Stir well to coat the macaroni evenly. Pour it into a 13x9x2-inch baking dish and sprinkle remaining ¼-pound of grated Jack cheese over top. Place the baking dish in the upper part of the oven. Allow the macaroni and cheese to bake for 15 minutes. Sprinkle remaining 1 ounce of blue cheese on top. Return to oven and bake for 15 minutes more or until top is golden browned and bubbly. Remove from the oven and allow the macaroni and cheese to rest 5 minutes before serving.

Chef Donald Barickman
Magnolias Restaurant
185 East Bay Street
Charleston, South Carolina

Chef Barickman's talents have been recognized by Esquire, Gourmet, Smithsonian Magazine, Southern Living, the James Beard Foundation and the Food Network, among others. Magnolias was awarded status as one of the Distinguished Restaurants of North America.

Pimiento Cheese Grits with Pepper-Seared Sea Scallops and Red Pepper Sauce

This dish brings together five of my favorite ingredients: pimientos, grits, sharp cheddar cheese, sea scallops, and black pepper. The creamy grits take on the flavors of the pimientos and cheddar cheese and make a great accompaniment for the pepper-seared sea scallops.

SERVES 6

PIMIENTO CHEESE GRITS

Makes 6 cups

- 6 cups water
- 1⅔ cups coarse stone-ground white grits
- ½ cup heavy cream
- 1 tablespoon butter
- 1 cup roasted, peeled, seeded, and chopped sweet red pepper
- 8 ounces sharp white Cheddar cheese
- ½ tablespoon salt
- Dash of white pepper

Bring water to boil in a heavy-bottomed stockpot or large saucepan. Slowly pour in grits, stirring constantly. Reduce heat to low and continue to stir so that grits do not settle to the bottom and scorch. After 8-10 minutes, the grits will plump up. Cook grits over low heat for another 25-30 minutes, stirring frequently. Add cream, butter, roasted peppers and Cheddar cheese. Cook an additional 10 minutes to melt cheese and allow peppers to flavor the grits. Add salt and white pepper. The grits will have a thick natural creamy consistency, and will have become soft and silky. Keep covered and warm until ready to serve. If the grits become too thick, add warm water to adjust the consistency.

(continued)

Pimiento Cheese Grits, continued

RED PEPPER SAUCE

Makes 1¾ cups

1 tablespoons plus 1 teaspoon olive oil, divided	½ cup red pepper flesh from 2 large roasted red peppers, chopped or 2 (4-ounce) jars pimientos, drained and chopped
¼ cup roughly chopped yellow onion	
½ teaspoon roughly chopped garlic	2 tablespoons chopped fresh basil
2 tablespoons all-purpose flour	Salt to taste
1¼ cups chicken broth	Pinch of cayenne pepper

Heat olive oil in a heavy-bottomed saucepan over medium heat. Add onion and garlic and sauté for 1 minute. Reduce heat and make a roux by adding flour and stirring until well combined. Continue to cook over low heat for 2 minutes, stirring constantly. Do not let onions or flour color. Turn up heat to medium and, stirring vigorously, add ¾ cup chicken broth. Continue stirring vigorously until the broth thickens and is smooth. Gradually add the remaining ½ cup chicken broth, red pepper strips or the pimiento and basil, stirring constantly until the broth thickens into a sauce.

Bring sauce to a low boil, then simmer over medium heat for 10 minutes to cook out the starchy flavor of the flour. Skim off any skin that may come to the top and discard. Remove sauce from heat and let it cool, stirring occasionally, for 10 minutes. Purée the mixture in a food processor or blender until smooth. Add salt and cayenne pepper. Use at once or place in a storage container, let cool to room temperature, cover and refrigerate. Red Pepper Sauce will keep for a week in the refrigerator.

(recipe continues on next page)

Pimiento Cheese Grits, continued

SCALLOPS

12	large sea scallops
1	tablespoon freshly ground black pepper
2	teaspoons fine sea salt
4	tablespoons light olive oil

½ cup white Cheddar cheese, cut in a small dice for garnish

½ recipe Red Pepper Sauce

Season sea scallops with black pepper and salt on the flattest surface of each scallop. Heat olive oil in a heavy-bottomed frying pan to the smoking point. Gently place scallops seasoned-side down in hot oil. Sear for 1 minute. Carefully lift scallops so that oil can get under each one. Continue to sear, adjusting the heat if necessary, until a golden crust or sear is obtained. Gently turn scallops over and cook them on the other side for 4-5 minutes. They should still be a little translucent in the center. Remove from heat and allow to rest for a moment.

Divide grits between 6 warm serving plates. Arrange two scallops beside the grits and sprinkle with the Cheddar cheese and a drizzle of Red Pepper sauce.

Chef Donald Barickman
Magnolias Restaurant
185 East Bay Street
Charleston, South Carolina

Sautéed Grouper with Artichoke and Creamy Crabmeat over Sautéed Spinach with Lemon and Leek Butter

Black grouper and many other fish are now being protected in many ways through the efforts of the Sustainable Seafood Initiative. It is one of the best quality bottom fish in our local waters, and my preference, but it has become scarce lately. Hopefully, through these conservation efforts, it and all of our local fish will always be available to us.

SERVES 4

CREAMY CRABMEAT

½   cup heavy cream

½   pound lump crabmeat, gently picked over for shell and drained of any liquid

1   tablespoon minced chives

Fine sea salt and white pepper to taste

Heat cream in a small saucepan over medium-high heat and reduce it by half. Add crabmeat and chives. Gently fold them together to warm crabmeat. Add salt and white pepper. Keep warm.

SPINACH

2   tablespoons butter

12   ounces baby spinach leaves

Fine sea salt and white pepper to taste

Melt butter in a large frying pan. Add spinach and cook over medium-low heat until just wilted. Add salt and white pepper. Drain. Keep warm.

(recipe continues on next page)

275

Sautéed Grouper, continued

LEMON AND LEEK BUTTER

Makes 1 cup

12 tablespoons unsalted butter	1 teaspoon lemon zest
1½ cups leeks, washed and drained very well, ¼-inch dice	¼ cup warm water
	Pinch of white pepper
1 tablespoon white wine	Fine sea salt to taste
¼ cup heavy cream	

Heat 4 tablespoons butter, add leeks and cook them for 2-3 minutes or until they have softened. Add white wine, cook for a moment, then add cream and reduce by one third. Add lemon zest. Gradually whisk in the remaining 8 tablespoons butter in small amounts over low heat. If the sauce gets too hot, it may separate. The sauce is also at risk if it gets too cold. It should be kept at approximately 120 degrees at all times. When all of the butter is incorporated and melted, the sauce will be thick and creamy. If too thick, adjust the consistency with up to ¼ cup of warm water. Add salt and white pepper. Keep warm.

(continued)

Sautéed Grouper, continued

TO FINISH THE DISH

1 **(14 ounce) jar artichoke hearts**

4 **tablespoons light olive oil**

4 **(4 to 5 ounce) grouper fillets**

1 **teaspoon coarse sea salt**

½ **teaspoon white pepper**

½ **cup all-purpose flour**

Preheat oven to 300 degrees. Drain artichoke hearts. Slice each heart vertically into ¼-inch thick slices.

Heat olive oil in a heavy ovenproof frying pan until almost smoking. Season the fillets with salt and white pepper. Lightly dust in flour and pat off excess. Gently place fillets in heated oil with the skin-side up. Sauté for 2-3 minutes, lifting fillets occasionally to let oil help to cook the fish evenly. Gently turn and sauté other side for an additional 2-3 minutes or until cooked through and the inner flesh of the fillet is white in color with no translucency.

Cover each fillet with a few slices of artichoke heart and place in the oven to warm artichokes for 3-4 minutes.

Divide spinach between four warmed plates. Place a grouper fillet on top of spinach. Top with creamy crabmeat. Spoon a few tablespoons of Lemon and Leek Butter around the spinach and a little over the crabmeat. Serve immediately.

Chef Donald Barickman
Magnolias Restaurant
185 East Bay Street
Charleston, South Carolina

Shrimp and Rice Salad with Lemon, Garlic, and Dill Vinaigrette

A great refreshing chilled summer salad. The lemon, garlic, and dill vinaigrette adds a great flavor enhancement to the rice and the celery and corn give it a sweet flavor and a crunchy texture.

SERVES 10-12

RICE

Carolina Plantation Aromatic Rice

I made this rice a staple at Magnolias shortly after I met Campbell and Meredith Coxe. They had just started to grow the heirloom Della variety in small amounts and asked me to try it out. I was immediately hooked by its aromatic qualities and the fact that it is the only rice produced entirely in South Carolina in retail quantity. I had not used Carolina Plantation Aromatic Rice prior to the publication of the original Magnolias Southern Cuisine, but you will find it in many of the new recipes. Carolina Plantation also grows and mills their white and yellow corn grits, brown rice, rice flour, and cowpeas.

2 cups Carolina Aromatic Rice (about 1 pound)	**3¼ cups water**

Rinse rice with cold water until water is clear. Place rice and water in a deep, heavy-bottomed pot and cover with a lid. Place pot over medium-low heat and allow it to slowly come to boil. Reduce heat and cook rice slowly for 12-15 minutes. It is best not to peek and allow the steam to escape. When the rice has finished cooking, steam holes should be present at the surface of the rice and all of the water should have been absorbed by the rice.

Remove pot from heat and fluff the rice with a fork. Spread rice out on a large pan or bowl to cool, fluffing frequently to release the steam. Cool to room temperature. Reserve.

(continued)

Shrimp and Rice Sallad, continued

LEMON, GARLIC AND DILL VINAIGRETTE

Makes 2½ cups

3 tablespoons spicy Dijon mustard	1½ cups light olive oil
2 tablespoons crushed fresh garlic	⅓ cup fresh dill sprigs, picked from the main stem and cut in medium thin slices
⅓ cup fresh lemon juice	Fine sea salt and ground white pepper to taste
¼ cup rice wine vinegar	

In a mixing bowl, combine mustard, garlic, lemon juice and rice wine vinegar and mix well. Slowly whisk in oil until all is incorporated. Add the dill. Add salt and white pepper.

SALAD

1 pound large shrimp, peeled, deveined, split lengthwise, cooked, and chilled	1 cup finely diced celery
1½ cups sweet corn kernels, cooked on the cob, cooled, and cut off	1 cup thinly sliced green onion, using entire green onion

Mix together rice, shrimp, corn, celery and green onion. Add 1½ cups of vinaigrette and toss to coat. Season with salt and white pepper to taste. Refrigerate at least 2 hours or overnight. Add remaining vinaigrette as needed to refresh the salad just before serving.

Place a small amount of salad in the center of a plate. Garnish with a drizzle of vinaigrette, a sprig of fresh dill and a lemon wedge. May also serve this salad family style for a picnic or large function.

Chef Donald Barickman is author of Magnolias Southern Cuisine published in 1995 and Magnolias Authentic Southern Cuisine in 2006.

Chef Donald Barickman
Magnolias Restaurant
185 East Bay Street
Charleston, South Carolina

Magnolias' Spicy Shrimp, Sausage, and Tasso Gravy over Creamy White Grits

These grits are not the same if reheated after they are refrigerated. They should be cooked within hours of serving.

SERVES 8

GRITS

Makes 12 cups grits

12	cups water	2	tablespoons butter
3¼	cups coarse stone-ground white grits	1	tablespoon salt
1	cup heavy cream	¼	teaspoon white pepper

Bring water to boil in a heavy-bottomed stockpot or large saucepan. Slowly pour in grits, stirring constantly. Reduce heat to low and continue to stir so that grits do not settle to the bottom and scorch. After 8-10 minutes, grits will plump up. Cook grits over low heat for 30-35 minutes, stirring frequently. Add cream, butter, salt and white pepper within last 15 minutes. The grits will have a thick natural creamy consistency and become soft and silky. Keep covered and warm until ready to serve. If the grits become too thick, add warm water to adjust the consistency.

TASSO GRAVY

Makes 3½ cups gravy

4	tablespoons butter	4	cups chicken broth
½	cup sliced tasso, cut in 1-inch strips	2	tablespoons finely chopped fresh parsley
½	cup all-purpose flour		Salt and white pepper to taste

Melt butter in a heavy-bottomed sauce pan over low heat. Add tasso. Sauté for 1 minute, browning slightly. Make a roux by adding flour and stirring until well combined. Continue to cook over low heat for 5 minutes, stirring frequently or until roux develops a nutty aroma. Turn heat up to medium and gradually add 2 cups chicken broth, whisking vigorously. Keep whisking constantly until broth begins to thicken and is smooth. Gradually add remaining 2 cups broth, whisking constantly until broth thickens into gravy. Reduce heat and simmer over low heat for 15 minutes to cook out the starchy flavor of the flour. Add parsley. Simmer for another 5 minutes. Add salt and white pepper.

SHRIMP AND SAUSAGE

½	**pound spicy Italian sausage**
1	**tablespoon light olive oil**
2	**pounds medium or large shrimp, peeled and deveined**
1½	**cups chicken broth**
1	**recipe Tasso Gravy**
2	**tablespoons finely chopped fresh parsley**

Preheat oven to 400 degrees.

Place sausage on a baking sheet with raised sides. Place it on the top rack of oven and bake for 10-15 minutes or until it is firm and its juices run clear. Cool and cut into small bite-size pieces. Reserve.

Heat olive oil in a heavy-bottomed frying pan over medium heat. Add cooked sausage and sauté for 2 minutes to brown slightly. Add shrimp and sauté until just beginning to turn pink, no longer than 1 minute. Add 1 cup of chicken broth to de-glaze the pan. Add Tasso Gravy and 1 tablespoon parsley. Bring mixture up to a gentle boil and simmer for 1 minute, stirring. Use remaining ½ cup chicken broth to thin the gravy, if needed.

Divide hot grits among eight warm bowls. Spoon shrimp and sausage mixture over grits. Sprinkle with the remaining tablespoon of parsley and serve immediately.

Donald Barickman is Founding Executive Chef and Vice President of Hospitality Management Group, Inc. which owns Magnolias Uptown Down South, Blossom, Cypress Lowcountry Grill. He and his wife, Jennifer and twin sons, William and Stuart live in Mount Pleasant.

Chef Donald Barickman
Magnolias Restaurant
185 East Bay Street
Charleston, South Carolina

PENINSULA
GRILL

Lowcountry Benne-Shrimp Stew with Wild Mushroom Grits

SERVES 4

BENNE-SHRIMP STEW

2	tablespoons (¼-inch diced) smoked bacon	2	tablespoons benne seeds, toasted
¼	cup diced Vidalia or other sweet onion	16	(26-30 count) shrimp, peeled and deveined
½	teaspoon minced garlic	2	tablespoons chopped fresh basil
2	tablespoons finely diced, mixed red, bell and yellow peppers		Pinch freshly ground black pepper
1¼	cups dark chicken stock or broth	4	warm soup bowls
¼	cup heavy whipping cream		

In a medium saucepan over medium-high heat, sauté bacon for 3-4 minutes or until fat is rendered and the bacon is beginning to brown. Add onion, garlic and peppers. Reduce heat to medium and sauté for 2-3 minutes or until the vegetables are translucent.

Add broth, cream and benne seeds, simmer, stirring occasionally, for 2-3 minutes, just to thicken slightly. Add shrimp and basil and simmer for 1-2 minutes or until shrimp are just beginning to set and are slightly curled around the edges. Stir in pepper. Serve immediately.

WILD MUSHROOMS

2	tablespoons unsalted butter	¼	pound shiitake mushrooms, cleaned with a damp towel, stems removed and caps sliced into ⅛-inch slices
¼	pound button or cremini mushrooms, cleaned with a damp paper towel, stems removed and caps quartered	¼	cup dark chicken stock or broth
		½	teaspoon kosher salt
		1	teaspoon freshly ground black pepper

Chef Robert Carter, a Johnson & Wales University graduate, started his culinary career as a private chef and later as a caterer in his own business called Rent-A-Chef. After graduation from the Charleston culinary school, Chef Carter apprenticed under Certified Master Chef Victor Gielisse in Dallas and later worked at The Inn at Blackberry Farm, Cafe Marquessa in Key West, Blue Ridge Grill in Atlanta and Richmond Hill Inn in Asheville. Drawn back to Charleston, Chef Carter returned to open Peninsula Grill in 1997.

Lowcountry Benne-Shrimp Stew, continued

Heat butter in a medium sauté pan over medium-high heat until foaming. Add button mushrooms and sauté for 1 minute. Add shitake mushrooms and mix well. Increase heat to high, add chicken stock or broth, salt and pepper. Cook over high heat for 2-3 minutes, or until all the liquid is evaporated. Set aside.

GRITS

3½	cups water	1	teaspoon kosher salt
1	cup heavy whipping cream	¼	teaspoon white pepper
2	tablespoons unsalted butter	1	cup stone-ground white grits
2	teaspoons minced garlic	1	cup milk
		¼	cup grated Asiago cheese

In a medium heavy-bottomed saucepan over high heat, bring water, cream, butter, garlic, salt and pepper to boil. Stir in grits and bring back to boil, stirring constantly. Reduce heat to medium-low and simmer, stirring frequently, for about 20 minutes or until grits are tender. If the grits need more liquid, whisk in some milk. Fold in Asiago cheese and wild mushrooms. Set aside in a warm place.

TO SERVE

Divide grits among four warm bowls. Spoon shrimp stew around grits, making sure that each serving gets its share of shrimp.

Chef Robert Carter
Peninsula Grill
Planters Inn
112 North Market Street
Charleston, South Carolina

Peninsula Grill is located in the Planters Inn on Market Street in Charleston. Planters Inn built around 1844 is one of the oldest inns in the City Market.

PENINSULA
GRILL

Spicy Buttermilk-Cucumber Soup with Grilled Shrimp Salad

SERVES 6

Peninsula Grill has received many awards including the DiRoNa Award, AAA Four-Diamond Award, Mobil Four-Star Award and Wine Spectator's Award of Excellence. Peninsula Grill offers innovative regional cuisine and impeccable service in a sophisticated, elegant setting.

SOUP

3	pounds cucumbers, peeled and cut into ⅛-inch slices
2	tablespoons salt
1	cup diced Vidalia onion
½	cup diced celery
1	cup spinach, packed

2	cups buttermilk
2	teaspoons chili paste with garlic (oriental condiment)
1	tablespoon rice wine vinegar
	Salt and white pepper to taste

In medium stainless steel bowl, toss cucumber and salt. Allow to sit for 30 minutes. Rinse thoroughly, drain in colander and pat dry. Place cucumbers, salt, onion, celery, spinach, buttermilk, chili paste and vinegar in blender and blend until completely green and no specs are apparent. Strain through small hole strainer and season to taste. Place soup in bowl of ice water to chill thoroughly. Serve within 8-12 hours.

GRILLED SHRIMP SALAD

12	(26-30 count) shrimp, peeled and deveined
1	teaspoon extra virgin olive oil
½	teaspoon minced garlic

	Salt and pepper to taste
½	teaspoon chopped dill
¼	cup small diced (⅛-inch squares) tomatoes
1	lemon

Toss shrimp in oil and garlic. Season with salt and pepper. Chargrill until just done, but still opaque. Remove tail and dice shrimp into ¼-inch diced pieces. Toss with dill and tomatoes. Squeeze lemon over salad to moisten. Season with salt and pepper. Serve atop soup.

Chef Robert Carter
Peninsula Grill
Planters Inn
112 North Market Street
Charleston, South Carolina

CHARLESTON GRILL

Camembert, Marinated Grapes, Roasted Pecans and Young Arugula in a Sherry Vinegar and Virgin Pecan Oil Dressing

SERVES 2

Salt and fresh ground white pepper to taste	6 ounces fresh young Arugula
2 tablespoons sherry vinegar	1 medium sized French Camembert cheese, cut into 1-inch pieces
6 tablespoons virgin pecan oil	½ cup roasted pecans
20 each red seedless grapes, cut in half	

In a small bowl, add salt and pepper to sherry vinegar until the salt is dissolved. Add pecan oil and then toss in the grape halves to marinate for 5 minutes. Arrange the arugula onto 2 plates. Place Camembert cheese over the greens. Sprinkle with roasted pecans and marinated grapes. Lightly spoon some of vinaigrette over each salad.

Chef Bob Waggoner, Executive Chef
Charleston Grill
Charleston Place Hotel
224 Kings Street
Charleston, South Carolina

Chef Waggoner has extensive experience working with many of the premier chefs in France. In 1988, at the age of 26, he became the first American chef to open his own restaurant in France, the highly acclaimed Le Monte Cristo. After working in France for 11 years, native Californian Chef Waggoner returned to the United States. He worked his culinary magic at the famous Turnberry Isle in Florida and The Wild Boar in Nashville before joining Charleston Grill ten years ago.

Charleston Grill Lobster Tempura with Creamy Stone Ground Grits

SERVES 4

Chef Bob Waggoner, Executive Chef for Charleston Grill, enjoys fusing Lowcountry cooking and his own French-influenced culinary techniques to create contemporary and sophisticated new southern haute cuisine. He uses the freshest seasonal ingredients from the local area and is known for his commitment to support local farmers. Chef Waggoner has been recognized by many culinary publications and received various awards.

LOBSTER

4	small fresh lobster tails, pre-steamed 5 minutes each	1	cup all-purpose flour
		1	cup heavy cream
	Salt and fresh ground white pepper to taste	1	medium sized green tomato, peeled, seeded, cut in cubes

Remove lobster meat from the shells. Salt and pepper each tail and cut them in half, lengthwise. Toss tails and tomato cubes in the flour, then heavy cream, then back in the flour once again. Set aside.

SAUCE

1	cup white wine Chardonnay		Salt and fresh ground white pepper to taste
½	Cup (Noilly Prat) French vermouth	2	tablespoons fresh tarragon leaves
3	shallots, finely chopped	1	large yellow tomato, peeled, seeded and diced
½	cup unsalted butter, diced into small cubes		

In a small saucepan, heat white wine, French vermouth and shallots until reduced to 3 tablespoons of wine. With a small whip, add butter cubes a little at a time over low heat. Whip slowly to emulsify the butter. Stir in salt and pepper. Add tarragon and yellow tomato just before serving.

(continued)

CHARLESTON GRILL

Charleston Grill Lobster Tempura, continued

CREAMY STONE GROUND LEMON GRITS

2½ tablespoons unsalted butter	1-2 cups heavy cream
2¼ cups chicken stock or broth	Salt and fresh ground white pepper to taste
½ cup Charleston Grill stone ground grits	1 teaspoon fresh lemon zest, finely chopped

Bring butter and chicken broth to boil in a thick-bottomed saucepan. Stir in grits and return to boil. Reduce heat, allowing the grits to cook for another 15 minutes at low boil, until grits are thick and have absorbed most of chicken broth. Stir occasionally to keep the grits from sticking. Add ½ cup of heavy cream to the pot and reduce the heat, allowing the grits to cook slowly for another 10 minutes. As liquid is absorbed, add more cream, cooking grits until the desired consistency. Add salt and pepper with a total cooking time of at least 1 hour. The grits should be thick and full-bodied. Fold in lemon zest just before serving.

PRESENTATION

Drop the lobster tails and green tomato in a small deep fryer at 375 degrees for approximately 1 minute until browned. Spoon 2 tablespoons of grits in a soup bowl. Spoon 1 tablespoon of the yellow tomato tarragon butter sauce over the grits. Gently set the lobster tempura and fried tomatoes on top of the grits.

Chef Bob Waggoner, Executive Chef
Charleston Grill
Charleston Place Hotel
224 Kings Street
Charleston, South Carolina

Shrimp and Grits, Charleston Grill Style

SERVES 2

SHRIMP

	Salt and fresh ground white pepper to taste	1	yellow tomato, peeled, seeded and diced
8	shrimp, peeled and deveined	½	cup dry white wine
1	tablespoon olive oil	¼	cup heavy cream
1	teaspoon garlic, chopped	1	tablespoon Opal basil, chopped fine
2	teaspoons chopped shallots		

Charleston Grill is located in the renowned Charleston Place hotel in Charleston, SC. Charleston Place is one of the finest hotels in Charleston and is part of the Orient-Express Hotels. Charleston Grill has been a continual recipient of the prestigious AAA Four-Diamond and Mobil Four-Star awards. It is also a Wine Spectator "Grand Award" winner.

Salt and pepper shrimp on each side. In a large pan, heat the olive oil and then add the shrimp. Cook for 1 minute on each side and remove from the pan. Add garlic and shallots and cook for another 30 seconds. Add tomatoes and white wine. Reduce the wine by half and add the cream. Reduce to a sauce consistency. Return the shrimp to the sauce and add the Opal basil.

Salt and pepper to taste and pour this over the hot grits.

GRITS

2/2	tablespoons unsalted butter	1-2	cups heavy cream
2¼	cups chicken stock or broth		Salt and fresh cracked white pepper to taste
½	cup Charleston Grill stone ground grits	1	teaspoon fresh lemon zest, finely chopped

(continued)

Shrimp and Grits, Charleston Grill Style, continued

Bring butter and chicken stock or broth to boil in a thick-bottomed saucepan. Stir in grits and return to boil. Reduce heat, allowing the grits to cook for another 15 minutes at a low boil and until the grits are thick and have absorbed most of the chicken broth. Stir occasionally to keep the grits from sticking. Add ½ cup of heavy cream to the pot and reduce the heat, allowing the grits to cook slowly for another 10 minutes. As the liquid is absorbed, add more cream, cooking the grits until thick and full-bodied. Add salt and pepper to taste with a total cooking time of at least 1 hour. Fold in lemon zest before serving.

Chef Bob Waggoner, Executive Chef
Charleston Grill
Charleston Place Hotel
224 Kings Street
Charleston, South Carolina

Jumbo Lump Blue Crab and Creek Shrimp Galette with a Zucchini Mousseline in a Noilly Prat Yellow Tomato Tarragon Butter

SERVES 4

Chef Waggoner has appeared on many cooking shows and has won an Emmy for his show, "Off the Menu" and filmed a pilot for a travel show featuring Orient-Express Luxury Properties. Chef Waggoner is currently host of a weekly cooking segment on a local network affiliate that showcases Charleston's culinary talent.

CRAB AND SHRIMP GALETTE

1	pound jumbo lump crabmeat, cleaned	1	teaspoon dry mustard
1	pound creek shrimp, peeled, cleaned and sautéed in grape seed oil, then diced	2	tablespoons mayonnaise
		1	pinch of celery seed
		1	pinch of cayenne pepper
2	egg whites	1	cup white bread crumbs
1	teaspoon Old Bay seasoning	1-2	ounces cracker meal
		2	tablespoons grape seed oil

Combine crab, shrimp, egg whites, mayonnaise, celery seed and cayenne. Form into cakes and roll lightly in a mixture of bread crumbs and cracker meal. Heat grape seed oil (vegetable may be used) in a skillet over medium high heat. Sear until golden browned on both sides and warm in the center (about 4-5 minutes). Heat in 350 degrees oven for 5 minutes.

(continued)

CHARLESTON GRILL

Jumbo Lump Blue Crab and Creek Shrimp Galette, continued

SAUCE

1	cup white wine Chardonnay		Salt and fresh ground white pepper to taste
½	cup (Noilly Prat) French vermouth	2	tablespoons fresh tarragon leaves
3	shallots, finely chopped	1	large yellow tomato, peeled, seeded and diced
½	cup unsalted butter, diced into small cubes		

In a small saucepan, heat white wine, noilly prat and shallots. Reduce to 3 tablespoons of wine. With a small whip, add the butter cubes a little at a time over low heat. Whip slowly to emulsify the butter. Add salt and pepper to taste. Add fresh tarragon and yellow tomato just before serving.

ZUCCHINI PURÉE

2	tablespoons olive oil	Salt and ground white pepper to taste
2	medium sized zucchini, sliced	

Heat a large sauté pan with 2 tablespoons of olive oil. Gently sauté zucchini. Add salt and fresh ground white pepper. Cook over medium high heat for 3-5 minutes. Do Not Brown. Cook until completely tender then blend in blender still hot.

Place the hot crab and shrimp galette in the center of the plate, spoon 1 large spoonful of zucchini purée on top of the galette.

Then spoon some of the sauce around the purée. Serve the plate hot.

Chef Bob Waggoner, Executive Chef
Charleston Grill
Charleston Place Hotel
224 Kings Street
Charleston, South Carolina

CHARLESTON GRILL

Sautéed Venison Tenderloin in a Port and Fresh Blueberry Reduction

SERVES 1

1	tablespoon vegetable oil	½	cup port wine
	Salt and pepper to taste	1	tablespoon reduced chicken stock or broth
4	ounces fresh venison tenderloin, cut into 3 medallions	1	tablespoon honey
1	tablespoon chopped shallots	¼	cup fresh blueberries

In a medium size pan, heat vegetable oil on a medium high heat. Salt and pepper all sides of the venison. Sear the medallions for 1 minute on each side in the hot oil. Remove the venison and lower the heat.

Add chopped shallots and cook for approximately 30 seconds. Add port wine and reduce the port to approximately 1½ tablespoons of liquid. Add chicken broth, honey, salt, pepper and blueberries. Cook for another 30 seconds to warm the berries. Spoon the sauce over the venison and serve immediately.

Chef Bob Waggoner, Executive Chef
Charleston Grill
Charleston Place Hotel
224 Kings Street
Charleston, South Carolina

Roast 'N Toast

SERVES 2

FISH AND ROASTED OLIVE MIXTURE

2 tablespoons extra virgin olive oil

3 garlic cloves, peeled and left whole

¾ cup Lucques olives, pitted

1 cup pine nuts

1 tablespoon rosemary, chopped fine

Salt and white pepper to taste

6 ounces of white flesh fish (swordfish, grouper, snapper, etc.)

Thin slice sourdough bread for each portion of fish

Large knob of French butter

2 sprigs rosemary

10 large green grapes, peeled

Chef Tarver King was named Executive Chef of The Dining Room at the Woodlands Resort & Inn in April 2006. He has been a chef at The Dining Room since 2004.

Warm olive oil and garlic in a sauté pan until the garlic becomes golden browned and smells fragrant. Add olives and fry until begin to wrinkle and barely color. Add the pine nuts and stir constantly until golden browned. Check seasoning and add rosemary. Spread pine nut mixture out on paper towels to cool.

Bring the fish up to room temperature and season with salt and pepper. Let the fish rest on a plate. When the fish begins to sweat, wrap each piece with a slice of sourdough bread. Melt the butter on medium-high heat in an iron skillet or non-stick pan. When the butter becomes foamy, add the wrapped fish and rosemary sprigs. Sauté for about 3 minutes or until toasty brown. Flip the fish only once as it will become soggy if rolled around too much. Drain the fish on a paper towel and keep warm. The longer the fish rests, the less crispy the final dish.

(recipe continues on next page)

Woodlands
RESORT & INN

Roast 'N Toast, continued

OLIVE VINAIGRETTE

1	cup black olive brine	2	tablespoons extra virgin olive oil
1	tablespoon red wine vinegar	1	tablespoon lemon juice
½	teaspoon Dijon mustard	1	tablespoon minced olives

Blend olive brine, vinegar, mustard, oil, lemon juice and olives. Store in a sealed container in the refrigerator. When ready to plate up, warm the olive mixture and add the grapes and spoon on the middle of the serving plate. Place the crispy fish on top. Spoon some of the vinaigrette around the dish and serve.

Chef Tarver King, Executive Chef
The Dining Room at Woodlands Inn & Resort
Summerville, South Carolina

Chef King has been cooking since the age of 15, inspired by his grandmother, Tatiana McKenna, recipes editor for Vogue magazine in the 1960's. He has worked at some of the country's most prestigious restaurants including the French Laundry, Le Bec Fin, Roy's in Philadelphia and The Inn at Little Washington. While working under renowned Chef Patrick O'Connell at The Inn at Little Washington, Chef King developed his fondness for comfort foods that utilize the best ingredients from local farmers. He continues the Woodlands' trademark of providing delicate dishes filled with deeply infused flavors.

Lobster Cappuccino

LOBSTER BROTH

¼	cup butter	2	shallots
2	pound lobster shells	¼	cup tomato paste
2	large onions, chopped	4	cups water
1	carrot, chopped	1¼	cups clam juice
2	stalks celery, chopped	3	cups cream
2	lemons, juiced	2	bay leaves
2	cups dry white wine	3	ounces lobster roe
2	tablespoons sugar		Salt and white pepper to taste
1	head garlic, crushed		Knob of butter

Warm a deep pot on the stove with butter and oil until butter begins to foam and bubble. Add lobster shells and crush with top of meat hammer. Once shells turn orange and the kitchen smells like lobster, add onions, carrot, celery, lemon juice, wine, sugar, garlic, shallots and tomato paste. Roll ingredients around in the pot being careful to avoid sticking. When aroma of alcohol is gone, add water, clam juice and cream, then reduce by half. Stir in lobster roe, salt and pepper. Add a knob of whole butter for flavor and shine.

GARLIC BISCOTTI

1	head garlic, sliced in half	1	egg
1	cup olive oil	1	egg yolk
½	teaspoon salt	1½	cups all-purpose flour
½	cup butter, softened		Pinch of baking soda
¾	cup sugar	1¼	teaspoons baking powder
	Coarse sea salt		

Place garlic, olive oil and salt in 1-inch square of foil and fold up to avoid leaking. Bake at 325 degrees for 30 minutes until garlic

(recipe continues on next page)

Woodlands Resort & Inn is located in Summerville, SC, a short distance from Charleston. It is an impeccably restored century-old mansion set among 42-acres of parkland grounds, featuring 18 beautiful guest rooms, guest cottage, day spa, clay tennis courts, swimming pool and many more wonderful amenities.

The Dining Room has received many national awards and has been voted the #3 restaurant and the "Best for Food" in North America by Conde Nast Traveler's Readers Choice Awards and has been highlighted on its Gold List with The only perfect food score in North America and Among the top ten restaurants for service in the world. Relais and Chateaux has named The Dining Room at Woodlands Relais Gourmand, the global organization's most prestigious designation. The Dining Room is the only Mobil 5-star restaurant in the state.

Lobster Cappuccino, continued

is a nice golden brown. Remove and allow to cool. Once cool, squeeze out soft cloves into a mixing bowl. Add butter and sugar and mix at low speed until butter looks light and shiny. Add egg and egg yolk and mix until combined. In a separate bowl, combine flour, baking soda and baking powder. Mix the dry ingredients with the wet to form a moist dough. Let rest for 10 minutes. Form into a loaf 3 inches wide 1 inch high and 8 inches long on a greased baking sheet. Bake at 350 degrees for 15-20 minutes. Let cool on a rack. Slice with serrated knife in ¼ inch slices and place back on a baking sheet. Bake a second time at 350 degrees until golden brown (about 5 minutes). Let cool on a rack before serving.

TO ASSEMBLE

½	cup cream, whipped firm	Fennel pollen
	Salt, sugar and white pepper to taste	

Ladle the hot lobster broth into espresso cups or coffee cups. Top with whipped cream. Let the cream sit on the broth for just a few seconds until it melts. Sprinkle, salt, sugar, pepper or a little fennel pollen and serve with the Garlic Biscotti.

Chef Tarver King, Executive Chef
The Dining Room at Woodlands Inn & Resort
Summerville, South Carolina

CUCINA ITALIANA

Involtini di Melanzane

SERVES 4

1	large eggplant (approximately 12 slices)
	All-purpose flour for dusting
4-5	eggs, beaten
	Oil for frying
	Salt to taste
12	prosciutto slices

	Sharp provolone (cut into 2-inch blocks)
1½	cups blanched spinach or escarole
4	cups tomato sauce
	Grated Parmigiano-Reggiano cheese

Peel and slice eggplant into thin slices (lengthwise). Dredge in flour and dip into beaten egg. Lightly fry in hot oil, remove and place on paper towel to dry. Season with salt.

To assemble, lay one slice of prosciutto, one block of sharp provolone and a pinch of blanched spinach in the middle of fried eggplant slice. Roll and secure with a toothpick. Place in a casserole dish and lightly cover with tomato sauce. Sprinkle with Parmigiano cheese and bake at 350 degrees for 10 minutes. Serve hot.

Chef Michael Cirafesi
Michael Anthony's
37 New Orleans Road
Orleans Plaza, Suite L
Hilton Head Island, South Carolina

Michael Anthony's is a family restaurant started by Hilton Head Island residents Becky and Tony Fazzini and relatives, Chef Michael Cirafesi and Jill Boyd. Originally from Philadelphia, they longed for the authentic Italian eateries found in the Italian neighborhoods around the city. These quaint restaurants were patterned after the trattorias found in the small towns of Italy.

CUCINA ITALIANA

Penne alla Boscaiola

SERVES 4

1	pound penne rigate
	Olive oil for sautéing
½	cup chopped prosciutto or pancetta
1	tablespoon minced garlic
2	cups sliced mixed mushrooms
½	cup sweet green peas
4	cups tomatoes
1½	cups heavy cream
	Salt and pepper to taste
	Parmigiano cheese to taste
3	tablespoons fresh basil (finely sliced or chiffonade)

Cook the pasta in boiling salted water as directed on package. Heat olive oil. Sauté pancetta, garlic, mushrooms and peas. Add tomatoes and cream to create pink color. Add salt and pepper. Add pasta and finish with cheese and basil.

Chef Michael Cirafesi
Michael Anthony's
37 New Orleans Road
Orleans Plaza, Suite L
Hilton Head Island, South Carolina

Michael Anthony's offers classic Italian cuisine prepared with a creative touch, paired with a nationally recognized wine list and served in a comfortable, cozy setting.

Blue Marlin Collard Greens

SERVES 4

3	slices bacon, diced and sautéed, reserve bacon grease
½	onion, julienne
2	bunches collard greens (we use Rawl Farms from Lexington, SC)
1	quart chicken broth
1	ham hock
1	teaspoon Tabasco sauce
	Salt and pepper to taste

In a stock pot, render bacon. When brown, add onion and sauté until translucent. Add picked collard greens, chicken broth, Tabasco and ham hock and cook for 2-3 hours until collards are thoroughly cooked. Finally add salt and pepper to taste.

We buy collard greens whole and pick them ourselves. May buy collards pre-picked from the grocery store.

Chef Brian Dukes
Blue Marlin
1200 Lincoln Street
Columbia, South Carolina

The Blue Marlin has been serving A Taste of Southern Lowcountry for more than 10 years from the heart of Columbia's Congaree Vista District. Lowcountry cuisine features fresh seafood such as shrimp, oysters, crab and crayfish and local grown produce such as greens, corn and tomatoes. These fresh ingredients are at the heart of the dishes served at the Blue Marlin. As you enjoy their signature dishes, you will experience the finest blend of African, West Indian, Caribbean and Cajun flavors. Specialties include Shrimp and Grits, Crispy Fried Flounder with Jalapeño Salsa, Salmon Ponchartrain and Oysters Bienville. All this delicious food served with a heaping portion of Southern hospitality.

BLUE MARLIN
STEAKS & SEAFOOD

Blue Marlin Shrimp and Grits

For the grits, use a heavy bottom stock pot and a large whisk.

SERVES 10-12

Chef Brian Dukes is Concept Executive Chef for all three Vista Life Restaurant Group restaurants, Blue Marlin, Willy's and Foxfire Grill. He is a graduate of Johnson and Wales University. Chef Dukes' experience includes working at Alan Ducasse in New York City, the French Market in Charlottesville, and Kingsmill Resort in Williamsburg.

GRITS

1	gallon chicken broth or water and bouillon cubes to equal 1 gallon	1¾	pounds stone ground Adluh grits
2	ounces kosher salt	2	cups whole milk
1	teaspoon white pepper	2	cups heavy cream

Bring chicken broth, salt and pepper to a boil. Add grits and reduce heat to medium low. Whisk steadily until grits and liquid are combined. Cook for 30-45 minutes on medium low heat stirring frequently to prevent grits from burning to bottom of the pot. Once the grits begin to soften to the bite, whisk in milk and cream. Taste and adjust seasoning if needed.

If you have leftovers you can pour into a shallow pan and refrigerate overnight and make grit cakes the next day. Cut grits with a cookie cutter, dredge in seasoned flour and pan fry on a griddle or sauté pan in butter or olive oil.

TASSO GRAVY

4	ounces butter	½	cup all-purpose flour
6	ounces tasso ham, finely diced	3	cups hot chicken broth
		2	teaspoons kosher salt

For the gravy, in a saucepot melt butter and sauté the ham for 2 minutes to release flavors. Whisk in flour and cook for 5 minutes stirring frequently. This is a roux. Slowly add hot chicken broth to the roux and whisk continuously to prevent lumps of flour. Simmer for 5 minutes and taste.

(continued)

Blue Marlin Shrimp and Grits, continued

SHRIMP

½	cup butter	Andouille sausage, 4 pieces per person	
4	ounces shrimp per person for lunch (8 ounces for dinner)	Salt, pepper, Old Bay and chopped parsley to taste	

For the shrimp and sausage we use Carolina or gulf shrimp which ever we can get. We also sauté andouille sausage with our shrimp to add some spice.

In a sauté pan, heat butter until sizzling in pan, add andouille sausage and cook for 1 minute so the sausage releases it's fat and add the shrimp. Sauté the shrimp until they are translucent. Season with salt, pepper, Old Bay seasoning and fresh parsley.

To serve, place the grits in a bowl, the shrimp and sausage in the middle of the grits and ladle the gravy on top of the shrimp. Garnish with parsley. Enjoy.

Chef Brian Dukes
Blue Marlin
1200 Lincoln Street
Columbia, South Carolina

The Vista Life Restaurant Group is truly a family affair with Chef Dukes' uncle Bill Dukes heading up the restaurant group and cousin Ryan Dukes, also a chef, managing Foxfire Grill. In March 2007, Brian, Ryan and Ryan's brother Matt Dukes (who is currently a culinary student) were part of a culinary team invited to prepare dinner at the prestigious James Beard House in New York City.

steaks • seafood • wine

Foxfire Grill Meatloaf

SERVES 8-10

5	pounds fresh ground beef	¼	cup Worcestershire sauce
1	medium yellow onion, diced	1	cup ketchup
1	medium bell pepper, diced	1½	cups Panko bread crumbs
1	tablespoon garlic powder	8	eggs, whisk together to blend
2	teaspoons dried thyme	2	teaspoons black pepper
		1½	tablespoons kosher salt

We smoke the meatloaf at the restaurant for a unique flavor. If you have a smoker bake it for an hour and smoke it for the remaining 30 minutes.

We also use our meat trimmings from sirloin, tenderloin and rib-eye for the ground beef.

Mix ground beef, onion, bell pepper, garlic powder, thyme, Worcestershire sauce, ketchup and bread crumbs in a mixing bowl. Whisk the eggs in a separate bowl and add to the meat mixture, mixing thoroughly. Place the mixture in a baking pan and with tender, loving care press the mixture down until it is flat and even in the pan. Cut the mixture down the middle of the pan lengthwise and form into two uniform loaves. Bake at 350 degrees for 1 hour, 30 minutes. Let the meatloaf rest for 20-30 minutes at room temperature covered with foil.

Chef Brian Dukes
Foxfire Grill
1220 Bower Parkway
Columbiana Station
Columbia, South Carolina

Truck Stop Gravy

½	medium onion, diced	½	cup all-purpose flour
½	cup butter		Salt and pepper to taste
1	quart beef stock or broth or bouillon cubes and water to equal 1 quart		

Sauté diced onions in the butter in a saucepan. In a separate pan heat the broth. When onions are translucent add the flour and whisk, cooking for 3-4 minutes. Slowly add the hot broth with a ladle, whisk after you add ¼ of the broth. Continue to add more broth and whisk in between to prevent lumps. Add salt and pepper to taste.

Chef Brian Dukes
Foxfire Grill
1220 Bower Parkway
Columbiana Station
Columbia, South Carolina

The great American grills of the 1920s were the neighborhood restaurants of their day. They served simple food using old family recipes and home cooking techniques. Foxfire Grill, part of the Vista Life Restaurant Group, takes restaurant concepts from the American classics, combines them and adds a new personal touch for a truly American dining experience.

Braised Pork Shoulder with Dark Beer

SERVES 6-8

1	pork shoulder, about 4-5 pounds	4	garlic cloves, peeled
	Salt and fresh white pepper to taste	1	shallot, peeled
		1	(12 ounce) bottle dark beer
¼	cup vegetable oil	4	cups veal broth
2	carrots, peeled and large diced	12	ounces fresh tomato purée or a small can of your favorite tomato purée
1	yellow onion, peeled and large diced	1	teaspoon ground cumin
			Parsley, thyme, 1 bay leaf

33 Liberty Restaurant has been praised by Bon Appetit, Southern Living, Chile Pepper & Chocolatier Magazines. Chefs John and Amy Malik have been guest chefs at the International Food & Wine Festival at Disney World, the Charlotte Wine & Food Weekend, Salute to Southern Chefs in Paso Robles, CA and Tribute to the Great Chefs of the South in Beaufort, SC. 33 Liberty is the dining destination for the true food and wine enthusiast.

Season the pork liberally with salt and pepper. In a large, heavy bottomed stock pot over high heat, sear the pork in the vegetable oil. The pork should be crispy brown on all sides. Remove the pork then add the carrots, onion, garlic and shallot. Sauté until lightly browned. After cooking the vegetables remove from heat, strain off the cooking oil then place the pork and vegetables back into the pot. Add the beer, veal broth, tomato, cumin and fresh herbs. Cover, place in a 350 degree oven then allow the pork to cook for at least 3 hours. Taste the cooking liquid and if necessary add more salt or pepper. Remove the pork from the liquid, strain off the vegetables and discard. The pork can then be pulled, discard the chunks of fat and viscera and place the pulled pork back into the cooking liquid, simmer and if necessary add more fresh herbs, salt, pepper or hot sauce.

Serve over fresh whipped Yukon gold potatoes or slow simmered cheese grits.

Braised dishes such as this are best the next day. The pork can be reheated in the same liquid for approximately 1 hour.

Chef John Malik
33 Liberty Restaurant
33 Liberty Lane
Greenville, South Carolina

Brioche Tart with Lavender & Honey Peach Jam

SERVES 8-10

HONEY PEACH JAM

1¼ cups wild honey	2⅓ cups sugar
1 tablespoon dried lavender	5 sprigs fresh lavender
3 pounds peaches, peeled and diced	1 (10-11 inch) tart pan with removable bottom
1 lemon	

Prepare the lavender honey by heating the honey and dried lavender in a small heavy bottom saucepan until just simmering. Cover with a tight fitting lid, turn off the heat and allow this to sit for 10 minutes. Strain through a fine mesh strainer to remove the lavender.

Peel and dice the peaches. Place the peaches into a large heavy bottomed stainless steel stockpot. Squeeze the lemon then add the juice to the peaches. Remove the lemon seeds and add the lemon halves to the peaches. Add the sugar, honey and fresh lavender. Bring this to a gentle simmer and allow this to remain at a simmer for about 5 minutes. Remove from heat and let stand for 1 hour.

Strain off the fruit and set aside. Return the syrup to the heat and bring to boil until syrup reaches 220 degrees on a candy thermometer.

Add the fruit back into the syrup and return to a gentle simmer for 15 minutes. Check the jam's viscosity by drizzling on a chilled plate. When the jam is no longer runny, it is ready. Depending on the water content of the fruit, the last stage should be checked every 5 minutes. The amount of time cooking is not as important as the proper thickness of the jam.

33 Liberty features Global Comfort Cuisine with a dash of Southern Hospitality. The menu changes weekly to reflect the best of local foods.

(recipe continues on next page)

305

Brioche Tart, continued

Remove the jam from heat. If you are going to put up the jam in jars, immediately can in 3 boiling-water sterilized half pint jars. Place sterilized lids and rings on the jars. Tighten then turn upside down for 24 hours. The jam is sealed when the lid is depressed and a vacuum is created. If you are not canning the jam, simply store in an airtight container in the refrigerator for up to one month.

BRIOCHE TART

Brioche dough, see recipe

Egg wash

Vanilla pastry cream, see recipe

Spray pan release on tart shell. Remove the dough from the refrigerator. On a well-floured surface roll the dough to less than ¼-inch thick. Place the dough circle in the tart shell and stretch the dough just enough to cover the rim of the shell.

Brush egg wash on the outer rim of the dough, being careful not to let the egg drip between the dough and tart shell as this will cause the tart to stick after baking.

Fill the interior of the brioche with pastry cream. Cover the cream with a layer of peach jam. Place the tart in a warm space to allow the brioche to proof just enough to fill up the shell. The edges of the brioche should be light and puffy.

Bake the tart at 350 degrees for 20 to 25 minutes. Remove from the oven and let cool for 10 minutes in the pan. First remove the outer tart shell ring by pushing up the center from the bottom. Then carefully remove the bottom plate. Allow the tart to cool on a baker's rack at least 15 minutes before serving.

Vanilla Pastry Cream

MAKES 1 CUP

¼ cup sugar	Pinch of salt
2 tablespoons cornstarch	Thin wire whisk
2 whole eggs	Fine mesh strainer
1 vanilla bean, split lengthwise	Several 2-quart stainless steel bowls
1 cup half-and-half	High temperature rubber spatula
1 tablespoon unsalted butter	

Place mesh strainer over a bowl and keep this near the stove. Into a 2-quart bowl sift the sugar and cornstarch together then whisk in the eggs until light.

Using a small, sharp knife scrap the interior of the vanilla bean and place the pulp and remaining vanilla bean into a heavy-bottomed 2-quart saucepan. Add the half-and-half and bring to a boil then place saucepan next to the bowl of eggs and starch. Now gradually add about half of the warm cream mixture to the whipped eggs while whisking constantly. Now add this warm egg mixture back into the warm cream and place back on stove. Over medium heat, bring the mixture to a simmer while constantly stirring with a rubber spatula. When the mixture thickens to the consistency of thick pudding, remove from heat and whisk in the butter and salt. Carefully remove the vanilla bean then push the pastry cream through the strainer. Place the bowl of pastry cream over a larger bowl containing ice water and stir the cream to expedite the cooling process. Once cooled, cover the bowl of pastry cream with plastic wrap and place the wrap directly onto the cream. This will prevent a skin from forming. The pastry cream can now be refrigerated and will keep for several days.

Chef Amy Malik has made a name for herself as an exceptionally talented pastry chef. Chef John Malik continues to impress with his creative touches to classic dishes that will ensure an unforgettable culinary experience.

Chef Amy Malik
33 Liberty Restaurant
33 Liberty Lane
Greenville, South Carolina

Brioche

SERVES 8-10

1	tablespoon instant yeast	½	teaspoon salt
3	tablespoons sugar	¼	cup plus 2 tablespoons butter, room temperature
1¾	cups plus 2 tablespoons all-purpose flour	1	large bowl lightly coated with melted butter
3½	tablespoons whole milk		Kitchen Aid type Stand Mixer with Dough Hook
2	eggs plus 1 egg yolk		

In a bowl mix the yeast and ½ tablespoon of sugar in ¼ cup warm (100 degrees water). Let rest for 10 minutes or until a light foam forms on top of water.

In the bowl of a stand mixer fitted with a dough hook, add flour and remaining sugar. With the mixer on lowest setting, pour yeast water mixture slowly into flour. Mix until yeast mixture is evenly distributed through out the flour mix and is the size of small peas. It will look like biscuit dough at the stage that the butter is cut into the dough.

Slowly add the milk, eggs and egg yolk then salt. Allow the dough to mix for 3-4 minutes at which point you will need to stop the mixer, scrape down the sides of the bowl using a small rubber spatula and then resume mixing on the low setting. The dough will be yellow and coarse in texture. Allow this to mix for 5-10 minutes or until the dough becomes smooth, forms a cohesive ball and pulls away from the side of bowl.

With the mixer running add the butter, 1 tablespoon at a time, until all is incorporated. The dough will look like it is not going to accept the butter but it will, just be patient. After all butter is added

(continued)

Brioche, continued

once again stop the mixer and scrape down the sides and hook. Continue mixing (medium speed now) for as long as 15 minutes. The brioche dough will be finished when it has become smooth, glossy and elastic.

Remove the dough from the bowl and transfer to the buttered bowl. Cover tightly and refrigerate overnight. The brioche will last 2 to 3 days in the refrigerator.

Chef Amy Malik
33 Liberty Restaurant
33 Liberty Lane
Greenville, South Carolina

Butternut Squash Soup

SERVES 4-6

1 large sweet onion, chopped	1 quart chicken stock or broth
1 leek (white part), chopped	1 cup crème fraîche or whipping cream
3 slices smoked bacon	Salt and pepper to taste
3 celery stalks, peeled and chopped	2 tablespoons organic honey
1 large butternut squash, peeled, seeded, diced and cubed (1-inch)	Chopped chives and crème fraîche for garnish

Sauté sweet onion, leek, bacon, and celery. Add peeled and seeded butternut squash and chicken broth. Simmer until squash is soft. Add cream, salt, pepper and honey. Blend and strain. Garnish with chives and crème fraîche.

Chef Steven Greene, Executive Chef and Partner
Devereaux's
25 East Court Street, Suite 100
Greenville, South Carolina

Steven Greene's culinary career started at the age of 16 at the Marigold Market in Greenwood. He continued to develop his culinary talent at 82 Queen in Charleston, McCrady's in Charleston, and as Chef de Cuisine at the Mobil 5-star Dining Room at the Woodlands Resort and Inn in Summerville. Chef Greene has also worked with some of the greatest chefs in France and Las Vegas. In 2005, he transformed a century-old cigar factory in Greenville, SC to one of the hottest new restaurants, Devereaux's. The menu at Devereaux's is a mix of new age and southern classics. Devereaux's recently joined the highly successful Court Square Restaurant Group which includes Soby's and Restaurant O. In recognition of his talent, Chef Greene had the honor of cooking dinner at the renowned James Beard House in New York in January 2007.

RESTAURANT

Heirloom Tomato and Bread Salad with Roasted Garlic Vinaigrette

SERVES 1

ROASTED GARLIC VINAIGRETTE

2	garlic cloves	¾	cup water
	Olive oil	1	tablespoon Dijon mustard
½	cup white balsamic vinegar	2	cups vegetable oil
			Salt and pepper to taste

Cut ends off garlic cloves. Drizzle with olive oil. Wrap in foil. Roast in 350 degree oven for 45 minutes. Blend roasted garlic, vinegar, water and mustard thoroughly. Slowly drizzle in oil while blending. Season to taste with salt and pepper.

INFUSED BALSAMIC REDUCTION

1	(32 ounce) bottle balsamic vinegar	2	tablespoons honey
¼	cup sugar	¼	cup dry currants
1	teaspoon molasses	¼	cup dry cranberries
1	teaspoon Worcestershire sauce	2	black peppercorns
1	piece star anise	1	vanilla bean
		1	sprig of rosemary

Combine vinegar, sugar, molasses, Worcestershire sauce, anise, honey, currants, cranberries, peppercorns, vanilla bean and rosemary in saucepan and reduce slowly until syrup consistency.

(recipe continues on next page)

Chef Freidank started his culinary career at 16 in a New York style deli in his hometown of Long Island, NY. Later, he apprenticed under Chef Pete Herring (CEC) in Carolina Beach, NC. After three years of developing a serious appreciation for the freshest seafood of the Carolina coast, he was lured to Greenville, SC. He joined Soby's New South Cuisine in 1997. He and his staff have won several local culinary awards and accolades. In January 2002, he was honored to host a dinner at the prestigious James Beard House in New York City. Currently, Chef Freidank is Executive Chef and Partner of Restaurant O, one of the Court Square Restaurant Group restaurants and is very involved in various community projects.

RESTAURANT

Heirloom Tomato and Bread Salad, continued

SALAD

1	slice country French bread, cubed	1	cup Roasted Garlic Vinaigrette
3	heirloom (or vine ripened beefsteak) tomatoes, chopped		Salt and pepper to taste
			Mixed field greens
1	tablespoon basil pesto		Infused Balsamic Reduction

Combine bread, tomatoes, pesto, vinaigrette, salt and pepper. Press into a ring mold and top with field greens. Drizzle plate with some of the Infused Balsamic Reduction.

Chef Rodney Freidank, Executive Chef, Managing Partner

Restaurant O.
116 South Main Street
Greenville, South Carolina

Restaurant O is a Contemporary Regional American restaurant offering Southern hospitality in a contemporary atmosphere. They provide the highest quality meats and freshest seafood available with an emphasis on local ingredients. They feature a Wine Spectator award winning wine list.

Pan Roasted Trout with Deviled Crab Fondue

SERVES 2

1	cup plus ½ cup butter, divided	
1	cup heavy cream	
1	tablespoon Blackened Redfish Magic	

6	ounces lump crabmeat, picked and cleaned
	Salt and pepper to taste
2	(8 ounce) clear-cut trout
1	tablespoon olive oil

Heat 1 cup butter and cream in saucepan to 160 degrees. In another pan, heat remaining ½ cup butter to 160 degrees. Put butter and cream mixture into blender, slowly add ½ cup butter. Add Blackened Redfish Magic and crabmeat and season to taste. Keep warm.

Wash trout and pat dry with paper towel. Salt and pepper both sides of trout. Heat nonstick sauté pan to medium-high heat. Place oil in pan and place trout in for 2-3 minutes on each side until cooked. Serve warm with deviled crab fondue.

Chef Shaun Garcia
Chef de Cuisine
Soby's New South Cuisine
207 South Main Street
Greenville, South Carolina

Chef Shaun Garcia is originally from Spartanburg, SC. His interest in food started at an early eage in the traditional "meat and three" restaurant that his grandmother owned. Chef Garcia worked in restaurants in both North and South Carolina before joining the Court Square Restaurant Group in Greenville in 2003. He was made Chef de Cuisine in January 2007. His primary focus in dish development is to use seasonal ingredients and local products whenever possible. In this way, he is able to support local growers and to provide the greatest flavor and taste for the customer.

Soby's New South Cuisine offers a blend of contemporary cuisine infused with traditional Southern ingredients. The restaurant is located in a renovated, century-old building in downtown Greenville. The wine list is a consistent Wine Spectator and Wine Enthusiast award winner.

SOURCES

South Carolina Department of Parks, Recreation and Tourism
South Carolina Department of Agriculture
South Carolina State Museum
MySCGov.com – Official Website of South Carolina (www.myscgov.com)
South Carolina Chamber of Commerce

Chambers of Commerce

Greater Abbeville	Aiken	Allendale
Anderson	Bamberg County	Barnwell County
Batesville-Leesville	Beaufort	Berkeley County
Bishopville	Bluffton	Boiling Springs
Calhoun County	Camden	Charleston
Cheraw	Cherokee	Chester
Chesterfield	Clarendon County	Clemson
Clover	Columbia	Colleton County
Conway	Darlington County	Dillon County
Dorchester	Easley	Florence
Fort Mill	Fountain Inn	Gaffney
Georgetown County	Greenville	Greenwood
Greer	Hampton County	Hartsville
Hilton Head Island	Kershaw County	Kiawah Island
Lake City	Lancaster County	Laurens County
Lee County	Lexington	Little River
Loris	Marion	Marlboro County
McCormick County	Mount Pleasant	Murrells Inlet
Myrtle Beach	Newberry County	North Myrtle Beach
Orangeburg County	Pawleys Island	Pendleton
Pickens	Ridgeland	Rock Hill
Saluda County	Seneca	Spartanburg
Summerville	Sumter	Union
Walhalla	Walterboro	Westminster
Williamsburg County	Winnsboro	York County

University of South Carolina
Clemson University
College of Charleston
Pendleton District Commission
South Carolina Hall of Fame

INDEX

Please send_____copies of *Nothing Could Be Finer* @ $24.95 each_____

Shipping and Handling   @ $ 5.00 each_____

Additional copies to the same address   @ $ 2.00 each_____

                                                                        Total_____

Please Print:

Name _____

Address _____

City _____ State _____ Zip _____

Make checks payable to The Palmetto Cabinet and mail to:
The Palmetto Cabinet
P.O. Box 593
Columbia, SC 29202
All proceeds benefit the South Carolina Governor's Mansion.

- -

Please send_____copies of *Nothing Could Be Finer* @ $24.95 each_____

Shipping and Handling   @ $ 5.00 each_____

Additional copies to the same address   @ $ 2.00 each_____

                                                                        Total_____

Please Print:

Name _____

Address _____

City _____ State _____ Zip _____

Make checks payable to The Palmetto Cabinet and mail to:
The Palmetto Cabinet
P.O. Box 593
Columbia, SC 29202
All proceeds benefit the South Carolina Governor's Mansion.

Please send_____copies of *Nothing Could Be Finer* @ $24.95 each_____

Shipping and Handling   @ $ 5.00 each_____

Additional copies to the same address   @ $ 2.00 each_____

Total_____

Please Print:

Name _____

Address _____

City _____ State _____ Zip _____

Make checks payable to The Palmetto Cabinet and mail to:
The Palmetto Cabinet
P.O. Box 593
Columbia, SC 29202
All proceeds benefit the South Carolina Governor's Mansion.

- - - - - - - - - - - - - - - - - -

Please send_____copies of *Nothing Could Be Finer* @ $24.95 each_____

Shipping and Handling   @ $ 5.00 each_____

Additional copies to the same address   @ $ 2.00 each_____

Total_____

Please Print:

Name _____

Address _____

City _____ State _____ Zip _____

Make checks payable to The Palmetto Cabinet and mail to:
The Palmetto Cabinet
P.O. Box 593
Columbia, SC 29202
All proceeds benefit the South Carolina Governor's Mansion.